D1452704

# PRINCIPLES
## ⁊ FOR
# ORAL NARRATIVE
# RESEARCH ⁊ ⁊ ⁊ ⁊

# Folklore Studies in Translation
## GENERAL EDITOR, DAN BEN-AMOS

*German* Volkskunde: *A Decade of Theoretical Confrontation, Debate, and Reorientation (1967–1977),* translated and edited by James R. Dow and Hannjost Lixfeld.

*The European Folktale: Form and Nature* by Max Lüthi, translated by John D. Niles.

*The Fairytale as Art Form and Portrait of Man* by Max Lüthi, translated by John Erickson.

*Nordic Folklore: Recent Studies:* edited by Reimund Kvideland and Henning K. Sehmsdorf (in collaboration with Elizabeth Simpson).

*Kalevala Mythology* by Juha Y. Pentikäinen, translated and edited by Ritva Poom.

*Folk Culture in a World of Technology* by Hermann Bausinger, translated by Elke Dettmer.

*Folktales and Reality* by Lutz Röhrich, translated by Peter Tokofsky.

# PRINCIPLES
## ଈ F O R
# ORAL NARRATIVE
# RESEARCH ଈ ଈ ଈ ଈ

B Y ଈ

AXEL OLRIK

T R A N S L A T E D   B Y

KIRSTEN WOLF

A N D   JODY JENSEN ଈ

INDIANA UNIVERSITY PRESS
BLOOMINGTON AND INDIANAPOLIS

Translated from *Nogle Grundsætninger for Sagnforskning* by Axel
Olrik, edited by Hans Ellekilde,
© 1921 by Det Schønbergske Forlag, Copenhagen.

The English-language edition of this book was made possible, in part,
by a grant from the Danish Ministry of Education.

© 1992 by Indiana University Press

Manufactured in the United States of America

**Library of Congress Cataloging-in-Publication Data**
Olrik, Axel, 1864–1917.
  [Nogle grundsætninger for sagnforskning. English]
Principles for oral narrative research / by Axel Olrik;
  translated by Kirsten Wolf and Jody Jensen.
      p   cm. — (Folklore studies in translation)
    Translation of: Nogle grundsætninger for sagnforskning.
    Includes bibliographical references and index.
    ISBN 0-253-34175-2 (cloth)
    1. Oral tradition—Methodology. 2. Folk literature—History and
criticism. 3. Epic literature—History and criticism. I. Title.
II. Series.
GR72.O5613   1992
398.2′072—dc20                                        88-46034

1   2   3   4   5   96   95   94   93   92

# CONTENTS ❧

# Foreword
## By Dan Ben-Amos

The absence of Olrik's *Principles for Oral Narrative Research* from any major European language has been a setback for folklore theory, which this translation seeks to amend. At the initial research stages documentation and classification dominated folklore studies and overshadowed any theoretical formulation. When, at later stages, students of folklore impressed upon the field the necessity of theory, they either turned to other disciplines, such as anthropology, linguistics, history, and literary theory, for ideas, concepts, and models, or proposed to turn a new page in folklore by presenting a theory without antecedents in earlier works. For a discipline that thrives on tradition, folklore appeared to lack the tradition of theory.

The present volume is a clear demonstration that this has been an erroneous image, wrought in sad ignorance and clouded by linguistic inaccessibility. Indigenous folklore theory was "alive and well," albeit tucked away on the shelf of Danish books. In his *Principles* Olrik proposed a comprehensive theory for folklore, but for years it was possible to catch only a glimpse of it in the form of the "epic laws," a chapter of this volume (§57–§82) that appeared in German and English translations. The formulation of laws that govern folktales and distinguish them from other forms of narration influenced the analysis of folklore and had a great impact also on literary and biblical studies.

In spite of the numerous references to, and the virtually universal acceptance of, Olrik's "epic laws" as folklore axioms, it has not been possible to fully appreciate their theoretical significance in the truncated and decontextualized form in which they have heretofore been available. The present translation, hence, offers the broader theoretical framework of which the "epic laws" are a part, and at the same time affords knowledge and an appreciation of Olrik's conception of folklore in general. Olrik uses the concept of "law" in the spirit of his time, as an application of scientific principles in physics to a humanistic field, seeking in oral tradition the same type of regulatory mechanism found in nature. However, in fact, he formulates several sets of theoretical propositional statements about folklore that are subject to falsification and confirmation. In so doing, Olrik places folklore on a firm scientific ground, enabling subsequent scholars to refute, confirm, or modify his propositions. These sets of propositions become in themselves a deductive model which is applicable to the narrative traditions of different peoples in different languages and cultural areas. Only after tests and rigorous examination would it be possible to discard some and confirm others, to modify some and specify the conditions for the validity of still others. Olrik's principles are propositions for research and an invitation for exploration of their universal or conditional applicability. As such, they are not a doctrine but an agenda for research, requiring repeated testing under various circumstances.

In light of these propositions the "epic laws" disclose a conception of folklore that exceeds the boundaries of the Nordic, historic-geographic scholarly tradition that dominated the field at the time. Olrik's folktales are subject to systemic principles and regulatory rules that govern narrative creativity, and the transmission of tales from one generation to the next and from one country to another. The sheer assumption that verbal performance proceeds in accordance with discernible "laws" frees folklore from the arbitrariness of forgetfulness and the randomness of memory recalls. Instead, folktales are subject to discoverable principles of narration. From that perspective Olrik was a precursor of Russian formalistic analysis of folktale morphology, and a harbinger of modern studies of the poetics of folklore. He shares with current trends in folklore a holistic, systemic conception of oral narratives in prose and in rhyme.

Obviously, it would be an anachronism to place him out of his historical context. Yet his *Principles* set him apart among the many scholars of his period as a scholar with whom modern folklorists can establish an intellectual dialogue. Elliptic, at times even enigmatic, he stands out as a thinker in folklore whose ideas provide a basis for continuity and departure, debate and consensus, trends and countertrends that are a staple for the advancement of knowledge. In his theoretical propositions he bridges the historical approach of his time and the structural and semiotics analyses that emerged in folklore in the second half of the twentieth century.

Being a philologist and a medievalist, initially Olrik purported to offer a set of diagnostic principles with which to distinguish the oral segments in the manuscripts in which they occurred. This task required him to single out, describe, and compare the narrative attributes that are characteristic of oral texts. The "epic laws" are diagnostic tools with which a trained person can recognize the oral qualities of a text that is currently available in script or print. The propositions concerning them (§57–§82) present these traits of oral narration as inherent qualities of folktales. But Olrik is fully aware of the literary context in which medieval texts occur, and hence he places the textual responsibility for them squarely with the observers and recorders of traditions (§14–§23), many of whom commit to writing only incomplete and fragmentary narratives. Furthermore, any evaluation and interpretation of these texts must take into consideration the circumstances and purposes of the recording (§42–§46). The emphasis on the writing of tradition reveals a sensitivity with which modern anthropology has only now caught up (Clifford and Marcus 1986). Although Olrik's narratives are subject to, and examples of, the "epic laws," they do not have an independent existence, but owe their literary qualities both to their initial oral performance and to their final commitment to writing. The preservation of the former depends on the adequacy of the latter.

Olrik was fully aware of the role of literacy in the preservation and presentation of orality, devoting several of his propositions to the description and analysis of their co-occurrence in medieval texts (§24–§36), suggesting methods and principles for the distinction between them. As he develops his theory of folklore, synchronic and diachronic considerations intertwine. The nature and history of tradition are interrelated. Since Olrik proposes that there is an inherent difference between folk and literary narratives, he follows up this distinction with the logical question concerning possible transference of themes and forms from one cultural sphere into the other. Restricting himself to literature, Olrik does not assume a possible enduring influence of written literature upon oral tradition, unless, of course, the literary themes had their origin in folklore to begin with, and were governed by the same "laws" of composition (§47–§56).

The "epic laws" (§57–§82) are descriptive propositions concerning the literary qualities inherent in folk narratives. In their formulation Olrik resorts to Aristotelian poetics, focusing on the unity of plot (§66–§69), the opening (§76) and the closing (§77) of the story, and the features that distinguish folktales from literary stories, such as episodic repetition (§61–§62), sharp contrasts along several dimensions (§71), and the limited number of characters in any narrative scene (§70–§74). Olrik's use of the "epic laws" is diagnostic rather than prescriptive or normative. They served him, and others who followed, to identify the oral and orally derived texts in a larger literary corpus. In biblical scholarship, for example, they had a most critical influence in the search for pre-scriptural traditional narratives (Kirkpatrick 1988:55–60). But as part of the *Principles,* it becomes apparent that Olrik assigned these "laws" a broader role. With their aid he sought to explain the process of oral composition and to describe the aesthetics of oral literature. In that regard Olrik was a precursor not only of morphological but also of formula analysis in folklore (Foley 1985).

Obviously it would be impossible to point out in the space of this foreword all the areas in which Olrik anticipated subsequent developments in folklore studies. Many of these trends have had their own course of historical development and had no direct indebtedness to Olrik's writings. The translation of the *Principles* could not correct this omission, but it can restore the role of theory to the history of folklore and could provide current trends with clear statements from the past in forging their intellectual dialogues for the future.

## REFERENCES

Clifford, James, and George Marcus, eds.
1986 *Writing Culture.* Berkeley: University of California Press.
Foley, John Miles
1985 *Oral-Formulaic Theory and Research: An Introduction and Anno-*

*tated Bibliography.* Garland Folklore Bibliographies vol. 6. New York: Garland.

Kirkpatrick, Patricia G.
1988 *The Old Testament and Folklore Study.* Journal for the Study of the Old Testament, Supplement Series 62. Sheffield: Sheffield Academic Press.

# Translators' Preface

The present translation was undertaken at the request of Bengt Holbek in January 1988. According to his express wish, the translation is kept as close as possible to the original in an attempt to capture Axel Olrik's crisp and eloquent, if somewhat dense, style without doing actual violence to English usage. The translation makes little pretense to literary elegance.

As this translation is primarily intended for students not conversant with Old Norse and modern Scandinavian languages, all quotations have been rendered into English. For the quotations from a number of Danish ballads, we have relied on E. M. Smith-Dampier's translation *A Book of Danish Ballads Selected and with an Introduction by Axel Olrik* (Princeton: Princeton University Press, 1939); all other translations are our own. In the notes and in our preparation of the bibliography, we have retained most of the references to Danish translations of Latin and Old Norse sources. For an English translation of Saxo's *Gesta Danorum,* we draw the reader's attention to Hilda Ellis Davidson and Peter Fisher, *Saxo Grammaticus: The History of the Danes, Book I–IX* I: *Text,* II: *Commentary* (Cambridge: Brewer, 1979–1980). For Old Norse works in English translation, the reader should consult Donald K. Fry, *Norse Sagas Translated into English: A Bibliography* (New York: AMS Press, 1980). Among the works by Olrik which are frequently referred to in the notes and which have appeared in English, the following should be mentioned: *The Heroic Legends of Denmark,* translated and revised by Lee M. Hollander (New York: American-Scandinavian Foundation, 1919); *Viking Civilization,* translated by J. W. Hartmann and H. A. Larsen (London: Allen and Unwin, 1930); and *A Book of Danish Ballads* (see above).

Hans Ellekilde's detailed description in the notes of his corrections of Olrik's occasional errors in spelling have been omitted; this information would be of little or no interest to the English reader.

During the progress of this translation we have had the constant cause to thank Bengt Holbek, who has been more than generous with his time and help, and we hope we have made good use of his criticisms. We welcome the opportunity to thank Jørgen Veisland for his many valuable suggestions and for his help in our preparation of the bibliography. Lanae Isaacson provided us with a useful list of Scandinavian ballads and folksongs in English translation. Phillip Pulsiano kindly undertook the task of copy-editing the entire manuscript, thereby saving us from many errors.

Charlottenlund,
July 1988

# Introduction

Olrik's *Principles,* perhaps the most comprehensive methodology for research in oral verbal art ever devised by a single person, was composed between 1905 and 1917. It was left incomplete at his death that year, but the body of the work was published four years later by Hans Ellekilde, one of his pupils, who meticulously accounted for its history and as far as possible filled out the sketchy paragraphs on the basis of his own lecture notes. It appeared in Danish, a language regrettably inaccessible to most scholars. Only one part of the work, the famous "Epic Laws," became widely known, because Olrik had given a lecture on that subject at a congress in Berlin in 1908. An expanded version of the lecture appeared in German in 1909, and an English translation of that was brought out in 1965; but the larger work of which it was but one section remained almost a secret until now.

Who was Axel Olrik? There is such an intimate relation between the man and his work that familiarity with one is almost a prerequisite for understanding the other. An English edition of *Principles* may be regarded as a tribute, a monument, *to* Olrik; but it will at the same time be a monument *by* and *of* Olrik.

Axel Olrik was born in Copenhagen in 1864 and lived there all his life. After leaving school in 1881, he enrolled at the University of Copenhagen, where he studied Scandinavian philology and folklore with Svend Grundtvig, the leading Scandinavian folklorist at the time. After Grundtvig's early death in 1883, he concentrated on philology and history. He wrote his M.A. thesis in 1887 and his Ph.D. thesis in 1892. Shortly afterwards he became a teacher (*docent*) at the University of Copenhagen, finally to become professor of folklore in 1913.

He grew up in a milieu favorable to the arts and the humanities. His father was a painter, and in later life he kept up lively contacts with the leading artists of his day. This perhaps explains his intense awareness of the visual qualities of oral verbal art, of its almost palpable contrasting of man and monster, bull and serpent, etc., in what has here been called *tableaux*. He realized that the traditional storytellers and singers retained these tableaux in their imaginations and built their poetry around them. Literature, particularly national and romantic literature, was read in Olrik's childhood home. He learned early to appreciate literary quality, as may be seen, e.g., from his reconstructions of the "original forms" of tales and ballads. He published them in editions which became immensely popular. His own writing is characterized by elegance and clarity, a fact which must be ascribed to his preoccupation with literature from an early age.

There is another aspect to his writing that does not come across in an English translation: he was a purist; he strove to avoid words and phrases of foreign origin. This tendency expresses a national feeling that could be found in the bourgeoisie of most European countries in Olrik's lifetime. And he certainly had strong national feelings, like his entire milieu. Not only the novels, plays, and poems of the Romantic era, but also the great literature of medieval Scandinavia was eagerly read at home and in school for the express purpose of fostering pride in one's own national identity.

It therefore came as a shock to the young Olrik when Sophus Bugge, the Norwegian philologist, endeavored to show that the great Norse myths were nothing but Christian and Celtic tales, imported and adapted during the Viking period. Olrik writes:

> When I was in the top form at the Metropolitan School, sixteen or seventeen years old, the air was crackling with new theories on the age and origin of Scandinavian philology. One of these was Bugge's ancient Christian-Irish theory; another was Worsaae's interpretation of the golden horns, which tended in a directly opposite direction. They awoke in me an aspiration to penetrate into the heretofore hidden springs of culture, but also a dread of going wrong at the critical points. With this scholar's mortal dread in me, I came to emphasize the outlook which is really present in the sources themselves as they are, both individually and collectively; and I was subsequently faced with a tradition for the study of Scandinavian narratives the basic characteristic of which I may most concisely call the typological—the classification of uniform types in family groups, in which each individual deviation must be judged according to the whole series of

texts in question . . . the narrative not as a mosaic but as an organism was what I received as the fundamental idea. (Olrik 1907, 188).

What Olrik objected to even before his own scholarly education was the kind of comparative research that is based on superficial and accidental similarities. He needed a firm method and had the great luck to learn it from Grundtvig.

Svend Grundtvig (1824–1883), Olrik's predecessor as professor of folklore in Copenhagen, had begun his main work, the editing of the traditional Danish ballads, in 1847. He had developed a method for handling great numbers of ballad records belonging to the same type while working at his monumental edition (*Danmarks gamle Folkeviser* I–XII, Copenhagen, 1853–1976; DgF + no. refers to ballad type) and had, in 1881, published an exemplary study of DgF 47 in which the method was clearly explained and demonstrated (DgF vol. IV, 852–874). Olrik then studied with Grundtvig, the last half-year under his personal guidance, and thus was trained to observe the "life" of ballads in oral tradition with their incessant change and adaptation to ever-new local and cultural environments.

Nevertheless, a profound difference between the two men's views of ballad tradition evolved. Grundtvig's view of history was Hegelian; he saw it as a gradual emergence of individual character. The ballads had been created at a time when only nations, not yet persons, possessed pronounced individuality; the people "sang as one man." In later times, classes and finally individual personalities had evolved, and they were now the bearers of the nation's hopes and aspirations. But the ballads were the specific product of the "folk poetic" era, i.e., the Middle Ages, for which reason their history could be described in terms of a "Big Bang" followed by streams and trickles which would, in time, peter out—a devolutionary view, in Dundes's (1969) sense. By contrast, Olrik developed a Darwinist view (*Principles,* §§85–87): different forms of a type and different types compete, and the stronger and better forms prevail; thus, the general trend is evolutionary rather then devolutionary. Olrik himself mentions that when he took over the editing of the ballads (Grundtvig was half through vol. V when he died, and Olrik got almost through vol. VIII), he stressed the independent value of the ballads recorded from oral tradition in the nineteenth century, where Grundtvig had regarded them as secondary as compared to the great corpus of ballads recorded by the Danish (and Swedish) nobility between circa 1550 and 1700. Likewise, where Grundtvig had stressed the unity of Scandinavian ballad tradition, Olrik observed characteristic differences between Eastern (Denmark, Sweden) and Western (Norway, the Atlantic Islands) Scandinavian tradition. Finally, Olrik found differences in attitude, e.g., toward supernatural beings, which could be ascribed to different epochs or different social classes. The difference between the two men perhaps comes most clearly to the fore in their handling of the thorny problem of reconstructing original forms. To take but one example: in his study of the Ribold ballad (DgF 82), Grundtvig, in conformity with his "Big Bang" theory, included everything of value in all extant versions, to arrive at an original form consisting of 105 strophes. Olrik based his procedure on the principle that only those strophes which were found in all or nearly all versions could be confidently assumed to have been present in the original form; his reconstruction of the same ballad therefore contains but 32 strophes. The method is explained in *Principles,* §§161–179.

It is one of the curious quirks of history that the typological method that Olrik learned from Grundtvig was independently developed by Julius Krohn in Finland at the same time. His emphasis was somewhat different, however. On the one hand, there was almost no Finnish material prior to the nineteenth century that could be compared to the vast material available to Danish ballad scholars; on the other hand, the Finns had recorded far more intensively and evenly from contemporary oral tradition than had the Danes, for which reason geographical considerations were more prominent in their version of the method. One of the basic assumptions was that songs would change but little as long as they were handed down in the same area, whereas they would be adapted when they made their way into new areas; thus, the geographical distribution would reveal the history of their wanderings. It is no wonder, then, that the actual historical "life" of the ballads loomed larger in the historico-geographical approach of the Danes than in the geographico-historical approach of the Finns. The main proponents of the latter, Kaarle Krohn and Antti Aarne, tended to view the "handing down" in more mechanical and devolutionary terms; but the underlying typological concept was the same (cf. Taylor 1928; Holbek 1969–70, 261f.).

Modern folklorists have followed the general trend in related disciplines such as anthropology and linguistics—the transition from diachronic to synchronic approaches—to such an extent that the problems that were the primary concerns of earlier generations have been partly lost from view; but it is impossible to understand Olrik and his contemporaries until one realizes that they saw it as their main task to reconstruct the unwritten cultural *history* of the peoples, or, more often, of their own nation. The study of folklore was widely regarded as part of the national philology, i.e., the study of the spiritual history of the people as it appeared in their language and literature; the specific contribution of the folklorist was to incorporate the evidence of oral tradition in this effort. It is in keeping with this view that Olrik turned to the study of philology and history at Grundtvig's death. His history teacher was Kristian Erslev, whose *Principles for the Evaluation of Historical Sources* (1892) was to become the methodological model for Olrik's own *Principles*. Nor is it surprising that he chose to specialize in Saxo, the historian whose *Gesta Danorum* (Deeds of the Danes) from circa 1200 still constitutes a unique challenge to Danish scholarship. Both Olrik's M.A. and Ph.D. theses concentrate on the first nine of Saxo's sixteen "books," those which deal with prehistoric times (down to the tenth century). They consist largely of tales and euhemerized myths, and Olrik took upon himself the task of unraveling Saxo's sources for this material. Saxo had written in his preface that he had drawn upon the knowledge of learned Icelanders, and this became the starting point of Olrik's analysis: Was it possible to distinguish between Icelandic and Danish sources?

The answer, given in Olrik's thesis and in a companion volume from 1894, was an emphatic yes: it was indeed possible to discern two categories of sources. The method by which he showed that a story in Saxo was Icelandic in origin may be demonstrated by an example, the tale of Hadding in the first book:

The tale as a whole reveals a striking resemblance to Norse *fornaldarsögur* (tales of a mythical past), a genre that has no known equivalent in Danish literature. It appears that the narrator had next to no first-hand knowledge of Denmark, whereas he was thoroughly familiar with Norway (observations of this kind became the germ of the chapter "Horizon and Localization," *Principles,* §§109–134).

> The stage of the tale is . . . precisely those countries which play the most prominent role in the Icelandic adventure sagas, but which are almost never mentioned in traditional Danish legends. In its content, the tale completely corresponds to the Icelanders' medieval heroic sagas: numerous feats performed in Viking raids, or during wanderings from place to place; a throng of characters who make their appearance, soon to disappear again; men and supernatural beings by the score; the giants and Woden, appearing in the same way as in the Icelandic sagas, and . . . the giant maiden who is the hero's foster mother and lover. The whole strewn with numerous small poems.

A personal name such as *Guthorm* is Norse; the Danish equivalent would be *Gorm.* The saga itself is preserved only in Saxo, but all other testimonies to its existence are Norwegian or Icelandic. Besides, the more recent parts of the Icelandic *Örvar-Odds saga* correspond so closely to Saxo's story that they must be considered a retelling based on a lost Norse Hadding's saga. None of these criteria are met in the parts of Saxo which Olrik believes to be drawn from Danish folklore. "I base," he writes,

> no part of my decision upon Saxo, but (1) I define the Danish style from ancient legends . . . , (2) I establish the same style in contemporary historical tradition, and (3) and (4) I pursue similarities with this style in particularly typical features as found in Saxo's heroic tales and in folk legends. On certain later occasions . . . I have shown that the same rules which we meet in these legends are also found in the ballads; for I was anxious to reveal the individual features—just as in the Norse sagas—as elements in a whole national culture. (Holbek 1969–70, 268)

Later on, Olrik realized that the "Danish" narrative style was actually the style of oral narrative art and that the "rules" described the formal features imposed upon the narratives by their oral existence. From this insight he developed the epic laws which were, then, means of discerning oral material in ancient literary sources.

In the introduction to the second volume of his Saxo study, Olrik further develops his view that in order to understand the relationship between the sources one must penetrate into each individual tale's poetic character and its relation to other poetry, see it as "a living organism, borne along by its own fundamental ideas, corresponding to the stage of development of the people, and ceaselessly changing as these stages change; each individual narrative existing in an uninterrupted symbiosis with its great kindred, the thousands of traditions of the people." This view represented a step forward as compared to what he had received from Grundtvig. In 1892, he had met Moltke Moe, the leading Norwegian folklorist at the time. After he had defended his thesis, he spent a semester in Christiania (now Oslo) to study with Moe and Bugge and also to study Irish and Lappish (in order to be able to evaluate at first hand the folklore of these peoples which had, respectively, influenced and been influenced by Scandinavian folklore). In his biography of Moe, Olrik sums up the inspiration he received from him:

> Hitherto my development had gone in a critical direction, borne up by the exact lines of philology, and influenced perhaps still more by the critical method of historical research. From the day in spring 1885 when Saxo's sources opened themselves to me, through the Ballad edition, of which the distinction of the different nature of the aristocratic song and the rustic song had been my personal contribution, and until now, when my dissertation on "The partition of Saxo's sources" was in the press, and soon to be defended for the Philosophical Doctor degree . . . , since that day, I say, I had, one-sided as I was, gone in the same direction. Now suddenly a new point of view was presented to me, which, although fully appreciating the character of each detail, yet accepted it, from first to last, as representing the totality. Svend Grundtvig's ideal perception of the transmission as a living organism, hitherto existing in the conception of single tales, unveiled itself with a more solid foundation of common reasoning, which accepted the primitive thought of humanity as the decisive factor. (1915, 6–7)

It can hardly be doubted that Moe was influenced by the British evolutionists, among them E. B. Tylor, whose *Primitive Culture* inspired so many at the time; but Moe developed his own view of the "Basic Epic Laws" that governed the life and development of verbal art in oral tradition. It was presented in a series of lectures first held in 1889 and later repeated, to be printed posthumously 1914–17. Moe visualized the trend in verbal art as an unceasing striving toward perfection, a view that Olrik not only accepted but later worked into the larger body of his own *Principles* (§§83–108). Their Finnish colleagues and friends, Krohn and Aarne, took up the same problem, although in a more devolutionary vein (see *Enzyklopädie des Märchens* s.v. "Epische Gesetze"). It is characteristic of this generation of Nordic scholars that they were not content to observe local variation, but wanted to explain it as part of a historical process. Of the quartet, Olrik was perhaps the most "optimistic." He not only saw variant forms as the effects of a ceaseless struggle for survival, but also believed that it was possible to distinguish between "lower" and "higher" forms emanating, respectively, from "lower" and "higher" cultures. The folklore of the latter would generally prevail, and thus there would always be a trend toward ever more perfect folklore.

One question this theory would have to answer was, of course, what constituted stronger or better forms. Olrik's answer was based on his sense of the aesthetic qualities in oral narrative art. A narrative with a strong imagery, with a clear and generally accepted tendency, and with a sound structure would thrive and spread, whereas the weaker one would perish. These thoughts were included at various points in *Principles,* e.g., §§10–12.

Olrik borrowed the term "epic law" from Moe, but used it in a different sense. Shortly after the turn of the century (Holbek 1969–70, 290), he began paying more attention to the details of form in the narratives he was studying for his great work on the *Heroic Legends of Denmark* (1903–10); expressions such as "the natural laws of the supernatural" began appearing in his writings, and by the fall of 1906, most of the "laws" had been defined. A later reworking became chapter III of *Principles* (§§57–82).

By another of those quirks of history, virtually the same

discovery was made at the same time by Hermann Gunkel, the German theologian. Olrik gave a lecture on the subject in 1908 and Gunkel read it when it was printed in 1909. He was then preparing the third edition of his commentary to the book of Genesis in which he had applied much the same criteria to determine which of the tales in that book derived from oral tradition. He wrote a letter to Olrik, who in turn applied the laws to part of the material studied by Gunkel (see the Appendix below).

In time, Olrik realized that the epic laws did not apply to all oral narrative genres in the same way and to the same extent. This caused him to ponder the specificity of the various genres, and chapter VI of *Principles* was devoted to the subject. It is to be regretted that the work was barely begun when he died. This chapter would have constituted the first major genre analysis in the field of oral verbal art; instead, it became a list of promises. The paragraphs on heroic poetry and local legends were written, whereas the rest has to be inferred from the general observations in §§4–6.

After the work on Saxo, Olrik had proceeded to study the ancient heroic legends of Denmark as they could still be discerned in a variety of medieval sources. In time, this led him to the study of first Scandinavian, then comparative mythology and religion. His interests ranged ever wider, and the ardent nationalism of his youth was tempered by the wider perspective of the mature researcher. In 1905, when he had taught folklore for a decade, he felt a need to gather his experience in the form of a comprehensive methodological exposition in which all the leading ideas of his time were to be brought together in the form of a single structure. His *Principles* therefore began its existence as a series of lecture notes that were revised each time he gave the same course.

Olrik had no intention of offering novel ideas or passing himself off as an oracle. He simply intended to describe the methods every student of folklore ought to know. Most, but by no means all, of his copious examples were taken from his own studies, but he quoted others just as readily. The emphasis was, however, on the theses themselves rather than on the practical demonstration of their validity. He endeavored to express them in the form of terse statements, much like those of a grammar. And a "grammar of oral narrative art" is what he wrote. A brief summary of the contents may be given as follows:

In chapter I (§§1–12), the concept of oral narrative (*sagn*) is described and some basic questions are dealt with: What does oral narrative mean? How does oral verbal art differ from literature? Which are its main categories? What can be said about the question of individual authorship?

In chapter II (§§13–56), the character of oral narratives as sources is discussed: their place in relation to other historical sources, their value as historical evidence, the relations between oral narratives and literature, etc. In this chapter, the influence of Olrik's history teachers, particularly Kristian Erslev, is felt.

In chapter III (§§57–82), the epic laws are described. This is Olrik's most original contribution.

In chapter IV (§§83–143), Olrik gives his version of the "basic epic laws" first formulated by Moe. He then goes on to describe his own concepts of "horizon" and "localization," finally to devote a section to Tylor's concept of "survival."

In chapter V (§§144–184), which is incomplete, Olrik describes the historico-geographical method. (Fuller accounts were subsequently given in Aarne 1913 and Krohn 1926.) A special section is devoted to the various principles for the reconstruction of original forms, a problem that was later to be developed more fully by Walter Anderson (1935).

In chapter VI (§§185–196), Olrik makes an attempt to solve the problem of genre analysis.

The Appendix contains Olrik's analysis of the tales of the Patriarchs of Israel by means of the epic laws. In addition, Ellekilde has included a draft for a rejoinder to Friedrich von der Leyen, who had criticized the "Finnish-Danish" method.

The years between 1904 and 1910 were, on the whole, the most fertile ones in Olrik's life. By this time, he was a seasoned scholar at the height of his intellectual power and with a singularly rich and diversified production behind him. The *Principles* should be seen in conjunction with a series of organizational initiatives which he took at the same time.

In 1904, he founded the journal *Danske Studier* (Danish Studies) together with the philologist Marius Kristensen. It was to be the main stage for Danish folkloristic debate for several decades, and from then on, most of Olrik's minor studies, reviews, etc., were published there.

In 1904–05, he founded the Danish Folklore Archives, which was to become the main repository for recordings of Danish folklore, and he remained its director until 1915.

In 1907, he was a co-founder—together with Krohn in Finland, Moe in Norway, Johannes Bolte in Germany, and the young C. W. von Sydow in Sweden—of the international society "FF" (Folklore Fellows, Fédération des Folkloristes, Folkloristischer Forscherbund, Foreningen af Folkemindeforskere), which began editing the great series *FF Communications* in 1910. The first two issues described the Danish Folklore Archives and the system of folktales devised by Grundtvig.

In 1908, he founded the Society *Danmarks Folkeminder* (The Folklore of Denmark), the members of which were to collect folklore for the archives and to receive editions and studies of folklore in return. Only the second half of this plan was successful in the long run.

In 1909 and 1910, the society formed committees on dialects and place names. Both still exist, now as departments at the University of Copenhagen.

Olrik thus created or helped create a widely ramified and surprisingly durable structure for the collecting, preserving, studying, and publishing of folklore. He had a vision, shared with Krohn and the others (see Krohn 1907 on the founding of FF), of an international system in which each nation had its own society, archives, and university chair, and all were united in the international umbrella organization FF. The germ of these ideas came from Finland, where the Finnish Literature Society (founded 1831) and the Swedish Literature Society (founded 1885) had organized collecting, archiving, and publishing activities long before. It is unquestionably an effect of Olrik's and Krohn's influence that a folklore archives was founded in Lund (Sweden) in 1913 and another in Kristiania/Oslo (Norway) in 1914.

It is probable that *Principles* was to play a part in this structure. The FF had been formed to facilitate international cooperation in the comparative study of tales, ballads, etc., and the scholars who were to cooperate naturally had to be schooled in the same methods. There is no evidence that Olrik had planned translations of *Principles* into other languages, but he was still relatively young, only 52, when he died, and there is little doubt that the book was intended for an international public. He would have expected the users to supply their own examples from folklore familiar to them, but it is obvious that he regarded the methods described in the book as generally valid.

This idea is of course *passé,* at least in one sense. The concerns of modern folkloristics are fundamentally different from those of the early twentieth century. To mention but two points: Olrik paid little heed to individual performers or to the process of performance as such. His main interest was medieval *texts* of anonymous origin. Similarly, he was curiously oblivious to the persistent tone of social protest and criticism in folklore, not only because this tone was comparatively weak in his medieval sources, but also because he, like other bourgeois scholars of his time, tended to think of the nation as an organic whole rather than as a stage for strife and social unrest. The contemporary folklorist will find other omissions as well, but that is to be expected.

In another sense, however, Olrik's *Principles* is timeless. Those who turn to historical studies of folklore will find that his observations are astute and largely valid even today. The epic laws, which have been tested over and over, are hardly in need of any correction. The discussion of the relations between oral verbal art and literature in chapter II contains numerous observations of lasting value. And there is inspiration to be found even in theses that run counter to modern experience.

This edition is therefore justified in a double sense: on the one hand, it distills the essence of the achievements of folklore research just before the outbreak of the First World War; on the other, it offers a wealth of insight into historical studies of folklore, much of which is still valid.

Bengt Holbek

# REFERENCES

Aarne, Antti
1913 *Leitfaden der vergleichenden Märchenforschung (FFC 13)*. Hamina.
Anderson, Walter
1935 *Zu Albert Wesselski's Angriffen auf die finnische folkloristische Arbeitsmethode*. Tartu.
Bugge, Sophus
1881–96 *Studier over de nordiske Gude- og Heltesagns Oprindelse* I–II. Christiania.
Dundes, Alan
1965 (ed.) *The Study of Folklore*. Englewood Cliffs, N.J.
1969 The Devolutionary Premise in Folklore Theory. *Journal of the Folklore Institute* 6, 5–19.
Erslev, Kristian
1892 *Grundsætninger for historisk Kildekritik*. Copenhagen.
Grundtvig, Svend et al.
1853–1976 *Danmarks gamle Folkeviser* I–XII. Copenhagen.
Gunkel, Hermann
1910 *Genesis übersetzt und erklärt*, 3d ed. Göttingen.
Holbek, Bengt
1969–70 Axel Olrik (1864–1917). *Arv* 25–26, 259–296.
Krohn, Kaarle
1907 Första meddelande från förbundet F.F. *Danske Studier* 1907, 221–224.
1926 *Die folkloristische Arbeitsmethode*. Oslo.
Lunding, Astrid
1910 *The System of Tales in the Folklore Collection of Copenhagen* (FFC 2). Helsinki.
Moe, Moltke
1914–17 De episke grundlove. *Edda* II, 1–16, 233–249; IV, 85–126; VII, 72–88.
Olrik, Axel
1892 *Forsøg på en tvedeling af kilderne til Sakses oldhistorie*. Copenhagen.
1894 *Kilderne til Sakses oldhistorie. En litteraturhistorisk undersøgelse. II Norrøne sagaer og danske sagn*. Copenhagen.
1903–10 *Danmarks heltedigtning. En oldtidsstudie* I–II. Copenhagen. (English ed. of part I: *The Heroic Legends of Denmark*. Scandinavian Monographs vol. IV. New York, 1919.)
1907 Sophus Bugge. *Danske Studier* 1907, 180–192.
1909 Epische Gesetze der Volksdichtung. *Zeitschrift für deutsches Altertum und deutsche Literatur* 51, 1–12. English translation in Dundes 1965, 129–141.
1910 *Dansk Folkemindesamling (DFS). The National Collection of Folklore in Copenhagen* (FFC 1). Helsinki.

1915 *Personal Impressions of Moltke Moe* (FFC 17). Hamina.
Ranke, Kurt et al.
1975ff.   (ed.) *Enzyklopädie des Märchens* Iff. Berlin/New York.
Taylor, Archer
1928   Precursors of the Finnish method. *Modern Philology* 25, 481–491.
Tylor, Edward B.
1871   *Primitive Culture* I–II. London.

# PRINCIPLES
## ❧ F O R
# ORAL NARRATIVE
# RESEARCH ❧ ❧ ❧ ❧

# CHAPTER

### ❧ 1 ❧

## INTRODUCTION

### The Narrative as Folklore

§1. The primary task of oral narrative research is to understand the narrative as part of human intellectual life. The secondary task of oral narrative research is to use the narrative as evidence of external conditions, such as social structure, worship, and political events.

§2. Narrative, in the broadest sense of the word, designates a report of an event that is passed along by word of mouth without the informants' being able to check its origin or its previous authorities.

With this very broad delimitation of the concept of "narrative," we do not judge whether or not the report is true in itself, or whether or not the narrators regarded it as true, as doubtful, or as invented (a tale).

This type of narrative comes continuously into existence. A rumor is a narrative about a recent event, usually in a brief and ephemeral form. It is disseminated from the time the event took place until well-attested information about it is presented. Contemporary rumors can easily become narratives over a period of time.

Example. Óláfr Tryggvason's death in the battle of Svold. In his commemorative poem about the king, the skald Hallfreðr said that it was rumored that he had escaped, but that new and more detailed reports had proved this untrue.[1] Yet, two hundred years later, the monk Oddr wrote in his *Óláfs saga*[2] an account of the king's escape and of his later adventures in Wendland, Russia, and the Holy Land, according to what "a judicious man by the name of Sóti skald" had related.

§3. Most narratives are items of folklore, i.e., they are told over an indeterminate number of years within the non-book-learned classes of society.

"Folklore" is information handed down from generation to generation in a certain definite form, such as in verse (poem, jingle, melody, proverb, riddle), prose (narrative), play, and custom. In a broader sense, folklore comprises every customary practice within the non-book-learned classes of society, in sports, trade, management, etc.[1]

Comment. On the other hand, the undefined manifestations of the inner life of the "people" belong to ethnopsychology. Insofar as the whole physical condition of the human being is also included, it can all be contained under the designation of anthropology.

Language occupies a somewhat special position in the way it is used in the non-book-learned classes of society, or insofar as it is influenced by the world view of these classes. It is congruent with folklore, because vocabulary and linguistic structure are external forms for thought and pass by word of mouth. But these means of expression have no independent existence; they are constantly combined into new (i.e., personalized) phrases. Accordingly, linguistics does not belong to folkloristics, but is as close to it as any of the other related branches of scholarship. Of course, all forms of ethnopsychological investigation are of great importance for folkloristics.

Literature: A comprehensive exposition of the above does not exist. However, reference can be made to Hartland (1891), introduction; *English and Scottish Popular Ballads,* Kittredge's introduction.[2]

§4. Folklore offers scholars a valuable tool for research, because it leads into eras and classes of society whose intellectual life we would otherwise know only to a limited degree. Moreover, it offers material which, because of its richness and regularity, is suited to scholarly study.

In the following discussion, we will mean by the term "narrative" that which pertains to "folklore." Related accounts from more recent times and other classes of society can naturally be included to illustrate the creation of narratives.[1] In the same way, any empirical observation of the inner life of human beings is also important for understanding culturally or temporally remote conditions; but this is not the immediate concern of folkloristics.

§5. The most important categories of narratives are lay, saga, and narrative (in the more limited sense meaning "folktale").

(1) A lay[1] is a narrative in verse. In terms of content, it oscillates between saga and legend. Most frequently it has a rather simple plot, but offers a fuller account than prose renderings.[2]

(2) A saga is a narrative of considerable length and with a more complex plot. Its two main forms are the heroic saga (including the historical saga) and the tale. The former is regarded by its narrators as primarily historical, the latter as invented.

(3) A legend is short, with a single plot, normally one episode, and frequently culminates in a character's terse exclamation. Its two main forms are the origin legend and the anecdote. The origin legend (etiological legend) serves to explain the origin of a thing, and gains credibility by the actual existence of this thing (the reality of its existence evokes belief in the validity of the cause). The most frequent form of the origin legend is the local origin legend, i.e., a legend that explains the origin of a local phenomenon. (Cf. on this subject chapter IV B.) The anecdote is a narrative that is not localized; it shows a person (normally a well-known person) in a characteristic situation.[3]

Comment 1. Here as few divisions as possible are used. It would be more complete to establish a series of transitional forms between tale and legend. Within the supernatural realm and primitive culture, the series would be: tale proper—animal tale[4]—fantastic legend—nonlocal legend—local legend. Within more developed societies, the corresponding series would be: folk novella (e.g., *The King's Treasury, Rampsinitus*[5])—jocular tale—anecdote—local legend.

Comment 2. Note the meaning of the word "saga"; in most Scandinavian languages, it also includes genuine tales.[6] In both ancient and more recent times, the term is sometimes used—incorrectly with regard to folklore—to describe the purely learned historical account that is not shaped by oral tradition (e.g., *Sverris saga,* a contemporary biography of King Sverrir).[7]

Comment 3. Folk drama resembles legend when it does not give its audience the impression of being about contemporary events, but rather of being the reflection of something from the past (e.g., religious feasts that recall an event in the life of a god). The same applies to lays in dialogues (e.g., *Bjarkamál,* several lays of the *Elder Edda*):[8] their use of the present tense is only a convention.

Common to all these forms of narrative is the clear picture of the individual situation, often so distinct as to approach pictorial definition, and displaying a characteristic power in the speech of the characters. Apart from these forms, small, vaguer remnants of narratives exist that contain an account about something ancient, but not as a completed plot (e.g., that here there was a forest in the old days, that here a person drowned himself). Of a similarly simple structure are the remnants of beliefs from former times that express a perception about something contemporaneous (that here elves lived in the bog, that here the trees must not be cut, that wheels must not turn at Christmas, and the like). The remnant of a narrative is the form in which the consciousness of past conditions is generally preserved, even if increasingly blurred by successive generations. It continuously receives a strong influx of impressions from reality and, correspondingly, omits that which is forgotten.

Comment 4. In folk transmission, there is a need to shape the remnants of narratives with the same kind of palpability found in the narrative: "There once was so much forest that a bride could drive in shadow from Skovby to the church at Sevel."[9] By virtue of this need for palpability, for creating an impression of tangible reality within the folk transmission, the remnants of narratives can swell into a genuine narrative; or this need may cause an already extant narrative to become associated with a new place, namely, that place which until now had only remnants of narratives linked to it.

Comment 5. Prophecies are normally similar to remnants of legends in inner structure (e.g., at some time Elsinore will sink so low that it will become a fishing hamlet and Hornbæk will become a town);[10] but now and then they resemble full-blown narratives (the battle of Ogier the Dane against the Turks).[11]

§6. Myths about gods are not a special category of narrative, but are distributed among the above-mentioned forms. The "origin legend" and a rather tale-like form of "legend" are the most conspicuous categories. "Myth," therefore, designates not form but content. It is a narrative that concerns supernatural situations and whose main character possesses superhuman abilities.

Comment 1. A large number of present-day "narratives about supernatural creatures" are thus not myths. They probably fulfill the first of these requirements—i.e., they are set in supernatural situations—but not the second, because the characters with whom they are concerned are human beings who become involved with the supernatural (the charcoal-burner who receives a visit from the elf-woman, the girl who is lured into the mountains but set free, etc.).[1]

The "religious legend" is an account in which a divine creature or a person endowed with divine gifts plays an important role, and which is told in order to influence the audience (by emphasizing the power of the divinity, or its justice or goodness).[2] Therefore, it essentially belongs to the "higher" religions. With regard to form, it is sometimes saga-like in scope, sometimes a local legend (often, however, with a poorly developed setting and localization), or sometimes like a short origin legend from the animal world (the lapwing that said, when Christ was on the cross, "Torture him!").[3]

Comment 2. The expression "religious legend" belongs to Christianity. The word "legenda" means a passage to be read, i.e., an account that is read aloud at religious gatherings because of its devotional character. Therefore, it is different from "myth," which flourishes most prolifically in the somewhat lower religions and easily acquires an undertone of entertainment or tale.

As there are myths about gods, there are also myths about heroes. The adventures of the hero and his abilities surpass human limits (e.g., a fight against monsters, a journey into the otherworld, an ancestor's arrival from the otherworld, the creation myths of groups of peoples, e.g., Finns or Indians).[4]

Comment 3. A hero is a champion who possesses mythical characteristics. Skjold is a hero;[5] Hrolf and Hagbard, on the other hand, are not. Hercules is a hero, but not Achilles or Menelaus. (Note: Only the narrative concept is considered here. The historian of religion will understand by "hero" a worshipped ancestor;[6] his concept of "hero," therefore, will coincide on only a few points with the narrative concept.)

Comment 4. Note that the division of myths according to content and religious value only partly coincides with the formal classifications of oral narrative research. The narratives that belong to divine worship are normally origin legends, but not vice versa. (Note the strong tendency of several more recent historians of religion[7] to attach the term "myth" exclusively to brief narratives that display religious respect, or even just to origin legends, which are connected to some sort of divine worship; designations such as "legend" or "divine tale" are used in referring to the other myths about gods. These designations are, from a folkloristic point of view, unfortunate, because the religious value is neither constant in itself nor easy to demonstrate in individual cases.)

§7. Heroic narratives, like myths about gods, are not in themselves a category of narrative parallel to the main categories that have been delineated above, but are distributed among them—mostly among lay and saga,[1] and less frequently among local legend and remnants of narratives.[2] Their essential characteristic is found in the subject: they are about ancestors, i.e., about people from whom contemporary families are descended, or about members of the same group of people; they display the human traits of the present time, but on a larger scale (often with regard to size, even more often with regard to strength, and to spiritual abilities). The accounts are founded on a mixture of a belief in the truth of the narrative and a tendency to embellish it arbitrarily. The formal structure specific to the heroic narrative is that a composition about the same hero or about the same group of people has a certain uniform character (even though the narrative material is told, for example, in several different lays). Moreover, there is a tendency to create larger, integrated groupings, partly by having many ancient champions meet in the same royal hall or on the same venture,[3] partly by intertwining the fates of several generations and also

by repeating the most important motifs of the plot over generations; the latter is very conspicuous in Norse heroic composition.

Literature: Grundtvig (1867); Olrik (1903–1910) I, §56.

§8. Historical narrative stands even less securely as a narrative category. It is a term used especially about briefer narratives (origin legends, anecdotes, remnants of narratives) when
they contain the name of a historical person, or when they relate
something that is close to events that have actually taken place,
or at least relate something that, from a modern scholarly standpoint, could have taken place.[1]

§9. Some scholars have defined folklore in opposition to
individual production within a higher culture: items of folklore,
they maintain, are created by an entire group or succession of
people, with no single person identifiable as the author.

It is true that folklore reveals only a small degree of individual
imprint, and that it is more or less continuously reshaped by
those who recite it. It is likewise true that striving toward giving
one's rendering a personal imprint is the surest sign that we are
outside the realm of folklore. (Particular attention must be paid
to these phenomena by those who want to investigate folklore
in more detail, not least if one wants to test the authenticity of
the material.) But it is false to define the substance of scholarship on the basis of that which can be concluded only from
an extensive examination. Furthermore, it will lead to the construction of quite perilous and extremely impractical boundaries:
Are not some Danish medieval ballads composed by individuals,
while others are not?

Therefore, without embarking upon a theory of origin, we
can say that the lack of authorial imprint in individual works
stands as a distinctive feature of oral narrative composition.

Comment. There is a large group of scholars who regard the nature
of oral narrative composition as consisting above all in the fact that
it is produced by the people as a whole, rather than being the work
of an individual. This idea originated with the Grimms and those
influenced by them; it is seen very distinctly in Grundtvig ("Darum

ist das Volks-Individuum als solches, nicht das einfache Menschen-Individuum, als Dichter der Volkspoesie zu betrachten," etc.,[1] in *Dänische Volkslieder,* introduction, p. XXIII). Recently, it has been asserted especially by American authors: *Old English Ballads,* introduction; *English and Scottish Popular Ballads,* introduction; Beatty (1914). In opposition to this idea stand a substantial number of scholars, especially those who are concerned primarily with other aspects of literature and language and only to a limited degree with "oral narrative composition." With a certain disdain toward the contrary standpoint, they claim that every literary work must be created by an individual author.[2] This position is asserted by many literary historians, but an approximation of the same view is also found in the work of many contemporary folklorists, e.g., those folktale scholars who believe that the tales are created by individuals in a form that is the root of the entire existing tradition.[3]

One can restate these general controversies as a series of questions that focus on individual problems: (1) Have individuals composed a part (or all) of the works we designate as "oral narrative composition"? (2) Did these individuals form so close an attachment to the society to which they belonged that it was not a question of individual works in a way similar to literary compositions of more recent times? (3) Did the works come into existence during group performances (e.g., as improvisation during dance), of which no individual has the right to be called the author? (4) Has the work been transformed to such an extent that, for this reason, it cannot be considered as being produced by any individual author? (5) Has it, by its conscious composition, absorbed so much from the style and contents of older works that, for this reason, it cannot be considered the work of an individual?

Scholarship urges the following points: (1) Some items of oral narrative composition, e.g., many Scandinavian ballads, must have been produced by individuals with the deliberate intention of creating a literary work.[4] (2) It is certain that authorial contribution is found less here than in more recent literature, and even where it may exist, it eludes our investigation. (3) A spontaneous production on the part of several people can possibly be demonstrated in satirical ballads, where a whole group of people during a dance are known to have created ballads by alternating improvisations.[5] (4) Considerable transformation can occur during a lengthy oral transmission, especially with regard to the oral form of the work; however, even the most extensive revision leaves the plot intact, which provides evidence that the ballad retains its identity throughout its transformations (see, e.g., the *Elfshot* ballad discussed in chapter IV below). Transformations over a period of time can probably be severe and considerably reduce the imprint of the original author, but they cannot abolish the thought that created the essential artistic form. If the revision is thorough, a new literary work comes into existence that has most of its plot in common with its predecessor. (5) When a transformation of older contents and expressions (strophes) appears, it is designated as new oral narrative composition, with a conception and a treatment of the material different from its model.

Example (to 3 above). There is evidence that satirical ballads are often produced by improvisations within a whole group of dancers (*Old English Ballads,* pp. XXXIIff.). It will be more difficult to demonstrate this method of composition with regard to serious ballads. (When Gummere gives the ballad about "The Sold One"[6] as an example, at least as a construed example, this does not square with the character of the ballad: the refusals of her various kinsmen to buy her back consistently point toward the final solution that only the betrothed is willing to do this.)

Example (to 5 above). DgF 459 *Sir Oluf dies on his Wedding Day*[7] in relation to its model DgF 47 *Elfshot.* In the Scandinavian (and northern English and Scottish) ballads called *Hildebrand* and *Ribold* (DgF 82–83), it can be difficult to say where one ends and the other begins: the *Ribold* ballad with its slightly courtly color, the Danish *Hildebrand,* which, in terms of its form, gives the impression of being an independent composition, and the other Scandinavian ballads about Hildebrand without this characteristic.[8] But the heart of the matter is that to distinguish them as two separate numbers does not express the peculiar character of the matter: the ballad shows a number of minor revisions, but not distinct branching. The error is due not, therefore, to an imperfect theory, but to the imperfect application of different numbers (valid only for Danish material) to the various versions.

§10. There is no sharp distinction between folklore and the products of a higher culture. It is natural that a given age show transitions from the simpler intellectual life of folklore to the more complex expressions of higher culture. It is also possible that some social classes up until now produced transitional forms which, on the one hand, were colored by what was inherited through generations and which, on the other hand, were influenced by social classes of a higher culture.

In practical terms, however, the difference between oral production and oral transmission, on the one hand, and written production and written transmission, on the other, is profoundly significant, partly because the ability of literary works to enter oral tradition is surprisingly poor, and partly because their whole structure and external form will reveal their particular origin.

Comment. See chapter II C (below) for discussion of the transition of written products to folklore, and also for the special case when an original item of folklore is returned to it through literary means.

§11. Somewhat ahead of the general introduction of writing (i.e., still during the time of oral transmission), intellectual products appear that border on, or even transgress into, some broader and more personal conception than that found in folklore. We can term this category "fringe folklore."

To what degree fringe folklore follows the rules that apply to folklore in general is, of course, different for individual cultures, times, and works, and demands separate analyses. Some contributions to this subject will be given in chapter III. Concerning general rules, it can probably be stated that narrative material as a whole often follows the rules more closely than the various poetic genres (i.e., because they originate in an older time), and prose traditions follow them more closely than lays.

Example. In the oldest Scandinavian literature, one can see a number of such types: (1) Þrymskviða[1] bears above all the imprint of oral narrative composition. What could pass as a personal literary element is the brief episode in which the giant's sister asks the bride for a gift; it does not carry the action forward and is just a comic interlude. (2) A large number of heroic and, more rarely, mythological lays relate transmitted legendary material without substantial transformation; sometimes an entire series of stanzas is passed down directly from the predecessors (the two Helgi Poems,[2] Hamðismál and Guðrúnarhvöt),[3] but their predominant preoccupation with the inner life of feelings, emotions, etc., makes them increasingly seem like the work of individual authors. (3) Lays (especially mythological lays) with independent composition, often in a dramatic form. In some cases, the formal plot seems to be newly invented (Völuspá[4]) or created as a less traditional rendering of a popular narrative motif (the troll who is made speechless > Vafþrúðnismál);[5] others follow a traditional scheme (the troll is caught by daylight > Alvíssmál or Hrímgerðarmál),[6] and only a freer amplification within this framework turns them into the products of a particular author. Those mentioned last are closer to oral narrative composition. (4) The *drápur* of the skalds[7] are works created by individual authors (but they can give an indication of narrative conceptions that existed during the time of the author; see §16).

Other examples: The early heroic epic of several European and non-European peoples;[8] the Oriental and the medieval *novella*,[9] etc.

§12. "Higher" and "lower" folklore. The oldest literature testifies that along with the fringe folklore mentioned above, other material of unquestionably folkloristic character existed, to a large extent material that still survives today: proverbs, riddles (some of *Heiðrekr's Riddles*),[1] nursery rhymes (*Grýla*),[2] prayers ("The Angel's Prayer," "Þrándar-kredda"),[3] and magical formulas (the riding Odin),[4] along with a considerable number of prose narratives.

There are thus two levels of folklore: a higher one and a lower one. The higher items of folklore are contemporary. They belong to the more respectable people in society, and are characterized by the intellectual traits of the age. The lower items of folklore live in the shadows (in the lives of children, in everyday speech and communication); they only occasionally enter into literature, and then are often only alluded to. They do not have the characteristics of the age in which they are told, and nothing suggests that they were created at that time.

The same item of folklore can be higher for one age and lower for another. Danish chivalric ballads must have been produced by poets acquainted with the nobility of the Middle Ages, i.e., with the higher level, and still flourished among the nobility in the sixteenth century. But when they are sung in the nineteenth century by a smallholder's wife in Jutland to her babies, they have descended to the lower level.[5]

Many items of folklore belonged to the lower level as far back as we can trace them. The tale about Psyche was already an old wives' tale in the time of Apuleius.[6]

One must assume that there was a time in which those that are now lower items of folklore were accepted by society in general, primarily by its thinkers and leaders.

Example. A Negro tribe by the name of Fjort [in the French Congo], which exists generally at a low cultural level, has a number of narratives that fall outside the whole range of tales common in the European-Asiatic world and represent a considerably less developed stage both artistically and morally; they are short accounts (of which some can be considered the Psyche motif in an embryonic stage: a broken marriage with a supernatural creature). But these narratives are recited at public meetings and during legal disputes and are used authoritatively in decision making. They were approved by the tribe's leaders. No comparable use of items of folklore is attested in Europe (Dennett [1897], p. II).

# CHAPTER

## ‧ 2 ‧

## INDIVIDUAL RECORDINGS OF FOLKLORE

An Evaluation of Narrative Sources

Literature: Olrik (1892–1894); Olrik (1898), p. 47; P. Müller (1817–1820); P. Müller (1823); Erslev (1892); Erslev (1911), chapter II (§26–60), "Kildeprøvelsen" (§54–59 sagn).

### A. NARRATIVE AND RECORDING

§13. The scholar can only rarely observe the narrative in its natural state, i.e., as an oral recitation by a person who has grown up in a non-book-learned culture, and which is addressed to an audience of a similar level of education. Therefore, the scholar must usually rely on a record of the narrative.

Comment 1. In Danish, the words *optegnelse* ("record") and *opskrift* ("version") are almost synonymous. "Record," however, designates in particular that which is written down from oral transmission; "version" emphasizes that which is different from other extant written forms.
Comment 2. Scholars, especially younger ones, must be strongly advised that it is not enough to learn only about an item of folklore in its written form, but, to as great an extent as possible, to find it in its "living" state and observe the conditions under which it is transmitted.

§14. The record is valuable in relation to the accuracy with which it reproduces its oral source. Thus, e.g., older written works that reproduce narratives have value as sources, not when measured according to the standards of historical truth or those of aesthetic quality or elaboration, but to the extent they accurately reproduce oral tradition.

> The Science of Fairy Tales is concerned with tradition, and not with literature. It finds its subjects in the stories which have descended from mouth to mouth from an unknown past; and if reference be occasionally made to works of conscious literary art, the value of such works is not in the art they display, but the evidence they yield of the existence of given tales in certain forms at periods and places approximately capable of determination: evidence, in a word, which appropriates and fixes a pre-existing tradition. (Hartland [1891], p. 4; cf. Erslev [1892], §24)

§15. To an adequate record or oral transmission belong (1) an accurate reproduction of what is orally communicated, and (2) information about the name, time, place, social and educational level, etc., of the informant (e.g., all other oral narratives told by him).

Complete records in this category are normally extant only from the latter half of the nineteenth century. Many older records (e.g., songbooks, broadside prints) are close to the oral transmission but lack information about authority as well as external evidence about the accuracy of the record. Older versions of legends (e.g., reports by clergymen from the seventeenth century),[1] however, often contain either explicit or implicit information about the place where they were recorded, sometimes also about the informants[2] ("old men in this parish," "a woman told that in her youth...").

Comment. Older court records often give detailed and accurate information about custom and belief (e.g., witch trials), but only rarely about narrative (e.g., evidence in 1676 about Ebbe Skammelsen, DgF VI, p. 211).

§16. Also, extremely incomplete records (an indication of the main content of the narrative, a name, a curious detail, a metaphor) can be of great importance when we are able to fill in what is missing. This applies to, e.g., numerous allusions (kennings) in Norwegian-Icelandic skaldic poetry, and to indications in general from the time when few or no records are extant.

Example 1. The historian Torfæus (born 1636) says that during his childhood in Iceland, he heard a story about Amlóði told by old men and women, and considered it simply a tale. This information tells us of the popular basis of the "saga" (i.e., novel) about Ambales or Amlóði (Olrik [1899], pp. 364ff.).

Example 2. In a list of kings,[1] the Anglo-Saxon lay *Widsith* contains the words "Hagena Holmrygum ond Heoden Glommum," which show that the main characters in the Hilde narrative were at an early time considered kings of the peoples south of the Baltic. The younger Scandinavian (in particular Danish) tradition knows only that the battle took place on an island near Rügen, but regards the characters as Danish and Norwegian kings (Bugge [1896], p. 315).

§17. The incompleteness of a record can be due to accidental circumstances (e.g., a page is torn out, the scribe was interrupted, or the scribe's memory failed), or it can be due to a particular concern of the author: the author only wanted to indicate something, or he incorporated one part or another of a narrative into a longer account (e.g., from a literary source).

In order to be able to use such a record we must, within certain limits and with some degree of credibility, know the most important aspects of the main outline of the plot.

§18. The incompleteness of the record can be demonstrated partly by a comparison with other versions of the same narrative, partly and especially by its own lack of events *in toto* (cf. chapter III: "Epic Laws"). When incompleteness is due to external reasons, it will normally reveal itself as an abrupt discontinuation of the sequence of events. On the other hand, if it is due to a deliberate adaptation on the part of the author who commits it to writing, it often reveals itself by the fact that one or more elements appear that do not form an integral part of the chain of events.

Example 1. Of the accounts about Oddr, Saxo mentions only the single combat on Samsø (Book 5, p. 250).[1] That it was not the only one that was known at the time is revealed by the name of the hero,[2] which indicates that he was famous because of his arrows; but, on the other hand, only the cudgel was used in the Samsø battle. The correctness of this information is supported by the fact that the somewhat younger *Örvar-Odds saga* tells of a great number of other adventures in other places, and because an older source, the *Brávalla lay*, alludes both to his many travels and to his home on the Jäder.[3] The fact that only the Samsø battle was of use to Saxo in his *Gesta Danorum*[4] (it was the only event that took place in Denmark) suggests either that Saxo was selective in his use of source material, or that he had access to an incomplete narrative.

Example 2. *Helgakviða Hundingsbana* (*Helgakviða* I)[5] ends with the victory and marriage of Helgi, but a sentence in v. 5, "one thing became his misfortune," reveals that the author knows more about his fate. Moreover, the other lays about Helgi (*Helgakviða* II) and related sources describe his death, caused by the deceit of a relative, as the main event in his life. *Helgakviða* I is, then, in relation to the previously existing heroic narrative, to be regarded as an incomplete record (cf. Heusler [1905], p. 13).

§19. One of the most important ways to fill in an incomplete transmission is to retrieve the narrative from other, complete records. Even a small and unimportant feature in the course of events can often form the basis of an accurate definition.

Example 1. So-and-so can remember that during her childhood in Odense she heard "a tale in which women's milk was used in the bread." This phrase points to a well-known tale (i.e., connected with Hamlet):[1] in addition, the branch of transmission to which it belongs can be identified (Olrik [1892–1894] II, p. 165).

Example 2. An Icelandic skald[2] says that the waves "in the old days ground Amlóði's flour." Explanation for this image can be found in one of Amlóði's wise answers in the complete account in Saxo:[3] he calls the sand "flour" and says that is must have been ground by a large grinder.

For filling in a narrative, one must above all use evidence upon which all complete versions agree. Furthermore, special attention must be accorded the versions that are close to the fragment in terms of content. Often the versions that are closest with regard to time and place will provide the most likely supplementation.

Comment. The fusion of an account from two sources, A (which is known in an independent form) and B (otherwise unknown), is a special case. It is then probable that what is missing in B can be filled in from A, since the author has regarded their content as more or less identical. This conclusion is uncertain, however, and the rule must not be carried too far: it is possible that the author left out much of B just because it did not agree with A.

§20. A far more uncertain method is to fill in a narrative on the basis of the content of the fragment itself, paying general attention to the demands of the entire folk tradition, as well as to the individual era and narrative category. Such conjectural reconstruction easily leads to errors.

Example. The skaldic verse about "Amlóði's flour" mentioned above has been thought to contain the recollection of a sea-giant or a sea-grinder Amlóði. Saxo's account shows how senseless this assumption is. But without such a key we could not possibly guess what was correct. The mythical interpretation would then have been, under all circumstances, not quite compelling, but fairly probable. To put forward the free interpretation in spite of the interpretation supplied by the sources is reprehensible[1] (Rydberg [1886–1889] I, p. 428; *Ambales saga,* introduction, pp. XIIf.).

§21. Therefore a scholarly demonstration must have its point of departure and basis in records whose essential coherence is clear.

It is also of the greatest importance that the scholar form his personal opinion first and foremost on the basis of traditions about whose completeness and accuracy there can be no major doubts.

§22. It is important to know not only the oral but also the written authority, and to be able to investigate its reliability in the reproduction of what was heard.

§23. The condition of recording is most difficult when the narrative has been used as source material in a larger literary work.

Here the task is (1) to separate the individual transmission (i.e., to find the boundary of its scope), (2) to define its content (i.e., to as great an extent as possible make out all of the individual concepts that have formed parts of it), and (3) to define its authority.

§24. The more distinguished an author is with regard to the scholarly or artistic treatment of his material, the more difficult it will be to recreate his individual sources.

Example. In the *Lejre Chronicle,*[1] the material exists in an unrevised form, translated only into Latin; in Saxo, quite disparate transmissions are conflated into a progressive narrative. The *Lejre Chronicle* is thus superior in regard to the genuineness of the individual account (source genuineness). It is another matter that Saxo's sources were more numerous, fuller, and, in part, more original than those of the *Lejre Chronicle.*

§25. The methods by which to identify the author's source narratives are primarily (1) the author's own information about either the work as a whole or an individual part; (2) the unfailing agreement of an individual section with a known, genuine narrative, whereby it reveals itself as a variant of the same narrative;[1] and (3) the agreement of the structure of the tale with folklore, partly with folklore in general, partly and especially with an individual category (see "Introduction" [§§5–8]; chapter IV B: "Horizon and Localization"; chapter III: "Epic Laws").

Comment 1. A fourth, but far more uncertain, point can be mentioned: dissimilarity to historical reality, because historical mistakes can also be made through the misunderstanding of the author (Erslev [1911] §§41 and 38).

Comment 2. "Learned narratives" are oral accounts that have their origin in the conjectures of book-learned people. They cannot generally be confused with the "folktale" proper (§5).[2] On the other hand, they are sometimes similar to the popular "remnants of narratives." In some cases, as in the arbitrary interpretation of place names,[3] there may even be a strong similarity, because they both depend on the random association of aurally concordant elements. Moreover, one must be aware that what in everyday speech is called "learned narrative" is sometimes not a narrative but the conjecture of an author that has been repeated by later authors.

§26. In the demarcation of the domain of the individual narrative transmission, the same characteristics are used, although particular emphasis is placed on the last one. There must be a unity of plot as consistent as it usually is in the particular category of narratives with which the account must be grouped. If motifs are included without being used, or if they are mixed in an especially artificial way, something is amiss.

As a countertest, one must next investigate whether the work has a sufficiently coherent form when this narrative is (or these narratives are) omitted. If in what remains one finds, e.g., many of the same characters as in the narrative singled out, it is likely that we have not found the correct boundary. If in the following text the features of the plot that are found only in the "narrative" are further developed, then the demarcation is incorrect unless it is only the kind of small remark that an author creates naturally for supplementation and transition.

Example 1. When Saxo in Book 1 passes from Danish to Norwegian tradition, the connection is that the new king (Gram) is made "son" of the previous king (Skjold) and that they are both portrayed as joint kings, when the one was old and the other was young.[1]

Example 2. When Saxo in Book 2[2] again leaps from Norwegian to Danish tradition, the young king (Halfdan) is similarly made "son" of the previous king (Frodi). Furthermore, shortly after, the text says: "King Regnir in Sweden died, however, and his wife Svanhvit soon followed him in death because of sorrow . . . their son Hodbrod followed him"; i.e., new characters appear throughout (and new actions are set in motion), but Saxo considers the present actors to be the children of the previous ones.

§27. The methods by which to determine the source genuineness of the individual features are in part to ascertain their necessary, or at least fortunate, placement in the plot of the narrative, in part to ascertain their general narrative-like character (palpability, etc.; cf. §25), and in part to ascertain whether they reflect a culture and a mentality other than the one prevailing at the time of composition. Conversely, some individual features reveal their artificiality by containing more artificial reasoning or more modern characteristics than can be expected of a narrative tradition of that particular time.

Example 1. Saxo has Hotherus elected as the King of Denmark at Isøre.[1] But the election of a king at Isøre is not known before 1076 and never became a kind of established arrangement, even though during the time of Saxo a person was inclined to regard it as such. Therefore, the Isøre election must have been added by Saxo (or one of his contemporaries) in order to provide a suitable transition to the appearance of Balder and Hotherus in Denmark (cf. §33, 1).

Example 2. The narrative about Hagbard and Signe from Sigersted on Zealand was told in detail by Beyer (1791),[2] and is strongly mixed with Beyer's own fantastic conjectures. In this last category probably belong, e.g., "Signe's walk down a grove in Alsted where Habor met with and spoke to the princess several times," and "Pole-hill, so-called because from this place Prince Habor's valet was supposed to give a signal by raising up a flag on a pole,"[3] because both the walk and the signal stand outside the consciousness of common people, and because they totally lack a characteristic narrative-like event. "The handmaiden hole," where the wicked handmaiden was drowned, and "Signe's well," into which Signe threw her treasures, are, however, genuine; they recur also in a genuine version of a legend from Sigersted,[4] and Beyer himself attests to the latter: "With regard to this tradition, one commonly hears the adage that Sigersted owns more gold and silver than they even know about themselves, if they wanted to dig for it." Moreover, the notion of famous people's hidden treasures is one of the most common in local folk transmission[5] (DgF I, p. 260; DFS 1917/47–48).

§28. For a definition of the authority of the narrative, we have two bases: in part, in an investigation of the inner structure of the narrative (see section B, §45), and in part, in an examination of the time, home, and conditions of the author who committed it to writing.

§29. The investigation of an author's work thus has two purposes: (1) to provide information about the author's position in time and place as witness to the existence of the narrative, and (2) to examine his conception and methodology in order to locate a criterion for the reliability of his reproduction and for the character of his errors.

§30. One must beware of passing off an author's personal changes as narrative.

Example. Snorri's description of the introduction of Odin worship in Scandinavia (*Heimskringla,* beginning) is not a narrative in itself but the work of an author who adapted transmitted material to the prevalent theory of his time. He had almost all of the same tradition available to him that we know of; and where he diverges from it, he is without importance as a source. On certain points, he used otherwise unknown traditions; insofar as we are able to separate them from his account, they receive value as sources. To cite a section of his account as a "source," which is even called "Odin's laws," is, on the other hand, most reprehensible.[1]

Comment. Earlier scholars had the notion that all literary works that fell within a certain time limit were "sources." They are naturally sources to the historian who investigates the spiritual life of the time of their origin; but they are not necessarily sources as far as narrative material is concerned.

Similarly, these scholars held that certain authors possessed a special authority. Of course, an author cannot give the narratives a source value which the tradition does not already have; by his alterations, the source value can only become poorer. On the other hand, his scholarly revision of the material can, of course, be right—or wrong. For example, in Snorri's conception of the origin of the Æsir cult, the revision is absolutely incorrect, because all of his explanation is euhemerism,[2] a theory that most scholars now reject, and that no one regards as the only definitive theory. (Cf. Heusler [1908].)

§31. The obligation to prove the source value of a written work lies with the one who asserts it, rather than with the one who denies it; for the scholar is responsible for the genuineness of his material—not only its written genuineness, but also its source genuineness.[1] Obviously, a rash assertion about the valuelessness of a feature is also unjustifiable.

§32. The methods by which to define an author's originality and his general treatment of his (written) sources are dealt with in more detail by general philological-literary criticism and evaluation of historical sources (cf. Erslev [1892] and [1911] §§26–60). Here attention will be drawn only to some special characteristics that are often connected to versions of narratives, whether they are committed to writing in the distant past or in recent centuries. The most common characteristic is a tendency to elaborate the style so as to elevate it to the level of the reader's taste. The setting and the characters are also commonly elaborated. Conversely, what is vulgar or offensive is often omitted. Similarly, what is too unbelievable is avoided, or rather, it is replaced by something similar that looks less unreasonable (i.e., is rationalized).

The historiographic narrative is the most extensively revised literary form.[1] The narrative is matched with given historical events or at least with the author's conception of the political situation of ancient times, which is often colored by the circumstances and wishes of his contemporaries; political considerations are more conspicuous than the personal ones prevailing in the narrative, and rationalization is more pronounced.

Comment. The "naturalness" of the account (i.e., its agreement with everyday reality) is thus not a characteristic of its genuineness as a narrative, as it just as easily, or more easily, may be due to the rationalization of the editor.

The larger literary works of an author (especially the epics of the Middle Ages) are, in their authorial viewpoint, closer to oral narrative tradition. But a number of them transform it very freely, adding various motifs.

The most reliable records within older literature are to be found among the more naive historians[2] and in collections of entertaining and instructive short stories.[3]

§33. Until now, we have presupposed the simpler case, that the individual author in his account followed a single narrative. We shall now briefly discuss the case where an account contains several sources or has passed through the hands of several authors.

Sometimes the scope of an oral narrative is not sufficiently defined by pointing out where in the literary work the narrative begins and ends; several accounts can be conflated into one account, either several narratives with each other, or narratives with a historical account.

(1) This process of conflation is evidenced in the lack of

unity in the account, in the many characters, horizons, and strands of the plot that are intertwined. Even though each single feature perhaps belongs to a narrative, the narrative as a whole is non-narrative-like.

Example. Saxo's account of Balder and Hotherus[1] cannot belong to an individual narrative. Such a large number of battles and political events (which, in addition, have little or no influence on the progress of the plot) are not known in genuine narratives. Furthermore, the account is about different motives behind the action: the battle for Nanna's love, for the Swedish kingdom, and for the Danish kingdom.

Comment. The fact that an account is improbable as a narrative does not mean that it is improbable with regard to reality (§32, comment). It will, however, when measured on the scale of reality, easily reveal its diverse origin by the fact that contradictions between the sources have been left unresolved. The main characteristic will, however, always be a breach in the unity and in the obvious causality prevalent in the narrative. A breach of external verisimilitude is found to a much greater extent in narratives that have grown together orally than in those that are literary products (cf. chapter III: "Epic Laws").

(2) Conflation can also be demonstrated at times by means of an evaluation of literary sources. The account turns out to be derived from, e.g., an older written source "A," which is also extant, and an otherwise unknown source "B," which must have been an oral narrative.

Example. The information in the *Lund Chronicle* about the sons of Lodbrok in relation to its written source, Adam of Bremen:

Adam, *Gesta Hamm. eccl.*
lib. I chap. 37 (c. 1074)

*Annales Lundenses*
SRD I 229 (12th century)

In Hystoria Francorum Sigafrid cum fratre Halpdani regnasse leguntur ... Erant et alii reges Danorum vel Nortmannorum, qui piraticis excursionibus eo tempore Galliam vexabant. Quorum præcipui erant Horich, Orwig, Gotafrid, Rudolf et Inguar tyranni. Crudelissimus omnium fuit Inguar, filius Lodparchi, qui christianos ubique per supplicia necavit.[2]

In diebus illis erant ferocissimi et crudelissimi principes Danorum, *filii Lothbrochi,* qui piraticis excursionibus Galliam vexabant, quorum precipui erant Horich, Sighafrith, *Ulff, Byorn,* Ormyc (var. Orwic), Godefrid, *Iuar,* Rothwlf, Inguar et *Ubbi.* Crudelissimi fuerunt *Iuar* et Ingvar, filii Lothbrochi, qui ubique cristianos per supplicia necabant.[3]

§34. The methods by which to carry through the separation are chiefly given in what was said above. The main characteristic is that the individual narrative forms a coherent plot; and, in general, each source from which an account is fused will have a certain inner coherence.

Many detailed characteristics should be added according to the circumstances (for the sake of convenience, it is presupposed in the following that only the fusion of two sources, A and B, is considered):

(1) The one source is a known older work. One can then ascertain the other through deduction (B equals account minus A minus the author's alterations).

Example. The sons of Lodbrok in the *Lund Chronicle* (§33,2).

(2) In terms of plot, the one source is close to known genuine narrative tradition (or each of the two sources is close to corresponding folklore).

Example. The special names of the sons of Lodbrok in the *Lund Chronicle* (§33, 2) correspond to the Scandinavian, especially Danish, tradition known from elsewhere: the many sons of Lodbrok, among them Björn Ironside, Ivar the Legless, and Ubbe.[1]

(3) The one source is a historical account, the other legend-like. They can be distinguished by the contrast between historical and oral narrative representation.

(4) The two sources are narratives of different categories, nationalities, or horizons.

Example. The account of Sigurðr's and Brynhildr's conflict in *Völsunga saga* is composed of two lays, an older, shorter, and more energetic one (*Brot*) and a younger one that focuses more on inner thoughts and emotions (*Sigurðarkviða* [*en meiri*])[2] (Heusler [1902a]).

(5) The two sources are distinguished by different linguistic forms, e.g., by the names.

Example. The special names of the sons of Lodbrok in the *Lund*

*Chronicle* have a Scandinavian linguistic form; the ones taken from Adam normally have a German form.

§35. The distinction between several parallel sources often presents great difficulties, and the need for caution and circumspection on this point cannot be sufficiently stressed. The main principles must be (1) that one uses as many characteristics as possible independent of each other to see if they lead to the same result; and (2) not only that the result should be a narrative form coherent in itself, but that all the presumed sources must have an inner coherence and correspond to known categories of narrative, and that one does not ascribe to the author a share in their conflation, which goes against what we otherwise know about his work.

Example. Saxo's account of Balder's and Hotherus's fight was, according to Kauffmann (1902),[1] compiled from three sources: an extensive Norwegian narrative, an extensive narrative from South Jutland, and brief narratives from Zealand. But the supposed narrative from South Jutland displays the strongest characteristics of not being Danish, and has conspicuous similarities in regard to detail with Saxo's Norwegian sagas. And one must attribute to Saxo an arbitrariness and also an ability for epic composition that is completely at variance with what we otherwise know about him. (The correct point in Kauffmann's theory, on the other hand, resides in the identification of "doublets"; see below, chapter V B, and cf. §36.)

Generally, one must beware of arbitrarily assigning to the work of an author what can equally well, or even more correctly, be assigned to the oral development of the narrative.

§36. When two forms of the same narrative are told as independent events following each other without the narrator realizing their close connection, they present a special form of conflation called "doublets."

Doublets of individual features or sections are even more common than complete narrative doublets.

Example. The stories about the Christmas thief and the giant Dofri in *Haralds saga Dofrafóstra*[1] (*Flateyjarbók* I, p. 563), the former based on a written source (*Ágrip, Heimskringla*),[2] the latter based on oral tradition.³ Many ballads in Vedel's redaction (e.g., DgF 18). Of the sons of Lodbrok in the *Lund Chronicle* (§33, 2), "Ivar" is the Scandinavian doublet of the "Ingvar" drawn from foreign chronicles. Comment. However, doublets also appear frequently in oral tradition, especially when it develops into a saga-like or epic-like fullness (see chapter V B below).

§37. When a version of a narrative is recorded directly from an oral source, it is called a "first-hand" recording. Often, however, it has gone through one or more written intermediary stages that altered its content or presentation; it is then called "derived."

Example. Arngrímur Jónsson's *Rerum Danicarum Fragmenta*[1] (1597) is throughout based on what he himself calls a "compendium" of the history of Denmark, namely, the younger *Skjöldunga saga* (ca. 1260), whose section on ancient times is now lost (the remaining part is preserved under the name *Knýtlinga saga*);[2] this younger *Skjöldunga saga* is again based on the now-lost, older *Skjöldunga saga* (ca. 1200). This older *Skjöldunga saga* was in its turn based on oral tradition, i.e., was a first-hand recording; the others are derived. Also, *Heimskringla* (which cites *Skjöldunga saga* and the *Edda*),[3] is in certain sections based on the older *Skjöldunga saga*. A first-hand recording can be the ancestor of many derived recordings.

Comment. "First-hand" and "derived" recordings thus do not correspond to what the historians call "primary" and "secondary" sources. To them, "primary" means any account that is not derived from other extant ones; "secondary" means a recording based exclusively on known material (Erslev [1892], §13; Erslev [1911], §39). Arngrímur Jónsson's *Fragmenta* is, from a historical point of view, a "primary" account of Danish antiquity, but it is not a "first-hand" recording of the Skjöldung narratives. Furthermore, one must notice that for the historian a witness is "first-hand" when the witness has, with his own eyes or ears, observed circumstances or events in human life (especially life in a state and society [Erslev (1911), §43ff.]); to the folklorist, a witness is first-hand when the witness has observed the narrative as oral tradition. He is far from a first-hand witness to the circumstance or event that might be the basis of the narrative (cf. Erslev [1911], §53ff.). The folklorist has the advantage over the historian in that he has far more first-hand witnesses about his subject than the historian.

§38. Derived recordings have value as sources insofar as they provide us with the means by which to recreate lost first-hand recordings.

They will never be able to replace first-hand recordings completely, because they always add a new and obscure element. However, by a study of the idiosyncrasy of a written work (e.g., in relation to the works, still extant, that are its sources), we will often be able to estimate in what direction the most important deviation is to be sought. We are even more fortunate when several derived recordings each branch off from the same base. (Example. The *Brávalla lay* can partly be recreated with the aid of Saxo and *Sögubrot,*[1] DFS 1917/46).

§39. Even though no literary information can be found about the source of the derived recording, the basic difference between oral and written presentation can provide a number of bases for a definition of the previous oral tradition.

§40. A written work that is based exclusively on known sources has no source value.

Example. The account in the *Danish Rhymed Chronicle* of the sons of Lodbrok (cf. §33, 2, the *Lund Chronicle,* and Saxo's Book 9):[1]

> XV mynæ søner, som iek hadhe kær,
> them fek iek hwer sith righæ sææer,
> som wor Ornik och Godhefredh,
> Wlff, Biørn, Rawerth oc Sygefredh,
> Sywordh, Iwer, Radwlff, Erich wetherhath,
> Agner, Vbbæ, Ingwer, Frillæ och Dumwath.[2]

§41. Even though the derived recording has no source value, it may have a psychological value, because it shows how certain material is adopted and transformed in a human mind; it shows what is perceived most clearly, what is blurred, what poetic possibilities are hidden in it, and the like.

Comment. The scholar can obtain similar knowledge by telling the narrative, preferably to an audience that is close to its natural audience in intellectual development. In so doing, he will, so to speak, illuminate the narrative from within, partly through his own feelings, partly through the atmosphere and the thoughts that reveal themselves in the expressions and questions of the audience. Within such somewhat narrow limits, the scholarly experiment has its place in oral narrative research. At the present stage of research, however, it serves more as a probe and as a supporting proof than as a compelling argument in itself.

## B. THE INNER CHARACTER OF THE TRADITION

§42. After the content of the tradition has been determined, the next step will be to define its inner character in order to determine its degree and value.

The methods by which to define the inner character of a narrative reside partly within a comparison with other versions of the same narrative, partly within other similar traditions, and partly within the conditions of folklore in general.

The aim of the comparison is here to provide an estimation of the value of the individual tradition. A comparison between different traditions is employed provisionally only insofar as it leads to this aim (cf. chapter V A: "The Relationship between Narrative Traditions"). The examination is primarily concerned with (1) the time and place of the tradition, (2) its character and inner coherence, and (3) its connection with other traditions of the same time and place.

§43. The time of the tradition is determined by the time of the recording.

Comment. Insofar as it is found only in a derived recording, it may perhaps be shown only to be older than a given point in time, and to belong to a more undefined period of time within which the recording falls.

§44. The place of the recording is determined by:

(1) The recorder's explicit information about the authority, if it is extant.

Example. A collection of exempla composed by an English Franciscan in the thirteenth century: "While the talk is about unrestrained playing, I shall not omit to speak of something that I have from Brother Peter, who was previously in the company of Concedus, the supervisor of the order, and who later became his successor in that position. He has told me and several other brothers in Dublin that in Denmark, the land of his birth, it is the custom that" women at birthing parties dance in a chain with a straw doll called Bovi, and that the devil once got into the straw doll and uttered a scream so that everyone fainted (J. Olrik and Olrik [1907], p. 175).[1]

Comment. Earlier authors frequently offer rather superficial statements about their authorities and about the origin of their sources in general, because they aim more at having the account generally believed in broader circles than at verifying exactly the individual piece of information. Thus, Saxo says that he has unrolled and researched the works of the Icelanders,[2] even though his account is not close enough to any Icelandic work that it can be his source.[3] (On the other hand, his sparse statements about individual items of folklore appear to be reliable: that *Bjarkamál* is still remembered by heart by some of his contemporaries; that somebody told Absalon about the beam that had been plowed up on King Sigar's castle square,[4] and the like.) The Icelandic monk Oddr tells that King Edward in England had the last story about Óláfr Tryggvason in a book.[5] Faroese ballads often begin: "Frøðið (ríman) er komið frá Íslandi, skrivað í bók so breiða"[6] even when they do not correspond to any Icelandic literary work. Sometimes a vague or misleading expression is due to an author's desire for a finer style: when Saxo says that he has "unrolled the works of the Icelanders," it is untrue for the simple reason that the works of the Icelanders were not scrolls like the antique ones but ordinary books with leaves.

Contrary to works of attested authorship, the folk tradition normally begins with just a phrase identifying it as an item of folklore: "It is told that," "I heard that," "Heyrðak segja í sögum fornum,"[7] "It was in the olden days that," "Once upon a time." Occasionally an authority is mentioned, however, who through familial relationships or something else has some connection with the event.

(2) The recorder's own place. (This characteristic, however, is uncertain for authors who have collected their material from all quarters.)

Example. Saxo mentions Absalon and the Icelanders among his sources, and has probably used even more.[8] The above-mentioned

English Franciscan who often cites foreign brothers of his order as his authorities.

(3) The linguistic form of the recording, or, if the text is written down in a foreign language, the linguistic form of the names.

Example. Saxo's chronicle contains names partly with Danish, partly with Norwegian linguistic forms,[9] in addition to a number of indeterminate ones and a number that have been normalized into a Danish linguistic form.

(4) The horizon of the tradition (i.e., the sum of geographical perceptions that appear in it). Here the rule applies that the horizon of the narrative must fall within the horizon of the narrator, and that thorough knowledge of the horizon of the narrative normally falls within the scope of what the narrator is thoroughly familiar with. This intimate connection, which is called localization, often presupposes a knowledge derived from personal experience (cf. below, chapter IV B, §§109f., 118f.).

Example. The thirteenth-century *Liber Visionum* from the Cistercian monastery Fürstenfeld in Bavaria contains an account that begins: "There is a monastery of the Cistercian order in Denmark by the name of Vitae Scola, where we have heard that the following took place not long ago." The account here reveals itself as having originated directly or indirectly in Vitskøl monastery (Jørgensen [1912], p. 16).

(5) Agreement of the subject or the structure of an account with the category of narrative composition that is characteristic of a particular time and place. Apart from the impression of the account as a whole, many characteristic individual settings (e.g., a typical form of Odin's earthly appearance),[10] characters from a special narrative world, and agreement with popular belief or with an external reality, along with the whole spiritual horizon, also pertain to a particular time and place.

Example. The above-mentioned account concerning the monastery of Vitskøl deals with an evil spirit who, in the shape of a man, was received into the monastery but revealed his origin by his fear of the still-distant thunder and was hit by lightning when he tried to escape to the sea. In content, it is similar to a great number of older Scandinavian traditions about trolls who are destroyed by thunder.[11] The Franciscan account of the birthing party corresponds to many later Danish descriptions of the playful nature of these celebrations,[12] and the straw doll that becomes a devil is found several times in Scandinavian tradition.[13]

(6) The close connection of the tradition with other recordings of the same narrative whose locations are known.

Example. Saxo's account of Uffe is close to Aggesen's,[14] but his information that Vermund's son was called Olaf is found in the Icelandic *Langfeðgatal.*[15]

§45. In an investigation of the inner structure of a narrative, it must first of all be decided whether or not the narrative is verbose, terse, or languishing.

When the narrator is uncertain about the content of individual episodes or their placement, when he does not distinguish among individual characters and gives several characters in the narrative the same name, or the like, the narrative can be said to be in a languishing state. It is then in a beginning stage of dissolution, and often it dies out.

Example. The paternal revenge of the two princes in Saxo's Book 7[1] (compared with the corresponding section about Hróar and Helgi in *Hrólfs saga kraka,*[2] cf. Olrik [1892–1894] II, §13). Many examples are found in DgF, where the forgotten verse form is accompanied by uncertainty or innovation in the progress of the plot (cf. chapter IV: "The Life of the Narrative," §91).

Comment 1. Often a tradition is found in a defective state, but the error has been remedied on the basis of available materials. The weakness will, however, reveal itself, in verse form by padding or unclear thought (von der Recke [1906]),[3] in narratives by the use of trivial motifs.

Comment 2. A badly remembered tradition frequently appears to contain especially peculiar motifs. The reason is probably that since coherence fails, various notions flicker into consciousness, and the consciousness does not know for certain what to grasp or omit. Such incoherent features may be used only with caution as testimony about the content of the narrative.

A tradition can be characterized as terse when it contains only the main events of the narrative in a concise account.

The more amplified account, whether or not its fullness applies to the characters and the main episodes of the narrative itself or to subordinate characters and episodes, can be characterized as verbose. If the subordinate material is amplified, then the main plot exists in a rather languishing state; its verbosity must then lie somewhere in the past.

> Example. *Hrólfs saga kraka:* the warriors are put in the limelight at the expense of their king.[4] *Greasy Pants* (*Fra Bindestue og Kølle* I, no. 9): the interest in Christ and St. Peter and in the "Cinderella-like" character of the protagonist overshadows the plot (*The Good Sword, The Dragon Fight*).[5]

§46. (Comment to A and B) What role the evaluation of sources plays in the individual investigation depends upon the character of the material. A large number of recordings from recent times are accompanied by exact reproductions of the folk tradition and complete information about the narrator and the place where it was recorded. To a large extent, the investigation can then be based on this information; this applies, e.g., to most of the more recent investigations of folktales. The literary sources are then normally categorized as a special group ("book variants"),[1] and are used only to a limited extent to examine the development of the tale, whose value is briefly determined on the basis of the large amount of genuine material.

The situation is different with regard to heroic narratives, myths about gods, or narratives with a historical basis. The material is so limited that every version must be meticulously scrutinized and fully exploited. Here a thorough evaluation must take all sources into account: no version may be assumed in advance to be an accurate reproduction of oral tradition, nor may it be assumed to offer complete information about the place where it was recorded. Often the item forms part of a chronicle or some other source; in many cases it consists only of a reference, etc. But here, too, the investigation will move in the same direction as in the other cases: from the (completely or mostly) folk-transmitted forms to those adapted or merely alluded to in literary sources, because the former group elucidates the latter.

## C. TRADITIONS OF A LITERARY ORIGIN

§47. Can folk tradition originate in literary sources? To what extent does this happen, and under what specific circumstances? These questions concern (1) the evaluation of the individual account, (2) the life of the narrative in general, and (3) the basic concept of folklore. For practical reasons, it is natural to discuss this complex of problems here rather than parceling it out to be handled in three different places.

The questions are answered diversely by different authors. But it is mostly scholars of a general cultural-historical or literary orientation who ascribe great importance to the literary origin. Scholars who have studied in detail the history of the individual narratives in all their forms generally regard the literary origin as far more tenuous; in some areas they even more or less categorically deny it.

In general, we must bear in mind that true answers to these questions are gained only by detailed research that encompasses no small amount of material. In this connection, mention must be made of Grundtvig's and Child's comprehensive editions of the Danish and the English ballads[1] and the recent comprehensive examinations of individual tales, not least those carried out by Finnish scholars.[2] Whereas scholars of an older school remarked, e.g., that the more recent Danish ballad tradition originated in Vedel's and Syv's collections,[3] hundreds of more specialized investigations have led to a different result: the ability of a ballad to survive in oral tradition until recent times depends primarily on quite different circumstances from its appearance in print; even among ballads that have been printed, even under circumstances that to a large extent facilitate their dissemination, one finds far more frequently forms without a literary origin than forms that stem from or are influenced by what is printed.

§48. The more specific circumstances characteristic of adaptation from literary sources are primarily these:

(1) The purely literary production has little or no ability to be transmitted orally.

(2) Folklore which is committed to writing can return to oral tradition; however, its capability to be transmitted is weaker than with folklore in its natural state.

(3) Insofar as the collector has made alterations or additions, the transmission will usually remove them again.

Example. The narrative about Odysseus and Polyphemus belongs among the materials in which the possibility of a literary origin of narrative tradition is greatest. For many centuries it has been read by a large number of people in a poetically powerful account,[1] the main content of which was very close to folk tradition. Hackman (1904) shows, however, how little of the literary form of the narrative has been adopted by the people. The narrative is extant in 221 variants; not a single one has the Homeric chain of events (salvation both by sheep and by the trick with "No one"); the variants most different from Homer include melted lead (not a stick) in the eye and hiding in the sheep's skin (not under their bellies), both of which have unquestionably had the strongest capacity for reproduction. For the transmission in Attica (shrunken and transformed) and for the *Arabian Nights,* a pure descent from the Homeric narrative is probable; a strong influence from Homer is found in the Caucasus. For Europe, the following is the case: Lithuanian no. 1 has absorbed much from Homer; only a few other records reveal some slight traces of Homeric presentation in a narrative sequence that, on the whole, is far removed from Homer (the address to the he-goat, the arrival of the other giants, or the name "No one"; in folk tradition, the hero always gives his name as "Self"). The strongly mixed Lithuanian form is printed in a somewhat unreliable journal;[2] a couple of the minor features are found in legend-like West European forms (one is attributable to a medieval clerical recorder);[3] a Swedish one (with the name "No one") is, at any rate, not attributable to any actual folklorist.[4] A Hungarian form, which ends with the noisy giants on the beach, seems, from the evidence of the recording, to be quite genuine, but must raise suspicion because of its occurrence among the inland people; it descends via the *Arabian*

*Nights* from Homer. The ability of the Homeric narrative to disseminate into the broader classes of people has thus been poor. Earlier editors and scholars anxiously noted each time a form was very similar to the Homeric one. Now the richer material consistently reveals closer connections in the folklore of neighboring areas[5] (Hackman [1904], especially pp. 47, 179–188).

§49. The account that is read never leaves as clear a picture as the account that is heard; and the account meant to be read and based on a higher culture can never quite be reproduced in its uniqueness. Even though especially susceptible individuals of an adroit disposition are able to do this, the memory fails for succeeding narrators.

That there is such a difference is due to the compact and palpable composition of the oral narrative (and frequently also to its close relation to a vanished stage of culture). Moreover, oral tradition has had its assured childhood abode in the individual home, in smaller circles, and among the least book-learned people: here it is most adaptable, and even the most frequently repeated account is delivered in a manner that appears quite natural.

Example. "In none of Hans Christian Andersen's independent fairy-tales—except perhaps *The Ugly Duckling*—is there such a solidly constructed, compact plot as in the ones originating in folktales. One cannot remember the others. A situation, a type, a symbol perhaps—but not a sequence of events" (Christensen [1906], p. 106).

"Das beste Kennzeichen für die Echtheit einer Sage ist aber schliesslich das Verhalten des Volkes selbst, ob es eine Sage annimmt oder ablehnt"[1] (Wehrhan [1908], p. 10).

Correspondingly, in some storytellers' repertoire, a tale with a literary origin may appear now and then; but one will not get many versions of the same tale, unless one has a whole group of traditions that branches off evenly into various modifications from an original literary form.

§50. Within most categories of folklore, it is very rare that an unquestionably literary production becomes a lasting item of folklore. The main event in the late classical Greek novel about Apollonius of Tyre,[1] for instance, provided the subject for the Danish ballad *King Apollonius of Tyre:* the shipwrecked hero, disguised as a fisherman, wins the love of the king's daughter (DgF 88). The ballad however, is late and rare, and it hardly reached beyond the Danish nobility; it remained a "higher" item of folklore.

A special case is constituted by the intrigue or jesting tales, which appear early in Eastern literature; literary and oral tradition seem to have supplemented each other more than usual in this case,[2] particularly in Europe. However, we lack definite information about their origin (oral or written) and about their routes of diffusion. They must be treated as a special category of "fringe folklore," the position of which deviates from common conditions.

In all, the literary work that lies fairly close to folklore has some possibility of appearing as folklore, especially those works in which the plot is more important, not the presentation. On the other hand, the abundant multiplicity of plot, which the written novel so easily develops, is an obstacle to the oral transmission of material: the transmission tends to cut out what is superfluous; in this connection, the novel is in a more disadvantageous position than folklore in its natural state.

Example 1. From the plot in *Apollonius of Tyre,* only a short section, a single aspect of the plot, has been adopted by the Danish ballad.

Example 2. The ballad about *Ogier the Dane and Burmand* (DgF 30) treats only the single combat with the heathen champion; it does not say how Ogier got into the prison tower from where he was brought out as a champion. In some way or other the plot derived from the French epic about Ogier le Danois's exploits as a youth,[3] but could not, according to its category, include the entire chain of events.

§51. Sometimes the literary poem enters oral tradition and becomes a "folksong." But often it will have difficulty penetrating the classes of society where folklore proper thrives; and its life expectancy is short if it is not supported by constant reference to the book. Thus, in Denmark in the nineteenth century, one will hardly find "folksongs" that go back to the seventeenth, let alone the sixteenth, century. On the other hand, one will find a considerable number of ballads orally transmitted from the Middle Ages.

Comment. *Ljómur,*[1] composed by the Icelandic bishop Jón Arason around the year 1550, has endured exceptionally well in the Faroe Islands (*Ljómur,* p. 311, and Jensen [1871], p. 227; *Folkesangen paa Færøerne,* pp. 237ff.). But it stands alone among a couple of hundred ballads; so far, the exception proves the rule.

§52. It is somewhat different when old narrative material becomes the subject of a literary work. In this case, the literary work will have somewhat better prospects of becoming folklore, because the transmission peels everything away, leaving the original narrative core.

Example. The Shetlandic ballad *King Orfeo* (*English and Scottish Popular Ballads,* no. 19; notice the foreign form of the name) can be traced via a medieval French-Celtic poem back to the antique Orpheus myth, as can, in part, the Scandinavian *The Mighty Harp* (DgF 40; Bugge [1891], p. 97). Note also the Polyphemus records, which in their entirety or in part go back to Homer as their source (§48, example).

§53. Published recordings of folklore are disseminated in broader circles only after the appearance of the literary work—thus the short-story collections of the Middle Ages, broadside prints of ballads from the sixteenth century onwards, and collections of folktales, almost exclusively from the nineteenth century. Since they are produced with a readership in view, the text is normally more or less polished; sometimes, especially in older times, it is considerably amplified and rewritten.

Published recordings have had some influence on oral transmission, that is to say in reverse proportion to the amount of rewriting (since extensive editing places them in a literary environment). The broadside prints of ballads in particular prove capable of being transmitted, since they demand the least in the way of circulation: one can sing directly from the page.

Example 1. The folktales edited by Perrault[1] (end of the seventeenth century) and his closest imitators[2] had no influence on French story-telling even as chapbooks and broadside prints, according to van Gennep: "Thousands of parents have read them to thousands of children, and the stories have, thanks to their illustrations, penetrated into all these small brains; but in spite of that, none of the fairytales have taken root in the villages and again become oral tradition" (van Gennep [1908–1914] III, introduction).

Example 2. "Around 1840, when Hyltén-Cavallius and Stephens made their impressive collections of tales,[3] almost nothing had entered Swedish folktale tradition from the already rich chapbook literature. Most of Perrault's tales had been accessible in broadside prints as far back as the 1770s and 1780s, and more than a score of the best tales of the Grimms since the mid-1820s.[4] The fact that a very few isolated recordings, which clearly go back to these models (*The Juniper Tree, King Thrushbeard, The Jew Among the Thorns*),[5] are found in their collections proves nothing. Just because one individual remembers and repeats a tale heard in his youth, it does not naturally follow that this became a Swedish folktale.... To be sure, recent folktale collections contain more recordings which may evidently be derived at first or second hand from printed sources." (Example. *Historiegubbar*;[6] Ahlström [1895], p. 33; cf. Aarne [1913a], p. 19.)[7]

§54. The literary dissemination of ballads is greatest in Castile and Denmark. Denmark has Vedel's edition of 1591 containing 100 numbers and his supplement *Tragica* (1657) with 30, to which Syv added another 100 in 1695, along with broadside prints (earliest 1572, many from the seventeenth and eighteenth centuries); furthermore, large printed songbooks (1550–1700) were in ladies' rooms in manor houses, and the songs were sung during the daily work.[1] In spite of this dynamic dissemination (around 250 ballads in print, and even more in manuscript), the far greater part of the tradition of the nineteenth century is of a non-literary origin.[2] Syv's songbook has only to a very limited extent managed to give rise to transmission,[3] *Tragica* not at all (except in the Faroe Islands),[4] Vedel only slightly. Only the broadside prints have had any real influence on oral tradition.

When literary form becomes oral tradition, it is probable that moralizing end verses will invariably be dropped; also, non-popular expressions in the text will fade away, and the conspicuous length or verbosity of a ballad will be reduced. As a remnant of the literary treatment, it then retains such features as altered personal names, the fusing of several lines of transmission, or the arbitrary reshaping of individual features.

Example 1. The records of *The Mermaid's Spaying,* in which the queen is called Dagmar and the king, Valdemar, stem from Vedel's edition (DgF 42, IV 818).

Example 2. *Brother Slays Sister* (DgF 438) is extant in only one original recording, a broadside print from the eighteenth century "by a redactor who has added a whole series of strophes in a style quite different from the ballad style; he has partly misunderstood even the common expressions in ballads." "All of the (6) more recent versions from oral tradition go back to this broadside print as their source; but they all present the peculiarity that they have omitted the self-made verses in the broadside print and retained only the genuine core of the ballad; and they have given even these strophes a more natural and popular form." "In determining the genuine form of the ballad, these versions consequently offer only indirect help."[5]

§55. The methods by which to identify the literary origin of an oral tradition are, then, partly external, partly internal:

(1) When a scholar collects all the forms of a certain narrative, it will become apparent which of them are close to the literary texts. For ballads, which are primarily tied to one language, the material is relatively easy to survey. For tales with wider distribution, the case is more difficult; but it is facilitated by the fact that only a small number of folktale collections reached the broadest circles. Other external evidence is found when features appear in a single version that are not found in the versions of neighboring places.[1]

(2) The story's own features can reveal it as non-popular.

Comment 1. The anomalous features of a narrative need not be absolutely non-popular, but alien to the folklore of a given time and place. *Daughter of the Sun* in Kamp,[2] "told by H. P. Larsen from Møn," seems strange in the context of the Danish folktale, where such a personification of nature is unknown; but it probably stems from *Sicilianische Märchen.*[3] (Olrik [1890–1892a], p. 255).

Comment 2. Even though the fusion essentially disappears in the transition to oral tradition, traces of it will often remain. Example.

The Polyphemus narrative from Attica: the other trolls hasten to the spot at the roar of the cyclops but cannot get into the cave (part of the discarded "No one" motif; cf. §48, example).

§56. The version originating from a known literary source has no source value for the history of the individual narrative. On the other hand, because we know exactly the basic form from which the narrative stems, it has value in that it shows how folklore reshapes its material. In addition, it can serve to define the genuine components in the literary text (§54, example 2).

Comment to §§48–56. The extensive connections between folklore and certain categories of early literature (e.g., medieval chivalric literature) in terms of subject matter and individual features raise the question whether or not they could be due to the fact that literary works furnish folklore with material, just as vice versa. According to the exposition above, one must assume that the literary work loses a large part of its uniqueness by becoming folklore. Proof of the correctness of such an assumption, however, has not been demonstrated. And what we do know certainly argues against it: the greater viability of the tradition in its natural state in contrast to the one that is transplanted outside the greenhouses of literature; the natural coherence of the narrative as it branches off from simple basic forms; and the fact that literary works usually have their place at some fringe or other.[1] Moreover, it is improbable that a literary origin should not leave behind any trace. Finally, the whole hypothesis is futile, because chivalry will not be able to explain the origin of the fantastic features; it must be assumed that lost folk tradition is their source. But a hypothesis that gives an artificial explanation of the phenomena is worthless from a scholarly standpoint.

It is another matter that names are frequently adopted from the more fantastic literature; *The Green Knight* (Arthur's champion),[2] the horse "Bucephalus",[3] *Mastermaid,*[4] Isodd the fair and Isodd the dark (the Tristan legend);[5] probably also Arabia as a fairytale land. While there may be a general correspondence between the adopted name and the character, no such similarity obtains between the narratives. The storytellers have chosen the name as suitable for the fairytale character in question simply on the basis of a general impression of the name.

# CHAPTER

## ❧ 3 ❧

# THE STRUCTURE OF THE NARRATIVE

## The Epic Laws

Literature: Olrik (1908b); Olrik (1909a), an expanded form of a paper delivered at the Historians' Congress in Berlin in August 1908, revision of the aforementioned; Olrik (1908f) = Olrik (1919a), pp. 177–185, aforementioned paper; Olrik (1907e); shortened English translation in Olrik (1908d); *Genesis,* introduction (this edition also contains a comparison with Olrik's "Epic Laws");[1] Schütte (1907), pp. 94ff.: About enumerations and hierarchies: here "Initial Stress" and "Final Stress" are observed and named for the first time;[2] Lund (1908); Christiansen (1915); A. Christensen (1916); Pohlmann (1912);[3] Meyer (1913); *Sagen, Märchen und Lieder,* p. XIII (numerical ascent); Meyer (1906c); *Vore Folkeviser,* pp. 188ff.

§57. The "epic laws" of oral narrative composition. In popular narrative, storytellers have a tendency to observe certain practices in composition and style that are generally common to large areas and different categories of narratives, including most of the European narrative tradition. The regularity with which these practices appear makes it possible for us to regard them as "epic laws" of oral narrative composition.

Comment. Literary composition also offers a number of examples of the same epic laws, or at least of features that take the same direction. Literary composition distinguishes itself from oral narrative, however, in that it obeys the laws selectively and inconsistently. Universal validity, which makes the rules into "law," is thus wanting in literary art, which, moreover, lacks the most pronounced (detailed) epic laws. (This is discussed further in §81.)

Despite this deficiency, however, there is always a certain latitude within the individual genres at any given time and place. Some prefer a more interwoven plot, a larger number of characters, a less rigid unity of plot; others adhere more closely to the epic laws. In all, however, one will be surprised by the strength of the agreements with the epic laws in oral narrative. One can find traditions from remote areas and from countries outside Europe that will give the reader familiar with oral narrative composition an impression of something familiar, not by virtue of its subject, but by its arrangement of material. Beyond this initial sense of recognition stand the "epic laws," a set of conventional procedures used in the composition of a narrative.

Certain genres are more rigidly bound to the conventions of narrative composition, particularly legends and tales, and especially the latter, perhaps because their larger dimensions and more interwoven plot give the conventions an opportunity to display themselves more strongly. A large part of the poetic tradition is less rigidly bound, since, by its nature, it looks to the preservation of the production of the individual poet, and is viewed as a tradition developed among specific peoples and within specific eras. This situation corresponds to the fact that many of our poetic sources belong to some category or other of "fringe folklore."[1] On certain points, they approach the stage where the more rigid rules for composition are replaced by freer mental activity.

The special nature of the "Epic Laws" resides not just in the fact that the individual narrative makes such a limited selection from the real multiplicity of life, but that large quantities of narrative material make the same selective choices of number, of characters and their mutual relationships, and of methods for suspense—tools which, from our point of view, might appear to be a repetition of the same small circle of thoughts. Therefore, we may also call the rules for oral narrative composition rules for the narrow selection from life.

§58. The clarity of the narrative. The narrative does not reveal a multiplicity of features corresponding to real life.[1] It has fewer characters and, above all, fewer forces are simultaneously brought to bear on the fate of a human being. If something must be depicted as a result of many concurrent forces, the narrative brings them into play one by one.

§59. Among others, the so-called Law of Two to a Scene is a manifestation of the clarity of the narrative: the narrative only reluctantly brings more than two characters on stage at the same time; under particular circumstances a third (subordinate) character may be added for a short performance. The narrative prefers one of the performing characters to disappear from the stage, or at least to step outside of the action, before a new one appears.

Example 1. The tale about the little duck (JFm V, no. 16): the king's bride, who is transformed into a duck, comes waddling into the kitchen through a hole in the gutter and asks the dog about its master (and with that the dog is gone); the king has been lying in wait for the duck. Now he grabs the duck and holds it tightly until it is transformed back into a human being.[1]

Example 2. Sigurðr slays Fáfnir: (1) Reginn encourages Sigurðr to the murder; (2) Reginn forges the sword and Sigurðr tests it; (3) Sigurðr digs a pit in the dragon's path, and receives advice from Odin; (4) Sigurðr sits in the pit and thrusts the sword into the dragon's belly; (5) a conversation with the dying dragon ensues; (6) Reginn appears and asks Sigurðr to roast the dragon's heart, after which he "goes to sleep"; (7) Sigurðr roasts the heart and hears the birds in the tree; (8) Sigurðr kills Reginn; (9) Sigurðr rides to the dragon's abode and loads his horse Grani with the gold.[2] Active gods do not appear on the stage at the decisive moment, but prior to it.[3]

Comment. Even when the plot encourages the interaction of many characters with each other, the narrative maintains a certain simplicity. Thus, when Sigurðr's assassin comes home to Gjúki's court, the following events take place:[4] (1) Guðrún's and Högni's dialogue; (2) Brynhildr's speech to the ones who have arrived; (3) Guðrún's answer to her. There are still only two characters in the foreground.[5]

§60. The narrative schematizes its characters and incidents, i.e., gives them only the features most necessary to the plot. Several similar characters or similar episodes are intentionally made to resemble each other as much as possible. Therefore, the literary value of the narrative is to a great extent dependent upon whether those features alone express the character of the entire situation.

Example. The tale *The Good Sword* (GldM III, no. 83): every day the boy drives his sheep into a new enclosure, meets a mountain giant, has almost the same conversation with him, and kills him in the same way.[1]

Comment. The schematizing of the narrative goes so far as to put words into the mouths of the characters that are correct only in the context of the main situation of the narrative: "Pretty maiden, shed a shift"; "King Lindorm, shed a skin" (Olrik [1904b], p. 5).[2] Ederland shouts to the trolls: "Now I'm coming only one more time"; "Now I'll never come again."[3] (Here this exclamation heightens the poetic power of the narrative; one feels more strongly her ingenuity and the helplessness of the trolls.)[4]

§61. Oral narrative composition does not know detailed description and thus cannot use it to express the nature and meaning of the plot. What must be shown to be important is depicted through repetition: in this way thought may dwell longer on the same subject.[1]

Example. *The Good Sword:* The first day, the boy kills a mountain giant in the first enclosure. The second day, under the same circumstances he kills another mountain giant in the second enclosure. The third day, he kills a third one. Apart from the fact that in this way his exploit is given a larger scope, the performance receives the greater fullness needed in a main episode.

Literature. "The language of primitive or simple passion is iteration, not figure; and the ballads, poor in figures, are full of iteration. In fact, the chief mark of ballad style, as it is found in such survivals as are given in the present collection, is a sort of progressive iteration"[2] (*Old English Ballads,* introduction, p. XXXII).

§62. Normally, repetition is accompanied by progressive ascent: the hero fights three times, with each successive fight more difficult than the previous one; or he makes three attempts, and he succeeds only the last time; or first the eldest brother is unsuccessful in the attempt, then the second eldest, and then the youngest is successful. (The last-mentioned example could be called a contrastive ascent: the ascent lies in the difficulty of the undertaking, in light of the first two unsuccessful attempts; the contrast lies in the fact that their attempts do not prepare for his victory; cf. §§71–72.)

Example. The boy (in *The Good Sword*) first slays a troll with three heads, then one with six heads, then one with nine heads.

§63. Plot constraint on the narrative. Any ability of a character or a thing must be expressed in action; otherwise it has no importance for the narrative.

Example. The tale about the little duck (JFm V, no. 16) does not begin by saying that the young girl was "unhappy, but pretty and good." Such an accumulation of thoughts is avoided in the narrative world; each must be expressed in action, and these actions form a series of episodes in the plot: (1) The stepdaughter is sent out onto the heath to gather heather, and she is given only ash-cakes to take with her as food; (2) A little boy with a red cap looks up from the knoll of heather; she greets him kindly and gives him some of her ash-cakes to take with him; (3) The little boy presents her with gifts: pearls fall from her hair when she combs it,[1] and a piece of gold springs from her mouth each time she opens it.[2]

The characteristics of the narrative and its view of life lie in the plot itself. Sigurðr Fáfnisbani is valiant because he kills the dragon; Psyche or "The Dog Bride" is punished and restored in her long wanderings;[3] Hagbard's and Signe's simultaneous deaths are the victory of fidelity; the narrative itself, which points out the place of execution and the bower set on fire across from it, focuses on their companionship into death as the leading thought of the composition.[4] A detailed treatment (in a ballad or a later literary work) may put these features in a clearer light and give them a finer nuance;[5] or it may perhaps efface them. But it is not that which makes them works of art. Each tradition reveals a perception of the conditions of life, and a few tales have in themselves such a grandiose architecture and have succeeded in being reborn in the thought of human beings so consciously that the poets will compete in vain with the folk mind working here.

§64. The tableau of the narrative (the palpability of the narrative). The narrative permits each episode to form a clear picture in the imagination: it shows each character in an action or state where external form and internal aspirations correspond to each other, and by which it distinguishes itself from everyday life to such a degree that it is not confused with it.[1]

The narrative preferably places simple contrasts together: big against small, man against woman, human being against animal. The contrast itself must characterize the special nature of each.

The narrative also draws its characters into physically close interplay, which corresponds to their roles with regard to each other (the hero and his horse; Skjold and the bear; Thor drags the World Serpent to the surface; the warriors by Hrólfr's corpse; Sigmundr carries his dead son).[2] The narrative is—far more than in later literary works—a series of tableaux compositions. The short narrative is most often based entirely on a single constellation of figures; the longer narrative frequently has a single constellation that rises above all the rest.

Peculiar to the composition of the narrative is the preference for the lingering position over the momentary.

A great number of the most famous compositions are based not on impressions of reality but on fantasy. Thus there is a multiplicity of interactions between animal and human being: the hero thrusts his sword into the serpent, the girl stands on the back of the ox and surveys the scene, the woman sits on the mountain and squeezes her own milk into the beaks of the crane and the swan, the eagle carries the hero on its back, etc.[3]

§65. The logic of the narrative. The narrative is unwilling to adopt motifs other than those that will have influence on the plot;[1] and their influence on the plot is in proportion to their varying degree of importance with regard to the goal toward which the plot moves.[2]

The logic of the narrative moves in a plane other than that of external probability. Sometimes it is strangely inaccurate in this respect; often it appears to be concerned only with the probability regarding the motifs it places in the foreground. The world order of the narrative ("the natural laws of the super-natural," Grundtvig; cf. "The mythical way of thinking," Moe)[3] corresponds to the views of vanished eras; it especially believes that the word or the will has a power over the visible world to a degree we do not know.[4]

§66. The unity of plot.[1] The plot of the narrative will naturally aspire toward a single event as its conclusion and omit what does not concern this.[2] Several things, however, will counteract it. Some narrators and some peoples have a poorer sense of the unity of plot and the logic of a narrative than others. On the whole, these qualities are a product of culture, and are often lacking among peoples of low-level cultures.

To a certain degree, unity is also hampered by a fairytale-like tendency to digress into remote and fantastic conceptions. But normally the individual episodes do not stand detached; they merely bring about the protraction of the same situation, allowing the narrative to approach its goal more slowly.

On the other hand, the "romantic" forms of narrative indicating transition to a higher culture will dissolve the firm structure of a narrative (its inner necessity) in order to lose themselves among a multiplicity of events and experiences.

§67. The epic and the ideal unity of plot. The simplest form of unity of plot is the straightforward epic one: each feature works toward the development of an event, the possibility of which the listener has sensed from the beginning.

Example. *The Girl as Helper in the Hero's Flight:* from the moment the hero comes into the service of the troll, the listener hopes that the hero will get away from him alive; from the moment the troll-girl addresses him, one senses her importance in his rescue.[1]

The ideal unity of plot arises when several narrative units are grouped together so that characters and the personal problems in the narrative are emphasized, without, however, the units forming an epic unity.

Example. Numerous European heroic narratives and tales have combined two plots into an ideal unity. *The Girl as Helper in the Hero's Flight* has grown together with *The Forgotten Fiancée* (the ingratitude of the hero increases, because she has rescued him from the troll); the murder of Fáfnir and the ride through the flames to Brynhildr (she has been deceived so much more painfully, because only the most exceptional hero could solve the problem she gave to her suitor;[2] Sigurðr's external feat of valor forms the prelude to his guiltless relationship to Brynhildr and to Gunnarr); Kete and Vige together with Uffe's battle against the Saxons (his deed so much greater, because it also washed away the blame of having broken the law of single combat).[3] Note: in the last instance the unity of plot is based on the idea (this is a late, reflective feature); normally there is unity in the main character.

Comment. A category of ideal unity is the harmonization of familial relationships, which is conspicuous in Scandinavian heroic narratives: standardized characters and events increasingly repeat themselves within the same family.[4]

Literature: Grundtvig (1867); Olrik (1903–1910) I, pp. 336ff.

§68. The single-strandedness of plot. The plot of a narrative consistently moves toward the next causal or temporal step. It does not break off in order to return to something that has previously happened;[1] and it does not move the scene unless the progress of the plot forces such a movement.

Literature. Characteristic of the simple ballad plot is the single narrative stream. Synchronistic events are exceptional, and synchronism is never necessary for the working out of the plot. (Hart [1907], p. 39; with examples.)

This characteristic applies to most forms of narratives (legend, tale, lay) usually so strictly that the plot does not leave its main character for more than a brief moment, and then only so that one keeps clearly in mind his relationship to what is happening.

The more developed categories of saga form an exception, either (1) by interweaving a new story in the form of a speech, or (2) by explicitly stopping the main plot at a suitable point of closing to introduce new plots, which only at their conclusion flow into the main plot. This structuring results from an attempt to combine several mutually related narratives into a broader saga- or epic-like account.

Example 1. The longest *Marsk Stig ballad* (DgF 145 A), which otherwise adopts all the smaller Marsk Stig ballads to a large extent verbatim, does not include the episode where the murderers go to Ribe to buy cowls,[2] for this would demand the simultaneous change of scene and character. Similarly, it has adopted the traitor Rane as an active character only by including a conversation between him and Lady Ingeborg as a transitional link.

Example 2. (1) Reginn's account of Fáfnir in *Völsunga saga* and the *Elder Edda*,[3] (2) the champions' special stories in *Hrólfs saga kraka;*[4] "Now two plots proceed," *Sturlunga saga* (1878) I, p. 23.[5] The Danish heroic saga about Uffe obeys the single-strandedness in time, but not in content.

§69. The Law of Concentration on a Leading Character (The Law of Centralization). The narrative always arranges itself around a main character. It includes what concerns him and disregards everything else. It reshapes the given material, especially when it deals with the extraneous (e.g., historical occurrences), in order better to place all of the episodes in relation to the main character.

The experiences of the main character sometimes constitute a unity of plot, sometimes a somewhat looser connection of material where the unity of plot is weak or non-existent, so that only the relationship to the protagonist and his character ties the parts together.

Example (to 2). Accounts about strong, fearless, or ingenious characters (*Strong Hans,*[1] *New Courage,*[2] the Hamlet narrative in Saxo in the expanded form).[3]

§70. Two main characters may appear in a narrative, or, rather, a character may perhaps appear whose importance for the plot approaches that of the actual main character.

Sometimes the latter character may equal or surpass the original protagonist in the interest of the audience (thus Mastermaid over the king's son;[1] Brynhildr over Sigurðr; Áslaug over Ragnarr Loðbrók).[2] In such cases, the former will be the formal main character of the narrative: it takes its point of departure in his fate and follows it to its conclusion.

Comment. Notice that a woman often attracts the most interest, but that a man is the formal main character. A shifting of the evaluation of the importance of the female character, then, seems to have taken place during the life of the narrative.

§71 The Law of Contrast. When two characters appear at the same time, the narrative will establish a contrast in character between them, often also a contrast in action. The contrasts between good and evil, poor and rich, big and small, young and old, etc., are very common.

Example. "Two valiant maidens walked over the green banks; the one was so cheerful, the other, she was so sorrowful" (DgF);[1] "Two ladies sat and worked gold; the one, she was so sorrowful" (DgF 286); *Per the rich Merchant and Paul the poor Smith* (tale);[2] Gunnarr Gjúkason as the weaker character, his brother Högni as the stronger.[3]

Generally, the character who is the worse off of the two will invoke the sympathy of the listener.

A popular form of this type of contrast pits a big and strong character against a small but ingenious character. In an incredibly large number of narratives, it takes the stereotyped form of a meeting between troll and human being.[4]

Comment. In Scandinavian, it also penetrates into the world of the gods: Thor and Loki, often with the latter being superior;[5] Thor and Odin, in the same way (Olrik [1905], pp. 135ff.; with a demonstration of the fact that these contrasts are not original in the myth).

§72. The Law of Contrast emanates from the main character of the narrative down to subordinate characters (rarely vice versa).

The narrative also makes the adversary of the protagonist in the plot as different in character as possible, partly by generally making him a knave, partly by giving him more definite features.

Example. The generous Hrólfr Kraki against Hrörik (*Bjarkamál*) or Aðisl (later narratives), Sigurðr and Reginn.[1]

New subordinate characters also are created to function as qualitative contrasts to the protagonist.

Example. The fearful one next to the valiant one (Hervör and the shepherd by the grave mound;[2] Högni and the slave Hjalli when their hearts are cut out).[3]

A special type of plot created in this way turns on the treacherous death of the hero and the underhanded assassin.[4] Another type concerns the great king's inept successor, who rules for only a few hours.

Example (2). Hjarvard, Hjarne, Shorthair (Olrik [1903–1910] I, p. 130).

§73 The Law of Twins. When two characters appear in the same role, they are both depicted as being weaker than a single character.

Example. "... two Haddings, and together they did the work of one man, because they were twins and the youngest; but Angantýr did the work of two men" (*Hervarar saga,* chapter 2); Kete and Vige are weaker than Aðisl and less significant than Uffe, as are the two Saxon warriors against the lone Uffe (the Uffe narrative in Saxo)[1]; Gunnarr and Högni as brothers as opposed to the lone Sigurðr Fáfnisbani. This applies especially to the young king's sons whose lives are threatened: Hredric and Hrodmund in *Beowulf*[2] (the latter otherwise unknown); Erpr and Eitill as Guðrún's sons (only the former a historical figure)[3]. In the myths, the helping creatures often appear in twos: Odin's ravens Huginn and Muninn; his wolves Geri and Freki;[4] Þjálfi and Röskva as Thor's companions;[5] Byggvir and Beyla as Freyr's servants[6] (on the other hand, Skírnir is alone and thus a more independent character); "Göndul and Skögul sent Gautatýr" (*Hákonarmál*);[7] the Dioscures in relation to a higher heavenly god.[8]

§74. The Law of Three. The narrative has a preference for the number three in characters, in objects, and in successive episodes.[1] This applies especially to tales.

In a large amount of narrative material, three is the highest number of characters that can be distinguished as individuals. Five and especially seven mean "many," particularly of a mysterious or magical kind.[2] Twelve is used about a group of followers who belong together.[3] Higher numbers are not used unless one can build a graduated series leading up to them: a dragon with three, with nine, with twenty-seven heads.[4]

Example 1. *White Bear King Valemon* (*Norske Folkeeventyr* [1876], no. 30): the bear takes the king's 3 daughters with him 3 Thursdays in a row; he keeps the youngest one; she stays with the bear for 3 years and has 3 children; the bear takes them away from her; she visits home, and is then tempted to light a candle and look at the bear; he is awakened by the dripping of wax on his forehead and leaves her; she visits 3 different women, sees 3 children there, and gets 3 objects; she comes to the troll-woman's court 3 days before her wedding with the bear, buys for the 3 objects 3 nights with her lover, and is recognized by him on the last night.[5]

Example 2. A Swedish legend about "Kettil's mound," Liared parish, Västergötland: "But while Christianity became generally accepted, Kettil was angered by it and had his burial mound built. For *three* years they worked on this, and he had *three* surrounding walls placed around it, whereupon he went into it and lived for *three* years until he died, at which time the mound was closed after his horse that had been adorned with golden shoes and his sword were brought in there" (Hallström [1912], p. 41).[6]

§75. The Law of Final Stress. When several narrative elements are set alongside each other, emphasis is placed on the last in the sequence: the youngest of three brothers, the last of three attempts, etc. The epically important character is normally in the "position of final stress."

On the other hand, the most impressive character is placed first: the eldest of several brothers, the mightiest of several gods, and the like. This is designated as "initial stress" and does not concern narrative research.[1]

Example of three with "final stress": "Three maidens sit in a bower, two spin gold; the *third,* she cries about her betrothed under black mold" (DgF 90). Russian magical formula: "Three ladies sit under a pear tree; they are all sisters; one has learned to spin, the second to embroider, and the third to cast spells" (Mansikka [1909], p. 255). In both these instances, the first two characters are quite unimportant to the plot; they seem to be added only in order to create a sequence of three with final stress. Per, Paul, and Esben (tale).[2] Nori, Østen, Dan (Danish narrative about the origin of the three Scandinavian countries; cf. Olrik [1907e], pp. 196ff.; A. Christensen [1916], pp. 45ff.); notice that the best forms of the tribal legends comprise not only three brothers but also three generations with initial stress (mythical ancestors) and final stress (the ancestors of individual tribes). The triple Odin: High, Just-as-high, Third[3] (the last is in Snorri's *Gylfaginning* the wisest).

Example of three with "initial stress" and "final stress": Odin, Hœnir, and Loki (Odin is the most distinguished character, Loki the acting one).[4] Ár kváðu Humla Húnum ráða, Gizur Gautum, Gotum Angantý[5] (the *Angantýr lay* in *Hervarar saga*); the Huns are the mightiest [people], but Angantýr and his Goths are the ones who receive special attention in the poem (note that Angantýr is in the position of "final stress" and therefore after Gizurr, who, however, is a chieftain subordinate to him).

Comment 1. Where gods appear with little or no epic material (so that the religious consideration is the predominant one), they are in the position of "initial stress," not "final stress," e.g., Odin, Vili, Vé; Odin, Hœnir, Lóðurr (the only ones present at the creation of man).[6] Note, by the way, that in an artistic tableau, the middle element is the most important. The difference is due to the fact that an oral description demands a development in time; the tableau, on the other hand, offers an instantaneous impression, and the middle of what is seen comes exactly within one's line of vision.

Example of several with "final stress": Twelve sons of Arngrímr, ending with "Angantýr" (Saxo, Book 5; Icelandic, on the other hand, gives him final stress in the first alliterative group);[7] in *Hervarar saga,* however, Angantýr is the eldest of the brothers (thus an unusual use of initial stress).[8] The twelve robbers and Björn (Saxo, Book 6, *Friðleifs saga*);[9] Björn himself, who stands last, is the only one of them who appears as an individual, and he far outlives the others.

Example of several with "initial stress" and "final stress": The East-Gothic chieftains in *Widsith:*[10] first the singer visited Ermanaric's royal court; thereafter he wandered throughout the land of the Goths to 29 chieftains, of which the last two are Vudga and Hama: "I do not consider them the poorest warriors even though I mention them last" (i.e., they are the most legendary ones).[11] The list of kings in *Widsith:* beginning with Huns and Goths as the mightiest peoples and ending with the Angles as the author's own countrymen (note that the personal interest creates "final stress" also where no epic consideration asserts itself).

Example of two with "final stress": "Phol ende Wodan vuorum zi holza" (the *Merseburg lay*);[12] "Sir Iver and Sir Esbern Snare, they drank ale in Medelfare" (DgF 131).[13] In Danish ballads, however, final stress is counteracted by the desire to place a man in front of a woman ("Sir Villeman and his beautiful wife")[14] and to mention the main character of the ballad in its first words (DgF 40, 76, 271).[15]

Comment 2. The question of "initial stress" and "final stress" has been discussed especially by Chambers in an excursus to his *Widsith* (pp. 255–256). He admits that "initial stress" and "final stress" correspond to a general tendency among narrators (he mentions David's warriors [2 Samuel 23] and Arthur's 110 knights as examples), but refuses to believe that the *Widsith* poet was conscious of such a rule. The list of kings begins with Attila, not with Ermanaric; and it ends with Hrolf, or, if he is a later addition, with Alevih. The Gothic warriors begin with Hedka, who is otherwise unknown; and the author apologizes for ending with Vudga and Hama.

Of these objections, the ones that are directed toward "final stress" are absolutely worthless:

(1) That Vudga and Hama, according to their status as warriors, ought to be mentioned earlier. That the singer admits this to his audience is no revocation but rather a confirmation of the consideration of the epic composition. (2) At the top of the list of the Goths is not the unknown Hedka, but Ermanaric himself: first the singer stayed with him, and "next he wandered throughout all the land of the Goths." The sequence is in a way parallel to the list of Arthur's knights mentioned by Chambers, beginning with Arthur himself and ending with Lancelot. (3) The list of kings ends with Offa and Alevih, who are then compared; but their mutual position is determined by alliteration ("Offa wēold Ongle"[16] must be at the beginning of the long line), so that only Offa in the epic statement connected with this receives final stress. The statement about Offa's great personal deed was epically necessary; for otherwise Alevih would receive final stress. (4) The list of kings opens with Attila, because the Huns, by virtue of their great power during the era of the Great Migration, have a standing position of initial stress: thus in the list of kings, thus also in the list of kings in the *Angantýr lay,* and in the list of peoples in *Widsith;* everywhere the order of succession is Huns and then Goths; they are both in the position of initial stress, but in such a way that the Huns are always the stronger.

These examples offer the most perfect illustrations of initial and final stress; i.e., the old catalogue composer (or catalogue tradition) obeys the rules: we see him overcome the small problems that the material places in his way, and we see also that it is not an abstract rule, but that by virtue of the conventions certain binding requirements have been placed upon the composer.

§76. The Law of Opening. In the beginning of the narrative, one moves (1) from the individual to the multiple, (2) from calm to excitement, and (3) from the everyday to the unusual.

Example 1. The sons' father is mentioned even though he is quite an unimportant character: "Skammel, he dwells up north in Ty, and Skammel is rich and gay, five sons he has both fair and tall, but two went an evil way" (DgF 354).[1]

Examples 2 and 3. Ballads often begin with a conversation, a dance, or another everyday event from which the actual event evenly develops.[2]

In Danish ballad composition, this rule applies very strictly; only rarely can one find beginnings that relate, for example, the sudden disappearance of a king's daughter,[3] or the king's outburst of jealousy against one of his courtiers (DgF 295). In all folksongs, this type of beginning must be considered normal.

Comment. As an exception, the Spanish ballads often have a violent beginning (Example: *El infante vengador,*[4] *Primavera y flor de romances* II, p. 72; *Petit romancero,* p. 174: *De l'enfant vengeur*):

> Hélo, hélo por do viene
> el infante vengador,
> caballero á la gineta
> et un caballo corredor,
> su manto revuelto al brazo,
> demudada la color,
> y en la su mano derecha
> un venablo cortador.[5]

§77. The Law of Closing. The account normally ends after the decisive event, but preferably not so suddenly that the audience is startled; the atmosphere must have time to calm down and to disappear gradually from the main character and the main episodes. A short, concluding story serves this purpose, e.g., (1) the later fate of the main character, particularly in such a way that one follows him through to a lasting, often lingering or resting state; (2) the influence of the fate of the main character on others, e.g., that his mother or his betrothed dies from grief; (3) the fate of the subordinate characters, e.g., the punishment of the villain in the account; (4) visible memories of the event, such as the reappearance of the protagonist as a ghost (cf. "localization" in chapter IV B).

Example 1. "Oh, sore has he wounded his father, and struck off his mother's hand, and so roams Ebbe Skammelsen, the wild ways of the land" (Ebbe Skammelsen's murder of his betrothed and his brother gives way to his outlawed wanderings in the world, DgF 354).[1] "Now Bengærd lies in black soil, still the farmer has both ox and cow" (DgF 139).[2]

Example 2. "All so early dawn grew red, where three in Sir Oluf's hold lay dead, Sir Oluf lay dead and his bride also, the third was his mother who died for woe" (DgF 47 and elsewhere).[3] "Now that the Lord God, my bridegroom, has called, he will not let me stay behind! Suddenly she falls down in front of the emperor, pale, and dies instantly" (*The Song of Roland*).[4] The ballad about the murder of Erik Klipping ends with the queen thanking the boy who brought her the message: "Now thou art a trusty messenger, ill though thy tidings be; food while I live and fire in my court, this shalt thou have of me" (DgF 145).[5]

Example 3. "Now hold thy peace thou evil maid, for thou art a liar, tomorrow or e'er the sun goes down, thou shalt be burnt with fire!" (the *Harbor ballad,* DgF 20).[6]

Example 4. The king offers to bring little Kirsten's corpse to Vestervig[7] (DgF 126; belongs also to example 1). "Sir Luno sailed back to Greenland, that knight so bold, and there sits the mermaid, a stone so cold" (DgF 43).[8]

Example (mixed). "One of my colleagues (Mrs. Astrid Lund) wanted to know whether there were any exceptions to 'the Law of Closing.' She then went through a large number of unpublished Danish tales about the release from an enchantment; here one would expect an abrupt ending. But the tale never ended simply with the disenchantment of the main character. Sometimes, right after the disenchantment, it continued with a loosely attached episode; often, however, the main event was followed by the release of subordinate characters or an indication of the later life of the main characters; and if there was no other possibility for continuation, then the narrator always added a long, jesting closing formula in order to quiet the mood—hung, as it were, a fig-leaf on the tale in order to cover its nakedness. Thus 'the

Law of Closing' invariably holds in this area without exception" (Olrick [1919a], p. 178).

Comment. Note that the composition unwillingly tolerates many closings; a single one is best. In various versions of the same composition, different closings are often found (DgF 126, see §96). However, this does not mean that one has the authority to go back to a "basic form" of the composition, where they all had their own place;[9] this would only weaken the poetic effect. The larger epic-like production better tolerates several closings than oral narrative composition because of its scope (*The Song of Roland:* the hand of the dying character holding onto the sword, the revenge, the death of the betrothed, the punishment of the traitor).[10]

§78. To conclude the explanation of the "Epic Laws," some small samples chosen at random are mentioned here with regard to their appearance in individual sources or individual groups of related sources.

Example 1. *Hrólfs saga kraka,*[1] the passage about Fróði (chapters 1–4): The brothers Hálfdan and Fróði each have their own kingdom: one is kind, the other is a quarrelsome man (Law of Opening, Law of Contrast). At night, Fróði attacks his brother's royal throne, kills him, and forces the people to swear loyalty to him. Hálfdan's two sons (Law of Twins) are hidden by their foster father Reginn, who leads them to old Vífill on his small island. Fróði searches for the king's sons; sorcerers reveal to him that they are in his vicinity, probably on the island. Then follow Fróði's three attempts to catch them: (1) the men arrive; (2) they are immediately sent on a new search; (3) Fróði himself is with them (Law of Three, progressive ascent). Vífill sends the boys to Earl Sævill, who is married to their sister Signý. They are taken into service unrecognized and follow Sævill when he goes to a party in the king's castle; they are recognized by their sister and Sævill but are not revealed. A seeress reveals their presence to Fróði but is stopped by a gold ring given to her by Signý; they manage to escape and then to burn Fróði to death in his castle. "There Sigríðr also burned to death, Helgi and Hróar's mother, because she would not go out"; they reward Sævill and Reginn and take over the kingdom (Law of Closing).

One will notice how accurately the narrative maintains the unity of plot and, in addition, how rigidly the plot is bound to the two young protagonists (only Sigríðr appears to to be irrelevant).[2] It is interesting to observe "the Law of Twins," because all action is carried out jointly by the king's two sons. Only the saga writer (chapter 3) stresses the fact that Helgi, although two years younger, "was bigger and more valiant" (namely, as an introduction to the next section of the saga, where Helgi plays the main role); the comment does not belong to the plot, but to the description that "Hamr [Helgi] gets an untrained horse and turns his face toward its tail and behaves like an idiot in every way," but "his brother Hrani [Hróar] turns the right way." Only after Fróði is dead and the sons of Hálfdan are grown up is the "Law of Twins" replaced by the "Law of Contrast,"[3] in that Hróar is peaceful, and Helgi is warlike and violent and becomes, among other things, Hróar's avenger (chapter 9).

The rest of the saga is composed of the following parts: (1) the Helgi section, (2) the Svipdagr section, (3) the Böðvarr and Hjalti section I-II, and (4) the Uppsala campaign and the fall of Hrólfr.[4] One will find a large number of examples; thus the Law of Contrast: the small and weak Hjalti in contrast to the strong Böðvarr; the brave Hrólfr and the brave Svipdagr in contrast to the ingenious and cowardly Aðils and, similarly, the ingenious Hjörvarðr and Skuld. The Law of Three appears only in the Böðvarr section I (which has a tale-like structure)[5] and in the Svipdagr section (with "initial stress" between the brothers; but the one who is in the position of final stress, Hvítserkr, has the main role in the corresponding *Skjöldunga saga*);[6] in the Hrólfr section [during the visit of Hrólfr and his champions to the farmer Hrani on their way to Aðils:[7] the first night an attempt is made to see if the champions can withstand cold, the second night thirst, the third night heat; only the twelve berserks withstand the tests, and only these are therefore taken along to Uppsala, where Hrólfr and his champions walk on their shields over the fires in Aðils's hall].

Example 2. Numbers in Finnish oral composition.[8] Only 1, 2, and 3 are contantly used about real individuals; all numbers from 4 to 10 are generally used to express a number that is greater than 2 or 3 (4, 5, 6, and 10 refer to reality only in exceptional cases). "Many" is often designated by 100 or 1,000; all other numbers larger than 10 are extremely rare. The influence of alliteration: the use of many numbers is determined by alliteration: "4 maidens, 3 brides"; 4 (*neljä*) is always found with words beginning with *n*-. Numbers larger than 3 are almost always determined by alliteration, hence certain stereotyped examples: 4 maidens, 5 brothers, 7 uncles, 6 coachmen, 8 places, 9 lofts, 10 brothers-in-law. By varied repetition of expressions, the numbers become indeterminate, although the series of numbers in each place shows a progressive ascent (§62; rarely descent): "3, 4, 5, 6, 7 dogs." One and 2 are always used in a real sense, 2 often in a contrast (cf. §71): "the one plait combed, the other not"; or with progressive ascent: "do not strike because of one mistake, and not because of two either" (§62).

Three is the most common number of all (as in folktales). When the alliteration does not demand another number, 3 is used, often with progressive ascent: "painted once, painted twice, began painting a third time." Four is rare in expressions of reality: "with four feet," "the four corners of the house"; the number almost only appears in alliterative formulas. Five is used in a similar way (really only in the phrase "five fingers"). Six is found only in certain expressions: "a house with six pillars," "a boat with six compass timbers," "I was along as the 6th–7th man" (when the earth was created); the fox has six cubs. Seven and 8 are only used for alliteration. 9 is independent ("I was present as the 9th man"), but is usually followed by 10 (or 9½): "behind nine locks (and still a tenth)," "nine brothers, the tenth a sister," "nine fathoms deep, an ell on the tenth," "nine seas, and half a sea more." Of the larger numbers, 10 is very rare ("ten years," "ten coins"), except in the case of progressive ascent. The numbers 10, 12, 13, 14, 15, and 16 may appear in expressions involving trade; moreover, we see phrases such as "12 years old," "15 years old," "15 verst," etc., occuring in progressive ascent (15, 16, 18 years). The number 20 occurs more frequently, although it is used only for alliteration: "20 fathoms wide," "not even for 20 reasons," "a boy of 20." We also find "30 summers old" (not rare), "50 coins worth" (more often, rarely 500), "60 summers," "60 sacks of flour" (only two examples in all), and "around 90" (one example). The numbers 100 and 1,000 are used infrequently about a large amount: "100 men," "1,000 men," "the church has 100 boards," "with 100 eyes," "a fir tree with 100 needles," the big eagle with 100 feathers. The number 1,000 is used only for alliteration. Numbers over 100 are usually used only in trade: 107, 115 kopeks (in more recent song), 700, 800, 4,000, 5,000, "a million" (borrowed from Russian); exceptions are "200 sisters-in-law," "200 shirts," "600 sheaves," "700 years," "100 times 100 children." (Relander [1894], pp. 258–276.)

§79. The aesthetic-spiritual foundations of the Epic Laws.

§80. The historical foundations of the Epic Laws.

§81. The Epic Laws and literary works. To a certain degree, these "Epic Laws" also apply to literary composition.

The most sharply pronounced forms of "Epic Laws" are normally avoided in literary works, or if they do appear they are so concealed that classification of the different cases is avoided (e.g., the Law of Three). Such schematization is most likely to be found in lyrical composition, and an unconscious sense of poetic effect is perhaps most easily found in the important poetic work.

Example. Johannes Ewald's battle song *King Christian Stood by a High Mast:* "It is possible that to Ewald himself the poem stood as segmented into four parts focusing on the king, the nobleman, the officer, and the sailor respectively... but it definitely seems more like 3 + 1 verses.... The initial stress falls on *the king,* who undeniably is the most distinguished of the company; but the final stress just as clearly falls on *the dare-devil,* the special hero of the common man with his magnificently stormy name. One begins with what one respects the most, but ends with what one likes the best" (Kristensen [1914], p. 97). It may be added that the detached last verse has several of the characteristics of the Law of Closing: not only does it synthesize the atmosphere of the previous strophes, but it also distributes interest to include the whole naval rank, and it ends with the brave ones being put to rest in the enormous embrace of the sea.[1]

Literature. Kristensen (1914); Seip (1916).[2]

Comment. Meyer[3] (1913) lists the following as common to (?) the laws for oral narrative composition and literary composition: (1) "die Scheidung von Haupt- und Nebenvorstellung" (*"Mittelpunktbildung,"*[4] i.e., the Laws of Centralization and Unity of Plot), especially "der Held" with "die moralische Gruppenbildung" (everything that furthers the luck of the hero is good, everything that obstructs it is evil), and "die ästhetische Gruppenbildung"[5] (with the correct standard for main and subordinate characters); (2) Gesetz der Symmetrie[6] (stylizing, repetition, the Law of Three); (3) Gesetz des Kontrastes. The last two items may be combined: the hero between two women (Heracles, Sigurðr,[7] more recent novel composition). Finally, (4) die Vertiefung des Themas, führt fast unausbleiblich zu einer Erweiterung, ... kann bis zur Bildung eines Zyklus gesteigert werden;[8] (5) das Gesetz der *Ausbildung des Gattungsmässigen,* especially die Anählichung der Werke derselben Gattung, and, more specifically, Gesetz der Konvergenz, auf nachträgliche Annäherung begründet.[9]* (The single combat

---

*"Wir dürfen sagen: ein gewisses Mass von Stilisierung versteht sich für jedes literarische Werk schlechterdings von selbst; Stilisierung aber ist nicht anderes, als die Angleichung der geistig oder körperlich erschauten Gegenstandes an andere, die bereits durch die geistige Verarbeitung der Künstler hindurchgegangen sind.... Die Stilisierung gibt das Allgemeine, die Wiedergabe des persönlichen Eindrucks gibt das Besondere, und ohne beider Vereinigung ist kein Kunstwerk.... Dies aber genügt, um eine ganz allgemein giltige, also von historischen, nationalen oder individuellen Bedingungen unabhängige *Zwangs-*

in the dramas at the time of Dumas.) Of these points, (4) and (5), however, belong to "The Life of the Narrative."[10] For the other points, Meyer only partially explains what is common to oral narrative composition and literature.

## §82. The importance of the Epic Laws for research.

---

*läufigkeit der literarischen Formen* zu bewirken. Unter 'Zwangsläufigkeit' verstehen wir die Erscheinung, dass mit Notwendigkeit auf einen bestimmten Tatbestand ein anderer folgen muss" (Meyer [1913] pp. 707f.).

# CHAPTER

## 4

# THE LIFE OF THE NARRATIVE

Literature: Moe (1914); Moe (1915); Moe (1917);[1] Aarne (1913a), pp. 23–39; J. Krohn (1888); Olrik (1903–1910) I, introduction; Moe (1895); Feilberg (1894); Feilberg (1892–1894a); Meier (1909); Wundt (1908–1912) II:1, pp. 326ff.

## A. THE LIFE AND TRANSFORMATION OF THE NARRATIVE

§83. In folkloristics, one uses the expression that a narrative "lives," i.e., that it is an object of oral transmission among human beings. The narrative "dies" when it is no longer remembered and passed on by someone who heard it.

Comment. The narrative still "lives"—although in a languishing state—as long as the one who knows it brings it to his own consciousness, tells it to himself, so to speak.

§84. The closer the new recipient of the narrative stands to the one he receives it from, the better his prospects are of adopting the same narrative world as the teller.

There will always be many individual reasons why accurate transmission of a narrative cannot take place (unclear speech, deafness, loneliness, lack of aptitude or memory, etc.). But the defective forms of the narrative that come into existence in this way will most often soon die out. At any rate, their influence will be counteracted by the fact that other individuals possess the same susceptibility as the earlier narrators and can therefore acquire it completely.

On the other hand, there will be reasons for the death of the narrative of a more general nature. The two most important ones are: (1) that other narratives penetrate from the outside, whereby those already present are forgotten; (2) that individuals or societies reach a cultural level at which they do not—or only to a small degree—pay attention to narratives.

§85. There will always be a "struggle for existence" among narratives. More narratives are heard than can be held in one's memory; the narratives that in some way or other make a deeper impression than others will especially be remembered.

The strength of the impression is partly determined by external circumstances (frequent repetition; appropriation during childhood or youth; the more or less good narrator), partly by internal circumstances: the ability of the narrative to set fantasy and feelings into motion.[1]

Example. Weil die Märchen als Mittel zur Erheiterung gebraucht werden, ist es natürlich, dass die unterhaltenden Märchen, von denen die Hörer mehr angezogen werden, sich schneller als die trockenen verbreiten. Das Märchen "die Tiere im Nachtquartier" ist offenbar durch seinen fröhlichen Ton in den verschiedenen Ländern Europas so allgemein geworden, während das verwandte Märchen von den auf der Reise befindlichen Hausgeräten [which must be its source] sich mit einer viel unbedeutenderen Verbreitung zufrieden geben musste.[2] (Aarne [1913a], p. 20; see also Aarne [1913b], pp. 160f.).

§86. For this reason alone, a *selection* among the available narratives will constantly take place. The narratives that create the clearest imaginative picture and whose plots aim at definite and universal goals receive preference. Inasmuch as this happens, it seems that a (usually slow) raising of the entire spiritual level of the narrative world will take place. The narratives that die out will primarily be those that form a vague picture and contain unclear or conflicting fundamental ideas. In this way, too, the simple narrative may give way to the richer and more artistic narrative.

Comment. The evidence of the correctness of this sentence, apart from its *a priori*[1] probability, will be that among undeveloped tribes, narratives appear that are looser or poorer in their structure, lower in their moral ideas, and more arbitrary in their relation to the real world. One must assume that these narratives (similar to the general development of culture) represent a stage from which the "higher" cultures have moved away.[2]

§87. For these reasons, the narrative will more easily migrate from people at a higher cultural level to people at a lower cultural level, partly by virtue of its inner quality, partly by virtue of the fact that neighbors are generally inclined to imitate more distinguished people. Similarly, the narrative will more easily move from centrally located and communicative people than from those on the periphery.[1] But these circumstances may be counteracted by the greater or poorer poetic talent of the individual group of people; and especially with regard to oral composition, which has lasted for thousands of years, the concept of a higher culture is too vague to be compelling for the individual case.

Example 1. Dissemination from the periphery: the ballad *King Valdemar and his Sister* (DgF 126) is the original form of the German and the Wendish ballad, and probably also of the English ballad of similar content.[2]
Example 2. Diffusion from a "lower" culture located on the periphery: immigration of Celtic narrative materials in the medieval chivalric literature.[3]

§88. The conditions for the continued life of a narrative are always best where it actually has its home.[1] Here it is most easily acquired by people at an early age and adjusted according to the intellectual horizon and to the external culture and setting. Often the narrative is connected to this scene in a special way by location or even localization.

A change in culture (also a change in language) and the transfer of the people to another home (which is often accompanied by a certain change in culture) are dangerous to the existence of a narrative. The narrative will die out or possibly be adapted to the new conditions.

Example. The narrative about a giant bound in the mountain who will break away in order to destroy the world is found with extraordinary vigor in the Caucasus, where the enormous mountains with volcanic phenomena provide a suitable natural background. Moreover, one finds narrative forms in a wide circle around this country that reveal themselves as migratory forms of the Caucasus types, thus offering proof of the better conditions for the life of the narrative in its home region than elsewhere (Olrik [1902–1914] II).[2]

§89. The narrative is never passed on exactly the way it is heard.[1] The change in traditions in metrical form is often insignificant, whereas it is considerably greater in traditions in prose forms, despite the pains one often takes to retain traditions held to be historical as accurately as possible.

Example. In this way kind, old people in the heather areas told us children *såg-en, læmmiker* and *emtere*.[2] *Såg-en* was set up to be historically true and should be kept pure. The above ("About the Bishop and the Town Herd of Ribe for King Valdemar")[3] is a *læmmik;* these received changes, but the main features were not allowed to be altered. *Emtere* were fantastic, probably derived partly from the *Arabian Nights*[4] (Kierckebye [1866–1867], p. 172).

§90. While the linguistic form changes continuously, the content of the narrative is less changeable. The same plot of a tale can be followed through many countries and languages, often under circumstances where the gradual transitions in content provide proof of the continued oral transmission of the same narrative material.[1]

Example 1. The narrative about the human being who takes a message home with him about the old troll's death, which appears earliest in Plutarch[2] (*The Great Pan has Died*) and is now a common European legend.[3]

Example 2. *Elfshot* (Grundtvig, DgF IV 852):[4] "A ballad which has such deep roots in the popular soil, which, like this one, rests on an ancient and common popular belief, and whose engaging topic has such a simple structure that all the individual [epic] segments interlock so definitely with each other that misunderstanding and distortion become almost impossible, is, as long as it retains the sympathy of the people and touches their minds and consequently is transmitted from generation to generation, a living organism, which in a surprising way manages to retain its unity even through changes of time and language. It appears as a solid organic unity just as fully in the recent formations found among the people, in the Danish versions of 7 or 8 verses,[5] as in the old Danish chief form with 54 verses."

§91. The changes to which the narratives are most constantly subjected are "reduction" and "expansion." Reduction results from faulty memory or poor narrative ability; expansion is due to the desire for a lively and full presentation.

Example 1. *The Old Hag Against the Stream* (Moe [1895]): "It is as if such things cannot die; they turn out to hang tenaciously onto life. They can expand to comprehensive stories, they can increase and grow into an entire forest, and they can shrink so as to hide in a word, in a name,[1] just like a little dried seed, but they do live."

Comment. Closely related to reduction is the "narrowing" discussed by Moe (1914), p. 8, but by this he understands a more active transformation of the narrative: (a) richly developed narrative material is dissolved into smaller parts (his example, the Lapp epic, is, however, doubted by more recent scholars);[2] (b) in an older, rich presentation, everything superfluous is taken out; in the latter he claims to see the effect of the intervention of genuine individual authors, whether expressing themselves in writing or just in oral form.

Example 2. The ballad of the Danish peasants is often strikingly brief, e.g., the versions of *Elfshot* in 7–8 verses in contrast to the far more extensive older Scandinavian versions (see §90, example 2).

§92. Innovation in narrative material appears not only as an expansion, but also as an alteration of the existing plot.

Example: *Elfshot* (Grundtvig in DgF IV 852): "But next to the wonderful unity and firmness in the principal theme ... we also find a very lively variety, sometimes appearing in a different delineation of the topic: a partial abandonment of individual elements, subordination of some, stressing of others, sometimes in a multiple variation of individual narrative features—as when the elf-maiden brings death to the knight: with a word, with a kiss, with a drink, with a sign, with a stroke of her hand, or with a magic wand or with a stab of a knife: either by a single knife in the individual elf-maiden's hand, or by a shower of knives thrown from many hands, or finally: the life is sucked out of him while he is whirled in the dance of the elves; sometimes [variety is achieved] also by adding new narrative features (only some Danish forms of the ballad let him step into the dance of the elves; the Faroese forms alone have his leavetaking from his mother before the outward journey and an indication of his earlier relationship to the elf-maiden); and finally this rich variety appears to an extraordinarily high degree in the execution of all details and in the expressions and rhymes employed for this purpose."

§93. The alteration of the narrative may be conscious or unconscious. It is conscious (or at least half-conscious) when the narrator recites the narrative in one way, while he knows that it was told to him in a different way. Of these two categories, unconscious alteration probably plays a much greater role than conscious alteration; "generally the singer takes pains to reproduce the narrative as accurately as possible" (Moe).[1]

§94. A change will often cause further changes by later narrators, and thereby the total transformation of the narrative will be quite extensive, even though the individual changes are small.

Example. The ballad about little Kirstin, who is whipped or danced to death[1] by her brother (*King Valdemar and his Sister,* DgF 126): the role played by the "son of the King of England": (1) unknown in almost all Scandinavian forms outside Denmark; (2) character off-stage: the one to whom little Kirstin should have been married (Old Danish A); (3) character off-stage: named by the dying little Kirstin as the father of her child (Modern Funen I); (4a) named as the father of her child and appears in time to save her life (Modern Swedish F from Småland); (4b) named as the father of her child but appears only in time to avenge her death (Jutish F from the seventeenth century, Modern South Jutish H, more recent German versions); (5) he appears in disguise as a suitor to the king's daughter, thereby causing her punishment (Wendish).[2]

§95. One of the strongest reasons for change, especially for unconscious change, is that the narrative is partly forgotten[1] and that the narrator, while attempting to collect his scattered reminiscences, combines them in new ways.

This process of change can be seen especially clearly when

the content of a ballad is retold according to incomplete recollection.

Example 1. *Johnie Cock* (*English and Scottish Popular Ballads,* no. 114):[2] Johnie sleeps in the forest and is attacked by seven strange hunters who cut off his legs; still, he raises himself with his back supported by an oak tree and shoots six of them dead; he lets the seventh escape with crushed ribs so that he can bring back the news, or, according to versions D E F G (J), throws him with crushed legs onto a white horse that carries him home. According to a single version of the ballad (S), which has dissolved into prose, Johnie himself is killed and "thrown onto a milky-white horse."

Example 2. All versions of *Nilus and Hillelil*[3] relate that on the way home from his wedding, Nilus stays overnight with her family and is killed because of an old feud. On the other hand, a version from the Jutish heatherland, which is halfway dissolved into prose,[4] tells that he was on his way home from the holy grave, and that he drew his sword and killed her uncle. The beginning and the end of the ballad have been forgotten, and these lacunae have been filled in from the known strophes (i.e., "I promised that on the holy grave . . . ").

Thus a strong "reduction" and a sudden "expansion" occur here, one immediately after the other. Under other circumstances, these factors have a much slower effect on the narrative material.

§96. The tendency of the narrative to change will be kept in check by the clarity with which individual episodes are borne in mind and by the inner coherence that exists among the different parts of the plot.

The beginning and ending of the narrative ("the free ends of the narrative") offer the least resistance to change. Here, additions—forward or backward in time—are most easily made; but straightforward transformation also happens more easily here, because the narrative situation is not squeezed in between the given parts of the plot.

Example. *Valdemar and Tove* (DgF 121).[1] Ending in A: Tove's sons trample the queen to death with their horses; B: they hit her and threaten to drive her out of the country; C: the king's grief for Tove; D: the king casts off Soffi; Icelandic A: the king casts off Soffi and marries another; Icelandic B: the king helps carry Tove's bier. (Cf. under §77, "the Law of Closing.")

§97. The individual reasons for change are primarily the following (cf. Moe [1914], introduction):

(1) Within the narrative itself: (a) to clarify a blurred point in the plot; (b) to illustrate an important episode (cf. "the tableau of the narrative," §64); (c) to bring the acting characters in close connection with the protagonist and the plot of the narrative (cf. "the Law of Centralization," §69); (d) to provide fuller development, better argumentation, and further effects of the events mentioned in the narrative, especially when they in the given connection attract strong attention.

(2) In the mind of the narrator: (a) a need to shape the plot in such a way that it corresponds to the sympathy he feels for the one suffering, or to introduce "poetic justice,"[1] where the good are rewarded and the wicked are punished; (b) to bring the plot into agreement with what he considers reasonable (rationalism), either by removing what seems to him unreasonable, or by consciously emphasizing its incredibility.

(3) From other narrative material: the narrative is mixed with or on some points is brought closer to other narratives that the narrator knows.

(4) From the external world: the narrative is influenced by circumstances close to the narrator in time and place with regard to (a) the mentality of his period and (b) external reality.

§98. The forces working within the narrative can be described as a drive for continuation, i.e., as a development or adaptation of already existing elements. Most typical in this respect is the drive for logical continuation, the need to bring existing features into fuller use (the further implementation of "the logic of the narrative"; see §65).

Example. *King Valdemar and his Sister* (DgF 126): "The King of England's son," who is mentioned in version A, is brought into action in later versions (see §94). *Valdemar and Tove* (DgF 121): Tove's son or sons are mentioned in almost all verions; but only in some of the versions of the younger form of the ballad (transmitted in Danish) do they have an influence on the plot.

Comment. Cf. Moe's formulation (1914), p. 9: "Closely related to the need for assimilation is the drive for continuation. If some song or narrative contains an especially good feature, the singer likes to increase the effect by developing it further by an epic elaboration or by adding other similar features. The drive for logical continuation in particular asserts itself strongly. It is felt that there is a need to bring a narrative feature, an image, or a situation to a conclusion (with the circumstances it implies)." This terminology is first found in J. Krohn (1888), p. 63: der logische Fortsetzungtrieb; example: mention of birds in creation myths will be followed by myths about the creation of the world from an egg.[1]

§99. The reasons for changes within the mind of the narrator will, according to their nature, usually be associated with the given features of the plot, which are adapted in accordance with the narrator's wishes. But the reasons for changing the plot must be distinguished from the normal expression of the drive for continuation: they will not content themselves with thoughts already present; they will add new ones or at least tone down the already existing ones. This appears most clearly where a sad ending is replaced by a happy one,[1] or vice versa,[2] or where a sad ending is modified to a semi-happy one.[3]

Example. It is common for the sad ending of a narrative to take a happy turn: DgF 126; one more recent (common) version has "the King of England's son" arrive in time to save little Kirstin's life (see §94). *Carl the Foundling* (DgF 294), where the mother unwittingly marries her own son, ends sometimes with capital punishment,[4] sometimes with exile, sometimes with their separation, and sometimes with the king's forgiveness. The addition of punishment for the wicked characters and reward for the good characters is common: DgF 13 Mimering, who has saved the queen's honor in single combat against the slanderer and rides away (in more recent tradition, with her as his wife): the unselfish knightly deed evidently did not satisfy the singers.[5]

Comment. The narrator's transformation does not work with the features given in the narrative alone; on the contrary, it may result in loans from outside: example 1: *King Valdemar and his Sister* (DgF 126) Swedish version F: little Kerstin looks out the window and sees "the crown prince of England" come sailing with flags hoisted that she herself made for him, and he arrives in time to rescue her; loan from *Lovmand and Thord* (DgF 387) in order to create a happy ending. Example 2: In Jutish tradition, the *Agnete ballad* (DgF 38) has often borrowed the ending from *The Bride of the Mountain King* (DgF 37),[6] probably because the singers felt that a sad ending would better suit the given conditions.

§100. A particular reason for change among those features of a narrative originating in the narrator's own mind is rationalism, i.e., an endeavor to abolish the existing contrast between the fantastic way of thinking in the narrative and his own idea about what is sensible. Rationalism may develop in two directions:

(a) Historicizing, i.e., features that are too fantastic are supplanted by the closest possible features from what is considered the real world. This technique is used when the narrator considers the narrative to be essentially true.

(b) Ironizing or parodying, travestying, i.e., the narrator himself tells the unbelievable, but he intimates that he finds it unreasonable.

"In this rationalistic costume the traditions no longer represent the essential mental property—knowledge or poetry. From the minute rationalism has seized them, they are important only as conscious composition" (Moe [1914], p. 234).

Example (a). A lay from heathen times in Scandinavia has Odin wander to Mímir's well and receive an answer from "Mímir's head"[1] (that is to say, it emerges from the well in the same way water creatures usually reveal themselves). In Snorri Sturluson's medieval retelling from about 1220, this event has been developed as follows: "Odin had Mímir's head with him, and it told him much news from other worlds," for "then they [the Vanir] took Mímir and beheaded him and sent the head to the Æsir; Odin took the head and smeared it with herbs that could not rot, and sang incantations over it and practiced sorcery, so that it spoke to him and told him many secrets" (*Ynglinga saga,* chapters 7 and 4).

An ancient lay tells of the happy time when King Fróði ground gold in his grinder.[2] In the Icelandic *Skjöldunga saga* (*Rerum Danicarum fragmenta,*[3] chapter 3), this becomes: "at that time there was great wealth in corn and in bees, the fields grew of their own accord, and there were all kinds of metals, in the processing of which Fróði was a great master."

Example (b). See "Ironic Localization" (§121).

Comment. Even though Moe leaves the impression that rationalistic transformation deprives oral narrative composition of its essential character, and that this development corresponds to a cultural split within society, i.e., it is a historical rather than a purely mental premise (a view, however, that he limits to folktales and to a split within the lower social classes),[4] it may surely be asserted that rationalistic transformation occurs frequently within the class that produces folklore. Example. According to the legend, King Peace-Fróði is slain by the sea-king Mýsingr; but a comparison with other narrative material (in addition to his name)[5] shows that the narrative was once about how Fróði was killed by a sea-bull: the narrative has thus been rationalized toward more human circumstances (Olrik [1903–1910] II, p. 245). Such rationalization is not rare in heroic composition; it causes the narrative to develop new possibilities continuously. It may even apply as a general rule that mythical conceptions are gradually rationalized to become narratives about tribal ancestors.[6]

Generally, rationalism is something that appears sporadically in oral narrative composition. It is probably most cleary seen in tales. Example 1. *The Trickster,* from the Huron Indians, in two versions: A: "When the Trickster saw the old witch walking far away, he shook down his hair. Oh, how long and beautiful it became all of a sudden! The witch asked: What did you do to get such long, beautiful hair?" B. "The Trickster got hold of a pony's tail, made a wig from it, and walked with it on his head, etc." (Barbeau [1915], p. 20; cf. pp. 166 and 170); there exists an additional example of a "rational and sophisticated version";[7] however, the rationalized forms stem from an Indian living within a modern culture, the more naive ones from an older woman who speaks only her mother tongue. Example 2. The Polyphemus narrative: the story of the hero who hides under the sheep's belly appears to be a rationalistic transformation of the more common version, which relates that he hides in their skin (cf. §48). Example 3. [See IV C "Survival" §139, example 1.][8]

§101. Influence from other narratives is an important reason for the transformation of narrative material. In Moe (1914), pp. 235ff., (1915). pp. 85ff., it is designated as the tendency toward conflation.

Example. DgF 126, Swedish F: little Kerstin looks out the window and sees "the crown prince of England" come sailing with the flags which she herself sewed for him; he arrives in time to save her life and marries her; loan from *Lovmand and Thord* (DgF 387, cf. §94 and §99).

§102. This influence contains not only the regular absorption of foreign narrative material, but also the vaguer impact of the style and the treatment of material in other narratives (analogy creation).[1]

§103. Influence from external reality ("external adaptation," Moe [1915], pp. 89ff.) will first and foremost reveal itself in a change of horizon and everything pertaining to it (see IV B), and subsequently in a change or expansion in agreement with changed cultural circumstances.

Example 1. *Ebbe Skammelsen* (DgF 354): in certain versions the hero goes on a penitential pilgrimage clad in iron, and not until the iron bands burst does he receive forgiveness for fratricide. This narrative feature corresponds to common religious custom in the Middle Ages regarding fratricide.

Example 2. The heroic narratives of antiquity often appear in a medieval ballad form with courtly scenery.[1] (DgF 90 *Aage and Else,* and DgF 415 *Sir Hjelm* are both derived from *Helgi Hundingsbani*).

Comment. An external adaptation will frequently contain important elements of a spiritual adaptation, especially if it has been connected with a poetic influence. Example. Ebbe Skammelsen's penitential pilgrimage (also in a form of DgF 25 *The Avenging Sword*).[2]

§104. These four reasons for the transformation of the narrative rarely work independently. Usually two or more work together, but in such a way that only one is the primary determinant for the direction of the narrative development; the others only strengthen it or operate on individual features. The adoption of foreign material can be prompted by the drive for continuation, by the narrator's particular standpoint, or by an attempt at adaptation. The transfer of narrative material to a new country will generally attract not only the external adaptation, but all kinds of transformations (concerning the adjustment of the Danish heroic narratives to the Norwegian-Icelandic fantastic tales, see Olrik [1903–1910] I, introduction).

§105. Alterations most frequently appear by a gradual shifting, by "a glide," rather than by sudden innovation. Gradual transitions between certain extremes are usually found where a large number of versions are extant.

§106. More sudden transformations often occur in the case of loans from or contamination by other narratives. The contamination may, however, also take the form of a gradual adoption. Two narratives that are related in content will be especially susceptible to contamination whenever they meet; thus, there is not a single loan, but a gradual interpenetration.

Example. The *Benedict ballad* (DgF 474, i.e., the Norwegian form of the Hagbard narrative) has in Telemark, to a highly varying degree, taken strophes from the *Hagbard ballad*.[1] Similarly, the Danish *Bjørn in Sønderborg* (DgF 473) has sometimes taken only a single strophe, but often it has taken the entire execution scene from the *Hagbard ballad* with deviations that show that the loans occurred in several places.[2]

§107. Transitions in leaps (i.e., by the sudden movement in thought of an individual) thus appear primarily in loans from foreign narrative material or in a linking together of two different narrative plots.

But we can hardly deny that many medieval ballads and motifs in the heroic poems of antiquity carry more the stamp of a single operating authorial fantasy than of an even branching of older narrative motifs.

As far as we can tell, some cultural forms and eras have had a greater ability for independent poetic production than others. To a large degree, this ability corresponds to the fact that certain categories of composition such as lay and heroic narrative are more suited to innovation, while categories such as the tale and legend grapple primarily with transmitted motifs. The former stand in close relation to the upper layers of society whose independent creative production is largest; the broader stratum of people is bound more by custom (cf. §12 "higher" and "lower" items of folklore).

§108. A general rule for the aesthetic value of the transformation cannot really be given. Within the resilient categories of narrative, a rise and fall often seem to take place; e.g., a tale which in many forms has nothing conspicuous appears in a single version with an excellent presentation of the details.

Example. *King Lindorm* (Olrik [1904b], p. 6).

It is more justified to speak of definite periods in the case of genres (e.g., lay, heroic legend) associated with a specific culture: a time of beginning, of flourishing, and of verbosity or worn terseness. Within Danish ballads, for instance, the ballads of the nobility are often verbose, the more recent peasant tradition often terse.[1] The flourishing period and the time of beginning must, however, be distinguished by means of internal criteria, e.g., the *Tove ballad* in its Danish and preserved Icelandic forms.[2] One can often distinguish between several periods of flourishing, among these a younger one that approaches verbosity (the great *Marsk Stig ballad, Niels Ebbesen*).[3] One must be cautious, however, in connecting aesthetic value with an individual period: the German heroic composition receives not only a very full, but also a poetic second blooming in the epic of the Middle Ages;[4] the Danish ballad composition makes a similar attempt in the *Marsk Stig ballad.*

A single line of development cannot be determined for oral narrative composition, because the transmission can always revert to the simple form of oral narrative, whose beauty depends on the clarity with which the basic subject stands out, freed from superfluous additions.[5]

## B. HORIZON AND LOCALIZATION

§109. The place where the events of a narrative occur is its "setting"; the place where the largest or most important part of a plot occurs is its "main setting." One can also designate it in such a way that the plot is placed at this or that setting (note: not "localized"; see below).

Example. The Völsung narratives are in large part set by the Rhine; the William Tell narrative is set in Denmark, Norway, England, Holstein, or Switzerland.

§110. The "horizon" of a narrative is the entire compass of locations mentioned in it.

The perception of each human being makes up a certain horizon, i.e., the sum of the perceptions of places the individual has acquired. The more remote a thing is, the poorer and more unreliable the reflection of reality is in his horizon.

In practice, one can divide the horizon into four areas: home, where one has full knowledge on the basis of frequent personal experience and first-hand reference; an inner circle, where one has some personal experience and full second-hand knowledge; a middle circle, where one is familiar only with the main features; and an outer circle, where one is familiar only with a few of the real conditions and where the empty space is easily fleshed out with fantastic conceptions.

The horizon changes for individuals according to their living conditions; a cattleman has a broader horizon than a heathland smallholder. For a common peasant population, the horizon will be distributed in approximately the following way:

> *Home:* parish, county
> *Inner circle:* country, province
> *Middle circle:* neighboring country
> *Outer circle:* more remote countries

When an individual gains a more favorable position in society, the horizon will be expanded. The horizon will also be expanded with a rise in culture.

Exchange of the various horizons of individuals takes place continuously, because people exchange information of a poetic, historical, or geographical content; in this way, a horizon is created that is essentially the same for an entire people, or at least for the more advanced class.

The horizon of individuals corresponds to the people's sphere of communication. One has daily or frequent intercourse with one's home; some intercourse (trade, military service, etc.) with one's inner circle; and less frequent intercourse with one's middle circle (neighboring countries). The outer circle is the area from which one extremely rarely—and usually through intermediaries—receives goods or information.

The sphere of communication (and thereby the horizon of

individuals) is more specifically dependent upon conditions such as natural ways of communication or obstacles, similarity in culture, similarity in nationality, the ability of the larger cultural center to disseminate, etc. Further demonstration of this topic lies outside the present discussion.

Literature: Schütte (1903).[1]

§111. The narrative world of a people will on the whole have approximately the same horizon as the people themselves.

This is a natural consequence of the fact that narratives in large part determine the horizon of the people. This horizon comes into existence through the interplay between narratives and impressions of reality.

§112. The individual narrative is a larger or smaller extract from the horizon of its narrators.

The fantastic story will principally be placed in the outer circle (although with a certain preference for having the hero belong to the home or the inner circle).

Comment. Generally, however, such a scene is not created for purely psychological reasons, but is dependent on narrative models (which again go back to the impressions of reality taken over from other areas and eras). The Icelandic mythical-heroic sagas (*fornaldarsögur*) take place in the Scandinavian countries or in their neighboring countries during the time before the settlement of Iceland (the horizon of the Viking Age).[1]

§113. When a narrative migrates from one area to another, its geographical horizon will normally be adapted either totally or partially to the horizon of the new narrators.

Example. *Ebbe Skammelsen* (DgF 354), in Denmark placed at Ty in Jutland, in Swedish tradition at Tidö on Lake Mälaren.[1] Often the transference to the home scene occurs without any definite designation of place, only through local personal names and scenery (the Danish *Elfshot* [DgF 47], as opposed to the French form of the same ballad *Jean Renaud*).[2]

§114. Altogether, a Law of Approximation applies to the life of the narrative. The narrator will move its horizon, its scenery, and its setting within what he knows, giving the individual expressions, notions, and personal names a familiar color.[1] Cf. under "localization."

§115. More extensive compositions (especially the large narrative cycles) often retain their horizon essentially unchanged. Only newly invented characters and events will be an expression of the horizon of later narrators.

Example. The Völsung narratives have the southern Gothic world as their main setting, especially the Rhine areas. For almost every area where they have been told, one can point to subordinate characters and subordinate episodes that reveal the new horizon.
Comment. It is a popular form of adaptation that the characters of the narrative are regarded as belonging to the narrator's home (Bjarki, Starkaðr in Norwegian-Icelandic tradition),[1] or that new subordinate characters are invented and added as representatives of the contact of new peoples with the narrative. (Example. Margrave Rodengar in the High German expansion, Iring in the Low German expansion of the Nibelung battle.)[2]

§116. The narrative, therefore, offers names that are alien to the practical horizon of the narrator, and belong to a horizon that is remote in time and place.

Example. King Dietrich lives in "Bern,"[1] originally the Gothic royal castle Basiana on the Danubian plain, later perceived as Verona in Italy, or simply as the imaginary throne of a ruler.

§117. The most decisive proof that a narrative originated in a horizon alien to the narrator is found when he places it within one horizon, whereas its own proper names, incomprehensible to him, reveal it as belonging to another horizon.

Example. The home of the twelve sons of Arngrímr, "Bolm," is in Icelandic sagas located in Hálogaland or Flamland;[1] but the proper name can be paralleled only with a lake in Småland (Steenstrup [1897], p. 152; Lundell [1903–1906], p. 64).[2]

§118. The traditions of a people may to a great extent preserve the old horizon, even though the people emigrate. Thus the Anglo-Saxon heroic tradition has a horizon that corresponds to the ancient homes of the people in the areas by the North Sea and the Baltic.[1]

In their tradition, a people may also retain the memory of a horizon that has disappeared: the Eskimos in Greenland about their battles against the Scandinavians,[2] the Circassians in the Caucasus about their battles against the Goths,[3] and the Irish and the Scots about the attacks of the Norwegians.[4]

The condition of such a preservation is, however, that the subject is often brought back to mind, e.g., by frequent mention of the heroic poems dealing with it. And in the course of time, the image will become poorer in specific details, because it is not nourished by a supply of empirical material (or is supplied by empirical material that does not belong to it).

## §§119–134. Localization

§119. A narrative is said to be "localized" when it is not only placed at a certain scene, but also connected to certain places in such a way that they are perceived as evidence of the truthfulness of the narrative, since they explain the origin of some element or other, the actual existence of which contemporaries of the narrator can ascertain for themselves.

Example 1. "Thus Þorgils Snorrason, a skilled man, relates . . . and he said that he had seen the burr and the cloak that King Haraldr had given Þórir, and then the cloak was cut into an antependium" (*Fagrskinna*, p. 117;[1] about how Þórir secured Haraldr Hard-ruler the title of king at the Alþingi).

Example 2. "In this way the legend [about the fight between the serpent and the bull] was told to me by an old farmer when I visited Fårevejle church.[2] 'That it is a true incident,' he concludes, 'can clearly be seen, for not only is the entrance toward the south walled up, but the pictures of the serpent are still over there on the northern door'" (Løffler [1876b]).

Comment. Normally it is not bluntly stated in folk tradition that localization proves the truth of a story; for the audience will, of their own accord, perceive it as such by virtue of the connection.

Literature. Olrik (1892–1894) I §6; Olrik (1898), p. 76.[3]

§120. Localization is normally placed at the end of the narrative (in longer stories, at some point of closure) as a kind of reasoning or retrospective of the event.

In contrast, however, localization is frequently found at the very beginning of the story, especially in a large group of minor legends. The existence of the feature in everyday life and the desire to have it explained is then the point of departure for the transmission of the narrative; the evidential weight of localization for the truthfulness of the narrative then recedes into the background.[1]

§121. Localization is found both in accounts that are historically true and in others that are invented, although especially when something improbable is told, because there the need for confirmation is greatest. The addition of localization presupposes that the truth of the story will be doubted and that this doubt must be disarmed.

Example. Sigurðr Fáfnisbani cuts two molars out of Starkaðr's mouth. Norna-Gestr takes one of them as a keepsake; "it is now used as a bell-pull in Lund in Denmark and weighs six ounces, and people find it strange to look at" (*Norna-Gests þáttr*, chapter 6).[1]

Comment 1. While an added localization in the tradition is still felt as a guarantee of the truth of the story, its origin is usually due to quite different reasons (see §129ff.).

Comment 2. Ironic localization is found when the narrator himself wants to poke fun at the reliability of his account. The Icelandic Skíðaríma[2] (about the beggar Skíði's visit to Ásgarðr), the end: "He had a bag, as is proper; it was empty in the evening. Now very old butter had been put in it; it was from the Æsir era. They found a tooth in his clothes [namely, of the dragon Fáfnir]; it weighed twenty marks. *Now you can see that my story about the youth's deeds is true.*" Common end of a tale: "I was also at the [princess's] wedding, and they fired a salute so that it thundered; but they needed a wad and put me in one of the cannons and shot me out, and that is the way I got here. But in the fall I broke one of my thigh bones and will be lame from this the rest of my life" (or the like).[3]

§122. Localization, therefore, distributes itself unevenly among most of the different forms of tradition. In the short legend it is found very frequently, because it is often the only proof of the truthfulness of a story. (Cf. §119.) In heroic prose narratives, localization is often interwoven; similarly, it is added to ballads in the form of short legends. Localization does not appear in ballads or folktales, except, in the latter, ironically (see above).

Comment. The genuine ballad shuns localization just as it generally avoids a detailed designation of the scene. Even where a local legend is the source of the ballad, one avoids the explicit statement that what is discussed in the ballad still exists (fossilized giantesses, DgF 43, 51;[1] "you will stand as a ridiculous harbor sign," *Hrímgerðarmál;*[2] "we will lead her to Vestervig," DgF 126). Legend-like localization in a ballad is a sign that it has been tampered with by a writer (little Kirstin's grave in Vestervig, DgF 126A-E, the end; Valdemar's preference for Gurre, DgF 121 C;[3] even here the actual localization—the grave, Valdemar's wild hunt—is not mentioned). A local legend connected to the ballad only exceptionally slips into it as a newly made final verse ("Then he set fire to Kjølnes...thus it stands until today," DgF 474 Norwegian A).[4]

§123. Localization may be important or unimportant. It is important if the narrative would lose its coherence by the removal of localization, but unimportant if the total impression is not altered by its removal.

Localization is thus important when it aims at explaining the formation of a thing (origin legend, see §5). The legend about the giant So-and-So who throws stones at church X usually aims at explaining why a big stone is lying in the middle of a level field.[1]

In heroic legends and myths about gods, most of the instances of localization are unimportant, and the same is true of prose legends associated with ballads.

Example. The capture of Loki. "And as he sat in the house he took some linen thread and tied knots in it in the way in which ever since a net has been made.... Thor grabbed at him and got his hand round him, but he slipped in his hand so that the hand caught hold at the tail; therefore the salmon tapers towards the tail.... But as the poison drips into his face, he jerks away so hard that the whole earth quakes; this is what you call an earthquake" (*Edda;*[2] only the last instance of localization is important).

§124. Localization may be strong or weak. Localization that is intimately connected to the plot of the narrative is strong; localization that has a looser relationship to it is weak.

Example 1. The troll was interrupted when building a church; therefore a stone is missing, and since then no one has been able to fill the hole.[1]

Example 2. Hjarnø in Horsens Fjord derives its name from the burial of King Hjarni there (Saxo, Book 6);[2] but it is not associated with any characteristic event in his life.

(The designation "strong" and "weak" according to the category of localization will usually correspond to "important" and "unimportant" according to its relationship to the plot.)[3]

Weak localization will often occur when the narrative is told far away from the geographical site in question, or a simple location will take its place.

Example 3. A Norwegian coastal saga about King Peace-Fróði in Saxo, Book 5:[4] in order to show complete respect of ownership, he placed one gold ring on the rock, which is named Fróði-stone after him (strong localization), and another somewhere in Viken (a vague location far away from the main scene of the saga).

§125. False localization occurs when the criterion for the truthfulness of the narrative is a feature that does not exist in reality. This may happen when a narrative wanders away from its home and the narrator or his audience no longer knows the real features of the place.

Example 1. *Knýtlinga saga*[1] contains the statement that the place where Knud Lavard fell stayed green. From all Danish sources[2] we know that there was a well that rose at the place (which strangely enough is unknown to *Knýtlinga saga*). Here the Danish well has been exchanged with the notion common in Iceland that the state of being evergreen is a sign of the supernatural power of a place.[3]

Example 2. In 1695, Peder Syv wrote about little Kirstin's grave in Vestervig: "A big stone is said to lie on it, over which King Valdemar's queen rode, and the marks of the horseshoes can still be seen in it" (DgF III 80; the stone does not have these "marks"; Syv had no direct knowledge of the stone; what he thus asserts also goes against the content of the ballad itself).[4]

Comment. Ironic localization (§121, comment 2) is consciously created as a false localization.

§126. An extreme form of weak localization occurs when what is told has a genealogical connection with the narrator's contemporary time.

Example. "Hrólfr Skálmarnes told the saga about the Viking Hröngviðr and the warrior king Óláfr, about the breaking open of Þráinn's mound and Hrómundr Gripsson, to which many verses belonged. King Sverrir was once told this saga, and he declared that such lying tales were the funniest; but there are still people who can trace their family back to Hrómundr Gripsson"[1] (*Sturlunga saga* [1904] I, p. 25).

§127. Localization may be circumstantial, i.e., it may adopt many details in its account. In addition, it may be multiple, i.e., it may consist of a series of independent localizations connected with different episodes in the narrative.

Example. Saxo's localizations of Hagbard and Signe's death: the place of execution where he was hanged, the hill where Sigar's castle had been, along with the beam that had been plowed up there, the village named after Hagbard and the one named after Sigar;[1] all of these details come under the rubric of multiple localization. Moreover, the campaign of revenge, which gives names to a series of points on the way from the coast of Zealand to Sigersted, next mentions the place from where the attack was launched, the hollow into which the corpses were thrown, and finally the grave mound of the avenger himself.[2] These details offer examples of circumstantial localization. Circumstantial localization, although to a lesser extent, is also found in many folktales about Hagbard and Signe: the place where he was hanged and the location of her room so that in death he could see its flames,[3] the hole of the wicked handmaiden, etc. (DgF 20, introduction; also in DFS 1917/47–48). There is a considerable difference, however, between the fullness of the localization in Saxo's heroic narrative and that in the folktales.

§128. Even if the original basis of localization disappears, the narrative tradition often finds a new feature that suits the plot, or to which it may be adjusted.

Example. The narrative from *Sønderborg castle* about the princess's suicide: (1) Pontoppidan 1729: "The lady who stood by a window in the castle in order to observe the execution...suddenly thrust a dagger into her chest, so that a squirt of hot blood spurted out onto the nearest wall. This blood has stayed on the wall; someone tried to wash it off with water, and as that did not help to coat it with chalk, but after a short while it emerged again. Many eye-witnesses have assured me that the blood was visible until about 8 years ago when *the wall where it had been seen was torn down* by the above-mentioned restoration and rebuilding of the castle." (2) Pastor Hansen 1840: "In the third story one sees a brown spot, which is said to be blood, on the wall *under a window* in the big hall toward the northwest. The narrative about it is as follows.... I saw it in 1826, but whether it was blood I cannot say" (DgF 473, *Sir Bjørn in Sønderborg,* introduction).[1] Cf. DgF 311, introduction; DgF 354, introduction.[2]

§129. The origin of localization. Localization can come into existence in three ways:

(1) The content of the narrative may essentially be in agreement with the real events and be a real record of local conditions.

(2) The narrative may come into existence as the imaginative explanation of some conspicuous circumstance or other (origin legend, etiological narrative; cf. §123).

(3) An already existing narrative may be placed in a new setting and localized there.

Example 1. The narrative about the construction of the Danevirke by Thyre Danebod contains an essential fact about the building of the embankment.[1]
Example 2. An isolated rock is interpreted as having been thrown by a giant of ancient times, who intended to harm somebody with it.[2]
Example 3. The narrative about Hagbard's and Signe's love and death is localized in more than 20 places,[3] and cannot possibly have either really happened or been independently invented in so many places.[4]

§130. In folklore, the localized narrative is always derived from a real event, and its localization reveals a trace of what really happened. From a scholarly point of view, however, the two other modes of formation seem to play a greater role (cf. chapter VI D, "Oral Narrative and History").[1]

§131. All narratives that begin with localization and have the account follow as its explanation must, from the standpoint of tradition, be regarded as origin legends.[1]

Example. The Irish saga about Condla's outward journey begins with the question: "Why did Art receive the nickname Single-Man?" The story relates how his brother, Condla, was enticed into the otherworld by the elf-maiden. When the mourning king sees his other son arrive, he exclaims: "There is Art Single-Man," and in this way he got the name.[2] Etiological features seem to have played an extremely important role in the mythical and heroic compositions of the Irish.

§132. An innovative localization of an already existing narrative (3) appears by virtue of an unconscious need to bring about an agreement between what is told and what is visibly present.

Example. In Denmark, the narrative about the fight between the serpent and the bull is often associated with a serpent carved on the church building (cf. §119). That the picture is not the origin of the legend is proved by the fact that here, and still in the Alps, the narrative sometimes appears without being associated with a church (Olrik [1902], pp. 208f.) and that the localization does not contain any evidence that it was a bull who killed the serpent: bull and serpent together are unknown in pictorial art.

Comment. The power of localization is found with great vigor in the audience of the narrative, about which many conspicuous and unreflected remarks give witness. In school, a little boy heard the story about Goliath's fall and immediately cried, "Oh, that was the noise I heard in our attic the other night!" A common sense of relevance often seems, however, to have kept the development of such localization in check.

§133. When a localized narrative is told frequently, the need to localize it will manifest itself in further innovation. In this way, the "circumstantial" or "multiple" localization will come into existence (see §127), which testifies to the longevity of the narrative in the same place. These later additions of localization are generally far less important to the main plot of the narrative than the original one, and they disappear relatively easily in order to be replaced by other similar localizations.

Example. According to Peder Syv (1695), at "little Kirstin's grave" in Vestervig, one saw the hoofprints of the queen's horse in the stone (even though the queen, according to the ballad, did not ride over her grave); in 1802, one saw "the grave of little Kirstin's daughter" as a smaller tombstone next to her own (DgF 126).[1] Cf. the prolific changes within the many localizations of the Hagbard narrative (DgF 20, DFS 1917/47–48). A very unimportant (i.e., arbitrary) kind of localization is the assignment of old pictures to famous personages in the area (of Hagbard and Signe in the church at Urnæs, DgF 20;[2] of Sir Ebbe's daughters in the church at Højby, DgF 194, etc.).

§134. Often the new localization is not a complete innovation but a moving of an earlier localization to a scene which, by likeness in names or scenery, offers points of similarity with the previous one.

Example. The Hagbard narrative is assigned to Onguley in northern Norway, to Ongulsnes in western Norway, and to Angenes in southern Norway (DgF I, 264–266; other conspicuous similarities between the localizations of this narrative appear too).[1]

## C. SURVIVAL

§135. A conception that is retained in the tradition of the people, even though its actual meaning is forgotten, is called a "survival"[1] or "rudiment."

Example. In a village church on Zealand, the churchgoers always used to bow their heads when they passed a certain place without anyone knowing any other reason for this than that it was the custom. When the church was restored and the chalk knocked off the wall, a picture of the Virgin Mary appeared;[2] this was what the greeting first applied to.

**§136.** A survival may be downright incomprehensible or misunderstood.

Example. The fear of throwing away cut-off nails is widespread. In some places, no reason for this is known (incomprehensible survival); in other areas, many different reasons are given (Olrik [1902], p. 226).[1] Since such a uniform habit hardly has many different origins, most or perhaps all of these reasons must be due to a misunderstanding of the survival.

**§137.** Survivals within religious and magical customs are extremely common, because a special respect for old forms is retained, while the mentality as a whole changes.

**§138.** Within narratives, survivals may appear partly as epic survivals, partly as cultural survivals.

An incomprehensible epic survival is a part of a story that is retained even though it has lost its significance as a part of the plot.

Example. *Hrólfs saga kraka,* chapter 4: "There Sigríðr, Helgi and Hróar's mother, also burned to death, for she would not go out." She has not been mentioned previously, and the audience of the saga has no idea why she did not go out.[1] The explanation is found in *Skjöldunga saga* (Arngrímur Jónsson's extract): after the murder of Hálfdan, Fróði married his widow, Sigríðr.[2]

A misunderstood epic survival is a part of a story that is retained, but that has a different influence on the plot in the narrative than the original one.

**§139.** The survival is easiest to point out when we have several versions of the same narrative, of which some show the actual connection and others show the survival as incomprehensible or misunderstood.

Example 1. Among the many versions of *The Little Duck,* one (JFm V, no. 16) has the transformation of the maiden into a duck not as the result of the curse of the stepmother, but as a result of her rescue by a fairy when she is drowning.[1] This reveals itself as unoriginal (1) by its unique appearance; (2) by breaking the common fairytale notion that transformation into a beast is caused by an evil creature;

(3) by breaking the logic of the narrative: the plot focuses on how she can be rescued from being transformed into a beast; (4) the notion is rationalistic: in a proper tale, one never drowns in water, but enters another world or mode of life.[2]

Even where several versions of the same narrative do not exist, conclusions can be drawn from a study of how the same episode is treated in other compositions belonging to the same area and culture.

Example 2. What was just mentioned about Sigríðr, who burns in the house with Fróði, corresponds to Signý in *Völsunga saga*,[3] who in the same way follows Siggeirr, whom she was forced to marry, in death.

§140. Where external information is lacking, the survival can be recognized from the broken coherence: a plot is set into motion that should have given rise to a different or narratively more significant result.

Example. The Irish saga about the birth of Cuchulinn prepares through a lengthy plot for King Conchobar to marry his own sister without recognizing her, but suddenly breaks it off. Another story says that it was Conchobar who was believed to have gotten his own sister with child. Here the preoccupation of two narratives with the love between a brother and sister indicates that it is the original form of Cuchulinn's birth, which is confirmed by many other narratives about the birth of the great hero (Olrik [1903-1910] I, p. 156; "the Irish composition has, more than any other, the peculiarity that even if it gives up a motif in favor of a new one, the old features remain, but without an epic importance").

§141. Any break of the epic coherence must, at least for more poetically elaborated oral narrative composition, be considered a survival of a historical reality that has not been totally incorporated (this will, however, normally disappear quickly), or as a survival of a narrative form.

§142. Cultural survivals may be distinguished from epic survivals by the fact that they do not come into existence during the oral transmission of the already existing narrative, but belong to its very birth.

A narrative arises out of survivals from a vanished culture when a permanent or frequently repeated cultural feature ceases to exist, but is remembered as an event (or as part of an event) that once happened.

Example. Narratives and tales about the hero who saves the princess from being sacrificed to the dragon are (according to Hartland [1894–1896])[1] supposed to have their origin in the sacrifice of human beings to sea monsters.

§143. How a cultural state, a general condition, influences the fate of an individual character in the story eludes our investigation in most cases.[1] As a general rule, the motif appears as a narrative in the country (or province) that borders the area where it is a custom or belief.

Example. (1) In Jutland, the wild huntsman who chases a bull at Christmas is a narrative motif, in Oldenburg, a sacrificial custom (Olrik [1901], pp. 156–157). (2) The smiths' blows on the anvil in order to renew Lucifer's chains is a custom in southern Germany (an extreme offshoot from a Caucasian-Armenian custom), but in Pomerania there are only narratives recording that an earthly smith was brought to a cave and had to weld the chain (von der Leyen [1908], pp. 1f.).[2] (3) The old world-weary warrior who makes a young warrior kill him is a narrative in Scandinavia (Starkad) but was a custom among the Herules during the era of the Great Migration (Olrik [1903–1910] II, p. 157).[3]

# CHAPTER

## ﹖❧ 5 ❧﹖

# THE ORIGINAL FORM AND DEVELOPMENT OF THE NARRATIVE

Literature: Krohn (1910, 1912); Aarne (1913a).

## INTRODUCTION

§144. One of the most important aims of oral narrative research concerns the origin and development of the narrative. More specifically, the task is threefold: to find (1) the prerequisites of the narrative, (2) its original form, and (3) its development.

The prerequisites comprise (a) a possible basis in a real event, a cultural state, or a custom that has contributed to the formation of the narrative, and (b) any element of perception that has been contributory.[1] The prerequisites of the narrative may, in some instances, be determined purely on the basis of sources. Events that provide subjects for narratives will, for example, be known from history; cultural conditions may be recognized from old accounts, from archeological finds, or the like. In many cases, however, the scholar arrives at the conditions of older times only through an inference from the state of later times, or from a conclusion based on a resemblance to the state of other peoples.

The original form can never be observed in the sources; no one has recorded a folk tradition at the same time and in exactly the same form it had when it came into existence. Sometimes it is possible that a younger version lies so close to the original that it practically replaces it. But then evidence must be given to prove that it lies that close to the original form.

The original form must always be recognized through inference from one or more transmitted forms, and partly also through deduction from the prerequisites of the narrative, insofar as they are known.

Consequently, the theoretical original form cannot in practice be reconstituted with complete accuracy. Instead of designating the absolutely oldest form of the narrative, it must in practice designate the oldest form that we can reach through inference. For narratives of which there are many and widely scattered versions, the "original form" then means the common basic form of the extant variants.

Comment. One must beware of advancing a very abstract formula as the original form of a narrative.[2] The narrative is always expressed in concrete terms, just as language always consists of real words. It is another matter that we use abstract expressions ("a creature," "a bird," "a means of redemption") when we do not know the original form accurately; they are an $x$ that we insert when we do not know the concrete value.

§145. The development of the narrative is the least unknown of the three factors. Every existing version of a narrative is a link in a chain (or chains) of forms through which the narrative has evolved; sometimes a large number of such links are known. The task is then to infer those links that are now wanting in the existing ones.

With the aid of all extant versions, one can aim at inferring the original form (the first link in the chain). Generally, however, it will be safer to infer the common basic form of a small group of versions that are closely connected in time, place, and content, and when several such groups are investigated, then to look for the common original form.[1]

This strategy offers the advantage that one first looks for the unknown links that stand closest to the known ones. One will be able to work with a rather large amount of source material when investigating minor differences in content. In addition, one will be able to profit fully not only from a comparison of the versions, but also from an investigation of the individual version (cf. chapter II).[2]

§146. When scholars want to demonstrate a connection between two narratives, both (or one) of which are extant in several versions, they often employ the method of listing all features in which one of the versions in question agrees with the other narrative. This approach can be useful for a preliminary orientation to the narrative material. But when a large number of versions are extant (e.g., a tale in several hundreds of texts), there is an extremely great risk of accidental similarities. In order for the evidence to carry scholarly weight, one must provide additional indications that the feature in question either belongs to the original form of the narrative or belonged to it at the time and at the place where it reportedly came into contact with the other narrative. A feature in the tale about the three kidnapped princesses[1] that is found only in a Hungarian or an Indian version is little proof of the relationship between this tale and *Beowulf* (Panzer [1910–1912] I; von Sydow [1912], pp. 123f.).

§147. When the relationship between two traditions is to be demonstrated, the proof must above all be based on the similarities between what is constant in the narratives, i.e., the epic structure.[1]

Similarities in individual features, such as "verbatim similarities" in linguistic expression, played a predominant role in the early life of folkloristics (especially among philologists). Now it is generally recognized that proof cannot be based on these details: identical perceptions will easily create identical linguistic expressions; and within large areas of linguistic material and names, there will always be room for accidental similarities.

Often, certain expressions are not particular to the individual narrative, but to the presentation of a certain era: in *Beowulf,* all kinds of dragons and trolls live "under the grey stone" (under hārne stān);[2] one of its episodes is reminiscent of a Danish treasure legend from the Gråsten area; but it is the content that determines the relationship, not this "verbatim similarity" (Bugge [1890–1892], p. 234; cf. Olrik [1890–1892c], p. 240). The best-known example of a proof based on a similarity in details rather than in general coherence is offered by Bugge (1881–1889).[3] On the whole, this direction has been cultivated more by philologists than by actual folklorists (cf. Olrik [1903–1910] I, pp. 307–315: Siever's attempt at identifying Fróði's and Beowulf's dragon fights).

On the other hand, the most decisive evidence that two narratives with the same plot really are related can be demonstrated on the basis of a similarity in details when the detail is of such a kind that one can only with difficulty create it simply on the basis of a general perception of the nature of the event. Most personal names are details of this kind. If a hero is called Tristan, for example, the narrative must belong either to the Tristan narratives or in some way be influenced by them.[4]

Comment. This does not, however, apply to designations of names or ranks that are common to a whole genre, e.g., the typical designations in tales.[5] Such a name can serve as evidence of general contact with a foreign fairytale world. In Scandinavia, *The Son of the Widow* is a rare name for the fairytale hero,[6] in Celtic a common one; thus it is probably due to Celtic influence in Scandinavia.

## A. THE RELATIONSHIP BETWEEN NARRATIVE TRADITIONS

§148. That two traditions are related means that they are descended from the same narrative. The descent may be such that they have had the same narrative as their only or most important source, or that only minor parts of them are descended from the same narrative. In the former case, we designate them as the same narrative; in the latter, we say that one narrative has borrowed from another.[1] The decisive characteristic is usually that either the main part of the plot or only a smaller part of it is shared.

§149. It is impossible to determine in advance which

traditions are related and which simply have a topic in common, i.e., have as their source the same human conditions.

On the other hand, the fact can be established that certain traditions are one and the same narrative in a large number of cases. They are characterized by having the same episodes in the same order, often also by having a similarity in names or other accessories. In addition, with a larger series of versions one will also be able to demonstrate that even apparently quite different ones descend from the same basic form, because one has the transitions between them represented by other versions. Especially with the fairytales it has been possible to follow the same narrative through a large number of versions distributed throughout a large number of countries.

Confirmation that the traditions really descend from the same original form lies in the fact that they (or most of them) belong to a definite area, or that the forms that most agree in content are in the largest number of cases recorded close to each other. Here a common center of dissemination is the only natural explanation.[1]

§150. When the structure of the narrative does not provide decisive evidence about the descent of the tradition, the geographical evidence gains particular importance.[1]

§151. Normally it is even more difficult to prove that two narratives are not related.[1] The most likely procedure is to show that several versions are similar in their main features, but appear in very different places.[2]

It is a special case when a motif appears in many areas of the world, including among peoples of a very undeveloped culture. It is then not unlikely that it is formed at an early stage of human development out of psychological necessity.

Example. Narratives about the one who has stolen fire or water for mankind (Tylor [1871];[3] von der Leyen [1902], pp. 143ff.).[4] Similarly, narratives about a supernatural spouse who disappears after the breaking of a taboo.[5] The notion of a gate or a couple of rocks at the end of the world that continuously open or close.[6] Etc.

The proof, however, is not compelling. It is possible that the motif was inherited from ancestors in early times.

§152. It appears quite frequently that basic mythical conceptions are common to large parts of humanity, but that the narrative plots based on these conceptions have far narrower limits, and, further, that specific details have an even narrower distribution. In such cases, the basic notions appear to be common human ones, while the narratives based on them have been disseminated from a definite point of origin.

Example. The notion of colliding rocks at the end of the world or in the land of the dead is common to a large part of humanity. On the other hand, the notion that one travels through those rocks to fetch "the water of life" or "the mead of the gods" is common to only some myths or tales, mainly from the eastern part of Europe.[1]

## B. VARIANT AND DOUBLET

§153. Versions of the same narrative are designated as variants in order to emphasize a perceptible difference in the more specific execution of the thought. Individual sections of versions can also be designated as variants of each other in the same way.

Example. "In this lay it is told about Sigurðr's death, and it is described as if they killed him out of doors. But some say that they killed him in his bed while he was asleep; and the Germans say that they killed him in a forest" (*Elder Edda*).[1] In the Danish versions of the *Tove ballad* (DgF 121), the wicked queen is normally punished by Tove's sons; in the Icelandic ballad, the king divorces her.[2]
(Note: Variants may display considerable differences, especially in individual episodes, for the transmission makes room for new conceptions when they expediently fill a place in the narrative.)

§154. Often one recording contains variants because the recorder has added what others have told (the entire narrative or a single point) in a different way. In oral transmission, variants also appear frequently, especially in narratives that claim to be essentially historically reliable.

Example. Such variants occur often in saga literature, although normally these deviations are insignificant. "A man whom some called Finnr, but others say that he was Finnish" (*Heimskringla* I, p. 448). "There are some who say that Haraldr [Wartooth] was not driven by jealousy [i.e., Odin's underhanded game] or lust for power, but willingly sought his own death" (Saxo).[1]

Comment. Thus, one cannot with certainty infer from the existence of variants that the recording conflates several oral traditions; but one can infer that either the recorder or a recent previous narrator knew about several traditions. Note: In Saxo, the citing of several traditions does not coincide with his piecing together of Danish and Norse narratives, but revolves around smaller differences within the same main tradition.[2]

§155. When an account (i.e., the rendering of a single authority) contains sections that appear as different events but are close to each other in content and lead to the same result (or are suited for leading to the same result), they are called "doublets."

"Doublets" are variants within the same narrative. Normally they appeared because the narrator did not realize the identity of the two narratives. (If the narrator discovers the identity of the narratives, he will often try to weld them together; the welding together of narratives and the incorporation of doublets go hand in hand as important reasons for the expansion and transformation of narrative material.)

Doublets can appear partly in written, partly in oral tradition that aims at a fuller (saga-like, narrative cycle–like) account.

Example 1. The saga in *Flateyjarbók* about Hálfdan the Black contains the story about the prince who releases the thief twice. The story derives first from a written source (Odin's theft at Christmas) and later from oral tradition (the giant Dofri).[1]

Example 2. Saxo's account of the revenge after Hagbard's death contains three men named Haki: (1) Haki Hámundsson, Hagbard's brother, who carries out the revenge and escapes with "a third of the army," (2) Haki the Proud (*cognomine Fastuosus*),[2] who stays behind with the rest of the army, falls by the Suså, and is buried at Hakehøj, and (3) "Haki from Zealand, Viger's son," who together with Starkad, leaves no. 1 in order not to fight against his countrymen.[3] No. 1 is well known as Hagbard's avenger; nos. 2 and 3 never appear elsewhere.

Example 3. Saxo's Norwegian *Balders saga*[4] consists of two complete doublet accounts:

| I. scene: Norway | II. scene: Sweden |
|---|---|
| motif: Nanna's love | motif: battle for the kingdom |
| method: win sword | method: win Balder's food |
| decision: sea battle in Baldersvåg | decision: Balder is pierced |

§156. When two doublets are conflated in the same account, it usually necessitates changes in them. The narrator must take care to ensure that the result toward which they both lead is reached only by the one that is told last. This conflation, however, normally leaves traces; the narrator suddenly turns away from the goal at which the material itself aims, and the motifs introduced reach no or an insufficient conclusion.

Example. In the *Balders saga* I (mentioned above), not Balder but a subordinate character, Gelder, falls in the sea battle in Baldersvåg and is buried after a magnificent cremation[1] (which is otherwise attributed to Balder himself).

§157. Until now, doublets in the proper sense of the word or parallel doublets have been discussed, i.e., narratives that existed as independent traditions before they were combined. But it may also happen that a narrator imitates already existing ones out of his desire to create new episodes. In this way, a derived doublet comes into existence, whose characteristic feature will be that throughout it is weaker than its model.

Example. *Hrólfs saga kraka* contains two conflicts with Böðvarr and the champions of Lejre; the one, the bone-throwing (which is also found in Saxo and in *Bjarkarímur*),[1] has poetic preference; the other (the wrestling) is definitely weaker.[2] Also, Svipdagr's conflicts with the champions in Uppsala and Lejre are probably derived doublets from Bjarki's bone-throwing,[3] the latter entirely, the former partially.

Comment 1. While a derived and a parallel doublet differ in origin, it is not always easy to distinguish them. If a parallel doublet is weak, or if it has been reduced in the conflation, it will look like a derived one. The resulting incorrect conclusion, however, is of little importance for the history of the individual narrative. The really distinctive forms will easily be kept apart; and one must base one's argument on vague forms that are not even extant tradition, but appear only in the form of doublets.

Comment 2. The reason for our uncertainty in this case lies in the fact that so little genuine material exists in the narrative genres where the doublet flourishes most prolifically: the saga-, novella-, or epic-like compositions. It is difficult to delimit empirically the range of innovation of individual narrators with regard to these genres.

§158. When doublets have recently come into existence, it will generally not be difficult to demonstrate their nature. Often, one finds support in other traditions that show one (or both) in an independent state and thus provide a criterion for the character of the adaptation. Even without such a basis, the conflation and the rupture will reveal themselves as breaks in the even progress of the narrative plot.

§159. The narrative may, however, also contain double episodes, the similarity of which is nowhere near as conspicuous, but which must be understood as doublets from an earlier time. The heroic narrative in particular, with its fluid outlines and episodic style, offers the opportunity of their thriving prolifically.

Example 1. Sigurðr's ride to Sigrdrífa at Hindarfjall and to Brynhildr in the castle surrounded by flames.[1]

Example 2. Erpr, in part as Guðrún's son, in part as her stepson[2] (Sijmons [1906], pp. 156f.). The unusual name and the identification with Attila's son, Ernac, prove that from the beginning it is the same person.

§160. The demonstration of doublets or variants is one of the most important methods of reaching back to narrative forms older than the ones we know from the sources themselves. (The words "doublet" and "variant" no longer sharply diverge when one departs from the actual sources to investigate the general outline of the narrative cycle.) The method is to be used with caution, however. It is easy to find the weak or doublet-like place in the transmission, but difficult to ascertain the original narrative form with certainty.

## C. VIEWS ON THE STRUCTURE AND TRANSMISSION OF THE NARRATIVE

§161. To find the oldest form of the narrative stands as the greatest but most difficult goal for research. Once it is identified, a basis for clarifying which intellectual forces and external circumstances have determined its development may be established; and with great certainty the entire narrative development from the original form to the now-extant versions may be determined.

The methods by which to determine the oldest form of a narrative are obtained (a) from the structure and transmission of the narrative itself and (b) through a study of external circumstances.

Scholars have often attempted to establish the original form of a narrative according to a single point of view or principle. Thus, the original form has been seen as sometimes the most complete, sometimes the (logically and aesthetically) most perfect, sometimes the simplest, or sometimes what is common to all (or many) transmissions. At times, the oldest version is considered to be the most original and its traditions are generally evaluated chronologically. Sometimes they are arranged according to types or according to the locations of the versions, etc.

In the same way, a single point of view is made the basis of the narrative material, where the mythical material or the most peculiar cultural-historical material is regarded as the oldest in the narrative; narrative material that agrees with actual history has also been promoted as the oldest. Finally, features from culture or language have been used to determine the age of the narrative (and through this, subsequently, its original form).

Each of these views and procedures will be discussed in the following.

§162. (A) The most complete form. The view that appears earliest in scholarship is that the most complete form of a narrative is the oldest. This view applies both to the most complete of the extant versions and to the most complete text that can be created by conflating the various versions.

This view is found, naively, among the earliest collectors and interpreters of folklore. In this way, the oldest heroic sagas of Ireland have grown through the literary conflation of several parallel sources;[1] the romantic literature of the Middle Ages constantly increases in scope; Vedel's 1591 edition of the Danish ballads aims at including everything found in the versions he had access to, etc. Similar conditions exist for the Indian epic *Mahabharata* (Sørensen [1883], pp. 277ff.). With the romantic school, the view reaches the status of a conscious scholarly and aesthetic principle (e.g., *Kalevala* [1835],[2] Grundtvig's redaction of the Marsk Stig ballads).[3]

§163. On the whole, this standpoint had been abandoned. There is no *a priori* reason why the composite story must be older than the simpler story. And it has turned out that the most conflated forms are easily created by literary procedure. Vedel's redactions of ballads are "more complete" than the genuine texts now known from manuscripts. Where folklore becomes a literary product, the "completeness" is easily increased. For present research, "completeness" (viz., many conflated features) is a characteristic of the relative lateness of the tradition.

Completeness is never an absolute advantage. But it can be so in relation to other badly remembered traditions. (Cf. chapter IV, "The Life of the Narrative.")[1]

This standpoint is valid only for works of a literary origin that enter folklore. Here reduction is a strong form of change; increase is very weak. But their origin itself (appearance in literary form and the conscious work of an individual) offers conditions essentially different from those of folklore.[2]

§164. (B) The most perfect form. Many scholars propose that instead of the more comprehensive completeness, the original form of the narrative must be the most perfect, i.e., have the best inner coherence and the greatest aesthetic effect.

This idea presupposes that a single person has formed (or

consciously transformed) the narrative. It has a certain validity for some categories of folklore: those in verse and some fairytales (especially the ones based on a particular intellectual problem).[1] On the other hand, it is hardly out of the question that obscurity or leaps in thought stem from the individual author, peculiarities that are subsequently erased in oral transmission.

But this point of view has hardly any bearing on items of folklore in which a motif has gradually been shaped over a long period of time. We must *a priori* regard a development from the simple to the complex, and from the obscure to the clearly perceived, as probable. This position finds support in the traditions of primitive peoples, which certainly do not have their strength in clarity of perception. (It must be remembered, however, that we cannot with certainty infer the infancy of the cultured peoples from primitive peoples.)[2]

The more perfect form of a story certainly has a greater chance of being accepted than the poorer. But in reality the perfect forms are found so rarely that one can often only with difficulty imagine them as being the basis of the other forms.[3]

§165. Instead of the simple formula "the most perfect," it is more justifiable to propose the following: the original form of a narrative must, as a rule, exhibit features characteristic of folklore (palpability, emphasis on content, clarity in structure) to an even greater extent than other traditions; for only by virtue of these characteristic features will it be able to be transmitted through time. This definition, however, is of limited use in determining the original form of the narrative.

§166. (C) The simplest narrative. Nowadays, scholars are far more inclined to regard the simplest form of a narrative as its original form. This view is based on (1) the general preference of our time for "evolution," the theory of a gradual transition from "lower" to "higher" forms; (2) the fact that it is easier to explain the existing narrative forms as transitions from the simple to the more complex: the evolutionary series become simpler, and the dynamics of the material or of the conception of the narrators become easier to comprehend.

On the other hand, one must not attach an absolute validity to the rule. The "simple" form may be due to "reduction" (§91), or is perhaps just an incomplete recording (§16f.).

Example. "Saxo's account [of the single combat on Samsø] diverges in several ways from that of the Icelanders; it is far purer and simpler than theirs" (Steenstrup [1897], p. 152). What primarily distinguishes the account, however, is the incompleteness of the recording (§18; cf. Olrik [1898], pp. 79f., 90f.).

The form that has been subjected to "reduction" can naturally be shorn of later expansions and thus may have become similar to the original form; for the basic features of the narrative are less susceptible to "reduction" than are the expansions. But in such a case, the extant versions do not represent a regular continuation of the simple original form; they provide evidence only about what is enduring in the narrative subject. They only secondarily help to determine the original form.[1]

§167. (D) Instead of "the simplest" and "the most perfect," one ought rather to suggest "the most natural."[1] "When all is said and done, the scholar must rely on his own judgment in order to decide what most naturally corresponds to the original form. Underlying the criterion of naturalness, there is undeniably something subjective that can be reduced by a comprehensive knowledge of and total absorption in the folklore material, and which will constantly be reduced by the continuous progress of research" (Krohn [1910], p. 41).

"Are the products of folklore then composed in a natural and logical manner to begin with? Like any other discipline, folkloristics has had to accept as a principle the perception that the material with which it works emerges from sensible reasoning; for where there is no logic, there can be no scholarship. But it has, in fact, frequently turned out that this principle is based on reality"[2] (idem, with references to Aarne's demonstration of detailed, well-structured original forms of several tales).[3]

§168. (E) "What is common to narratives." The original

form of a narrative contains those features that all traditions have in common.

There can be only two exceptions to this rule: (1) that the same transformation has taken place independently in several places, or (2) that a later, developed feature has been disseminated by loan to all versions. But (1) it is unlikely that uniformity in intellectual preconditions will result in such uniformity in features as is the question here; and (2) a diffusion that is later than the original dissemination of the narrative will only with difficulty reach all versions.

Example 1. In the ballad about the Battle of Lena (DgF 136),[1] there is in all versions (except one)[2] a strophe about slaying the enemies "like farmers mow the field." So it probably belonged to the original form of the ballad. This view is supported by two arguments: (1) it contains a historically accurate detail, Count Engelbret's relationship to the sons of Sune, and (2) the very different wording of the versions shows that it is an epic survival, not a recently disseminated migratory strophe. Conversely, the single version referred to above has the names Ebbe and Lorentz in newly composed strophes that are entirely uncharacteristic of ballads; they were probably inserted by a book-learned man from one of the current chronicles.

In practice, one will rarely find full agreement among a large number of versions. (If nothing else prevents it, some versions will be incomplete because of memory lapse or supervening circumstances at the time of recording; cf. §84.) One should then formulate the thesis in this way: The features that most versions have in common often stem from the original form. The argument must, however, be supported by other evidence to gain acceptance among scholars.[3]

Example 2. Seven versions of the Danish ballad *Sir Bjørn in Sønderborg* (DgF 473) have the knight hanged and the princess burned in her bower; only two do not have this.[4] But these two versions agree with Icelandic tradition and a local legend from South Jutland, and partly with an allusion in a third version. This latter group contains the original; hanging and burning are borrowed from the *Havbor ballad*. It is the many traditions from different areas that reveal the original. A common basic form of the Danish and Icelandic ballad texts and of the legend from South Jutland must have had this content.[5]

§169. (E*) The original form of a narrative often contained only what all (or most) traditions agree on.

The decisive characteristic is that the common features form a complete plot, the coherence or presentation of which is disrupted by the addition of features from the individual traditions. (Example. *Ebbe Skammelsen*, DgF 354, introduction.)

§170. When one begins to examine narrative material, it is important to know from the outset what is common to all or most of the versions: (1) not until then does one derive a criterion for what in content pertains to the investigation; (2) since the original form normally consists of the common features, with or without additions, we can in this way form a basically correct impression of the content of the original form relatively quickly.

§171. (F) The chronology of versions. In critical literature, one often finds the opinion that the oldest version contains the original form of the narrative and that the chronology of the versions expresses the gradual transformation of the narrative. This perception, however, is less common among actual folklorists than among historians and literary historians who occasionally work with narrative material. As a general principle, it is to be discarded. Many circumstances other than the date of the version are decisive in determining its value. In many cases, there is a disadvantage in adhering to the oldest recordings that have been reworked by writers, e.g., the literary fairytales.[1] More recent scholarship designates such material as "book variants,"[2] and often treats them afterwards so that they do not confuse the results that are reached on the basis of genuine source material.[3]

§172. Only where the version is fairly close to the origin of the narrative (or the narrative form) does the chronology play a more important role. This statement applies especially to versions (1) where the narrative aims at accurately retaining the memory of something that has taken place (the historical legend), and (2) where the narrative has an especially close connection to a particular historical period ("higher item of folklore," see §12).

Above all, the statement is valid for heroic poetry: the chronology of the sources offers an important aid in establishing the development of the narrative (Olrik [1903-1910] I, introduction). The reason for this is found partly in its greater variability and immediate reflection of the life of its time, partly in the fact that we can date not only the recording but also the lays that belong to the culmination of the narrative and through which a large part of the development of the material has taken place.[1]

§173. (G) Since research only relatively seldom has access to versions that are distributed throughout the total lifetime of a narrative or a notion, it fills in what is lacking by observing the local distribution of the versions.

A notion that has come into existence late will generally belong to a smaller region, one that has come into existence early to a larger region. In addition, the dating must naturally take into account the individual category of folklore: a fairytale disseminates easily, a ballad more slowly (at least when it has to transgress linguistic boundaries), a legend likewise, and belief and custom even more slowly.

The appearance of a notion or a narrative motif in very different parts of the world suggests a very old age; dissemination throughout Asia and Europe suggests an extremely old age, etc. Dissemination within a single country suggests that it is younger.[1]

§174. Generally, the place of origin of a narrative lies within the region in which it appears.

Example. The following legends and tales, which are found (complete) only in Scandinavia, probably also have their origin there: the giant, Finn, who built a church,[1] the princess in the mound,[2] the gold-grinder which grinds salt at the bottom of the sea (von Sydow [1907, 1908]; Moe [1908a], pp. 263f.; Olrik [1903-1910] I, p. 299).[3]

§175. When a narrative occurs frequently in a single region

and more rarely the further one moves away from it, its place of origin must be sought where it appears most frequently.

Example. The tale about the grinder at the bottom of the sea: most frequent in Jutland, rarer in Norway, Sweden, Finland, Estonia; from the Greek islands comes a single, incomplete version (Olrik [1903–1910] I, p. 299).[1]

Comment. Naturally, special circumstances prompt dissemination at a relatively late period in a certain place. Thus, the narrative about the fight between the bull and the serpent (otherwise almost unknown) has become very common in Denmark because it explains illustrations of serpents and a walled-up church door (Olrik [1902], p. 208). Incidentally, we do not know if this narrative is not of a North European descent.[2]

§176. Also, the center of dissemination can be established with some certainty even without using the frequency of the narrative in a single region as a criterion. It will lie either at the center of the entire region of dissemination, or at least in such a way that the routes of communication facilitate its outward dissemination from this center to the entire region.

Comment. While dissemination will take place in a circle under identical circumstances, it will be reduced to only a small sector of particular size under special natural conditions (or other circumstances). Indian narratives are barred from migrating toward the south, Celtic ones toward the west, etc.

§177. This is as far as the purely geographical method can go. It does not lead to very clear results, and serves more to delimit the question than to bring about the actual solution. The method rarely appears in its pure form among actual folklorists; it is best suited to solve the problem when applied within narrow local boundaries, and when the material appears abundantly and uniformly.

The geographical method is of greater importance to the anthropologist and the ethnographer who investigate the dissemination of individual motifs, partly in order to demonstrate the number of contacts among various tribes, partly in order to clarify the oldest human range of ideas. Only when combined with the typological method does it become important for oral narrative research.

Example. Hartland (1894–1896):[1] of the motifs in the tale, he points out the supernatural birth, the turning into stone, and the life-token[2] as universally human; the motif of the maiden saved from the monster is common to ancient narratives.

§178. (H) For more recent oral narrative research, the most important method in discovering the development of the narrative is typologization.

After the scholar has collected all the versions that present the subject in question, he tries to group together those that agree in their overall structure and, if possible, in details. He will thus be able to divide them into certain larger groups and into a number of smaller groups that usually can be arranged under one of the large groups. In this way, he will be able to construct the genealogical tree of the narrative.

Example. Contrary to the ancient form, the more recent tale versions related to *Amor and Psyche* form a group in which all are about a prince who appears in the shape of a dog (wolf, bear).[1] Within this group, one can again recognize a large group that is similar to "Psyche" and a smaller group that strongly diverges from it (climbing over a glass mountain, the task of awakening her husband's memory). The large group can again be divided into one that is similar to "Psyche" and another in which she is to carry the bride-candle to the wedding of the witch's daughter to her betrothed. The latter group also contains a section in which she is rescued by her former husband after having entreated him by calling him her "beloved friend."[2]

The grouping looks like this in a genealogical table:

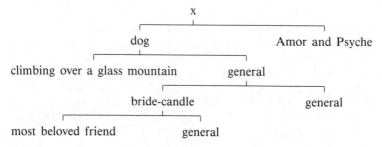

§179. Typologization is, however, preferably not used alone; scholarship combines the classification by location and type (and, in the same way, the classification by date and type). The classification by location offers itself as a point of departure for this type of work; it is contingent upon an externally given condition, the location of each version, while the typologization, on the other hand, rests upon the approach of the scholar, i.e., a subjective factor, even though this approach is nurtured by extensive study of narrative structures.

One begins with the simplest observations of the relationship and the local similarity of traditions, proceeding from the smaller groups to [the larger and observing how local distribution coincides with the typological differences. The investigation then turns to consider how individual main types and subtypes are related to each other, establishing the common original type of these different types and explaining why the diverging forms of the narrative have developed in different ways in different areas.]

The local distribution of versions has achieved significance only in recent times.

Comment. In 1881, Julius Krohn published the introductory chapter to his *Kalevala* investigation. Continued study provided the opportunity for new investigations, and in the sequel (1884) he stated that he, "by an altered method of research," had arrived at different results on a number of points, which were set forth in the second and third chapters, "The Places Where the *Kalevala* is Found" and "*Kalevala* Compared to the Myths of Other Peoples." His closest contemporaries did not understand the new methodology. "It is strange that in the discussion about the *Kalevala*'s Karelian origin, none of these individual investigations [the places where the individual lays are found and their development], on which my father's results were primarily based, were commented upon. It is just as characteristic that in not a single review is an attempt made to rectify these individual points. But the theory of the geographical development of the forms of the lays, which penetrated the entire chain of argument, was extraordinary at the time" (Kaarle Krohn).[1] At the same time as his father solidified his thoughts on the *Kalevala* lays, the son began to apply them to the fairytales. In 1887, the year before his father's death, his investigation of Finnish animal tales appeared;[2] later he applied the method to the lays of the *Kalevala* (Krohn [1903–1910])[3] and partly to a large number of questions concerning myths.[4]

## D. VIEWS ON NARRATIVE MATERIAL

§180. Often the view is put forward that the mythical content of the narrative is older than the realistic content. To a certain extent, this thesis is correct. Taken as a whole, the mythical narrative material is older than the realistic material. Similarly, of the individual narrative motifs, the mythical ones are usually the oldest.

§181. The validity of the thesis becomes much weaker when it is applied to various transmissions of the same narrative, or when it is used as a means of identifying older and younger parts of the same narrative. Above all this is the case with narratives that have their origin in historical personages and events, partly heroic epics, partly legends about historical characters: the realistic material is the oldest, the mythical material penetrates little by little.

Mythical material often appears as an addition to material that already in itself has its unity of plot.[1]

§182. [The view that the cultural-historically most peculiar is the oldest.]

§183. [The view that the material agreeing with real history is the oldest.]

§184. [The linguistic view that the date of the narrative is determined on the basis of linguistic or cultural features.]

# CHAPTER

## ❧ 6 ❧

# CONCERNING THE INDIVIDUAL
# GENRES OF FOLKLORE

## A. TALES

## B. HEROIC POETRY

Literature: Ker (1897); Heusler (1905); Meier (1909); Vedel (1903); Chadwick (1912).

§185. Heroic poetry[1] or heroic narratives (in the broader sense of the word "narrative" as it is used in the present work) are epic presentations with human beings as their main characters. These characters are presented as surpassing present-day human dimensions. They belong to a vanished time, usually a heroic time, during which most of the heroic figures known to the people lived. They belong to a certain tribe, normally the tribe in which the tradition is found, or a closely connected one.[2] The present-day leading families are frequently regarded as being descendants of these heroic figures.

Heroic poetry is associated with warrior life. It thrives in a warlike culture ("heroic age"; see "Literature"), which often exists somewhat before the earliest literate culture. In its most developed form, heroic poetry co-exists with a literate society.

Heroic poetry is often closely associated with the kings and their entourages of warriors. They constitute the audience for whom the heroic narratives are primarily, although not exclusively, told. Most of the heroic lays are about kings and, often to a lesser extent, the warriors in their service. This always indicates a culture with a rather well-developed political structure. Heroic narratives without a well-developed political structure are now found only among tribes isolated from the main roads of culture, such as the Finns and Kirghiz.[3]

The professional singers played an important role as the bearers of heroic poetry (and probably also as its creators); they were often connected to a king's court (all references to the antiquity of our race, references in the Homeric poems) or wandered from court to court (*Widsith*).[4] They are also found as wandering minstrels among the masses (French *jougleurs,* German *spîlmänner* in the Middle Ages).[5] Professional singers also play a role in simple cultural stages (the Finnish *kantele* singers are local singers).[6] A monotone accompaniment to the song on a stringed instrument is customary.

A pure "folk" transmission of heroic poetry exists, for instance, in Scandinavian ballads (sung to a dance) and in prose.


## C. FOLK LEGENDS


## D. ORAL NARRATIVE AND HISTORY


Literature: Feilberg (1892–1894a), p. 81; Nielsen (1892–1894);[1] Schwartz (1893), pp. 117f.; Neckel (1910).

§187. The formal character of the legends, which has its basis in historical events or impressions, is not generically different from what applies to the narrative world as a whole. The same rules apply to "the structure of the narrative" and "the life of the narrative"; the transformation just seems so much stronger because the historical reality, which the popular imagination must deal with and shape according to its needs, is so different from legendary material and, in particular, more variegated.

§188. The relationship between narrative and history offers an interesting problem to folkloristics, because here we know not only the result of the development, but also its point of departure; i.e., we can recognize the development of the narrative with greater accuracy than in most cases.

On the other hand, folkloristics can do historiography a favor: it can determine the narrative genre with greater accuracy than would have been otherwise possible and thus throw light on the reliability or unreliability of the legendary account.

§189. The divergence of the narrative form from the real world is due in part to selection and in part to transformation.

A selection from the multiplicity of real life will take place, determined especially by the demands of the narrative for palpability (single character and visible plot). This selection takes place not only at the time when an event gives rise to a narrative, but also later on, because some narratives—the least legendary ones—are forgotten, while others are remembered.

Transformation probably begins even before the concrete oral tradition exists; it lies in the very character of the popular perception of the event.

§190. It is, however, impossible to prove this last thesis by means of verified sources. We do not know (1) the historical basis, (2) the perception in its embryonic stage, or (3) the completed narrative. The middle stage will almost always elude our observation. On other occasions, we can often make observations of the method by which non-book-learned people perceive events.[1] Sometimes, however, we can come so close to the historical basis of the narrative that we can in all probability infer how the event was perceived by the eyewitnesses.

Example. In 1870, in Königsberg, it was told that a girl who had received communion the very same day went to a dance hall in the evening, where the devil, in the shape of a fine gentleman, came and danced with her. The musicians, who sensed that it was the devil, suddenly changed to a hymn at midnight, and the devil hurried out the window and threw the unconscious girl out onto the turf. For a long time, no girl dared visit this dance hall. The historical reality was that at midnight the musicians suddenly played a chorale in honor of the host, whose birthday was the next day. The sudden change in atmosphere had an effect on the listeners, especially because it was right before their departure (Feilberg [1892–1894a], p. 97). This account shows the ability of the "folk" to see a palpable event in which only the atmosphere and everyday conditions are present. The legend can only untypically be called historical; it is, rather, just a rebirth or, better, a renewal of a mythical episode.[2] But the part of it that treats a historical event very clearly shows the ability of the people to visualize episodes.

§191. The forces that operate on perception and narrative development are so completely identical with the "Epic Laws" and "the Life of the Narrative" that discussing them individually would be redundant. Only some of the more special cases of these general conditions will be emphasized here.

§192. A conspicuous peculiarity of historical legends is the accuracy with which they give information about some characteristic detail or other.[1] It cannot be determined in advance with complete certainty whether this accuracy in detail is due to impressions of reality retained by the individual's sharp observational sense, or to a later poetic reworking. The frequency with which such features appear would at best seem to indicate that they satisfy the demand of the narrators and the audience of the legend.

§193. Subordinate characters with identical roles in the narrative are merged into one character.

Example. Earl Sivard the Fat of Northumberland was a Danish warrior who came to England under Knud (Cnut) the Great and advanced himself.[1] He killed the Earl of Northumberland and received his earldom under Harda-Knud [in the year 1041, and at the same time received the earldom of Huntington]. He undertook a campaign against Scotland [in 1054], and died [in 1055] under Edward the Confessor. The story, which, in fact, was composed a hundred years later than the events it records, merges him with Earl Sigurðr the Fat of Orkney [d. 1014] and has Sivard's arrival and the murder of the earl happen at the same time (Olrik [1903b], p. 215).[2]

§194. Characters with the same name (1) are confused, or (2) are merged into one.

Example 1. In the Middle Ages, the emperor entombed in the mountain is Frederic II, and in a chapbook from the sixteenth century, it is Frederic Barbarossa.[1]

Example 2. In Northern English tradition, Earl Sigurðr the Fat of the Orkney Islands (d. 1014) and Earl Sivard the Fat of Northumberland (d. 1055) have become one [and the same person], who on his way to England slays a dragon in the Orkney Islands.[2]

§195. Original time intervals are completely disregarded insofar as they do not express a certain causal relation.

Example 1. *Widsith* presents Ermanaric (d. 375) as the ruler of the Goths when they fought by the Weichsel river against the Huns.[1] Generally, heroic poetry regards all its characters as living almost simultaneously during a specific heroic age.[2]

A special case is when original time intervals are increased or reduced according to what suits the economy of the legend.

Example 2. In the legend, the Northumbrian Earl Sivard the Fat dies "many years later,[3] when he began to feel his age"; in reality, it happened the year after the campaign in Scotland (1054, 1055), but the narrative could not place the events so close together when there was no causal relation (Olrik [1903b], p. 214).

§196. It is usually difficult to determine the historical basis of a legend on the grounds of the narrative tradition alone.

Just to declare that a legend has historical basis can cause difficulties. Within the actual "folk legends" one will, however, find support for such a claim in the features of the legend that approach verisimilitude, in its intimate knowledge of places and circumstances that are unimportant to the plot, and, finally, in the fact that people consider themselves to be descendants of the character in question (preferably with a knowledge of the intermediary links).

But the following may argue against a historical basis: (1) the character of the narrative as being purely folktale, (2) the character of the narrative as origin legend, created as the effort of imagination in order to understand the reason for a name or another feature, and (3) the localization of the narrative at several, especially many, places.[1] The last-mentioned point does not preclude a historical basis, but it does reduce the likelihood that the individual legend contains the correct placement in time and of characters.

# APPENDIX

## From the Domain of the Epic Laws

What I have to add to this study is an extract from conversations at the institute of the university during discussions of the principles for oral narrative research. We discussed subjects that stood on the borderline of folklore or on the periphery of its domain: the narrative tradition of Israel, the historical or less historical parts of our medieval saints' lives, especially in order to throw light on the structural relationship between the narrative and non-narrative parts of them. I prepared the section about the ancestors of Israel, but I incorporated comments made by Miss Ruth Gerner Lund, M.A. student. After my draft, we both read the relevant sections in *Genesis,* pp. 159ff.

### A. THE PATRIARCHAL HISTORY OF ISRAEL

The history of the Jewish patriarchs constitutes the main content of Genesis (the creation story and the more remote ancestors form chapters 1–11 of the book). The presentation is compiled from several sources. The two most important are usually called J and E (the Jahvistic source and the Elohistic source, according to their different designations of "God"); P (the Priestly source) plays a less significant role. J offers the fullest and most basic presentation, and probably the oldest; it is human, is descriptive, and displays an interest in good narrative plot; E has an even stronger religious coloring, with a tendency toward sermon-like style, and with an interest in the form of the worship of God. These characteristics are, however, present in J as well, if to a less overwhelming extent. The conflation of several sources is one of the main reasons why double accounts—doublets[1]—of the same motif or plot frequently appear.

It is obvious that folk tradition is the source of this presentation of material in Genesis. It is proved negatively by the fact that a people at a cultural stage of still being in part nomadic shepherds could not have written history on such a large scale. It appears positively from the general character of the account: its person-oriented and palpable plot, its interest in places and names that are explained by the narrative, and a number of other peculiarities in the presentation that are treated in the following discussion. (About this, see *Genesis,* introduction).

Taken as a whole, these stories must be considered as pertaining to the genre of heroic narratives. They are about eminent personalities who are believed by the people to be their ancestors and founders to a degree never surpassed by the preceding or succeeding ones. Three such ancestors are mentioned: Abraham, Isaac, and Jacob. These three are not main characters in separate plots, however, for Isaac completely lacks a section in which he carries the main interest. (1) Abraham spans the entire section in which Isaac's birth and Jahwe's promise are the main incidents, beginning with the genealogy of Abraham and ending with the delegated servant's obtaining a bride for Isaac. In this last incident, Abraham is also the main character. It is to him the servant commits himself; it is as his messenger that he relates the words of courtship. And even though Abraham seems to have died in the story (perhaps the compiler of the text removed this passage from J, because a little later he must have him die again according to another source),[2] it all concerns the fulfillment of the prophecy connected with him. (2) Jacob versus Esau: the birthright, the exile, the courtship of Laban's sister and the service in his household, and the flight and reconciliation with Esau form a well-structured plot that naturally combines the flight and the courtship journey; and each of the two episodes is introduced by a dream that portends God's help and thus a happy outcome. (3) The story of Joseph: sold to Egypt by jealous brothers, raising himself up as a powerful man there, letting his brothers feel his superiority, and finally revealing his identity to them. (4) The story of Jacob's other sons forms a looser series of narratives that are concerned primarily with the fortunes of the individual tribes in later times.

The form of the presentation is smooth narrative prose, occasionally sprinkled with lyrical pieces of a prophetic content, e.g., Jahwe's prophecy about Esau and Jacob (25:23) and Jacob's great prophecy about his sons' descendants (49). The prose progresses smoothly, beginning with genealogical tables or with a place of sojourn, and receiving fullness in the presentation when it approaches the climax of the event (e.g., Abraham's servant at the well when he sees Rebecca [24]: he first turns his prayer toward God, then the scene and the gifts he gives her are painted in detail; we see a similar progression in the detailed account of Abraham's reception of the three men [18]; etc.).

These descriptions are often palpable, sometimes with a tableau-like suspense, as when Jacob wrestles with God in the night and says, "I will not let thee go except thou bless me" (32:26);[3] or when Abraham raises the sacrificial sword over the bound Isaac, but is forced to stop by the Lord's angel and is told to take the ram tangled in the briars (22). Even though conversation or at least speech is the most important vehicle for expression, there is often a momentary glimpse of physical movement, as for example, when Abraham's servant, with his hand on his master's loin, swears to bring his son Isaac's bride (24); or when the old Jacob places his hands crosswise so that he can bless Ephraim with his right hand and Manassa with his left (48).

A single factor, however, breaks the palpability of the narratives: the immense power of the religious in the entire tradition of Israel. Only in individual characteristic episodes does the deity assume a visible shape (the men with Abraham, the angel on Mount Moriah, Jacob's dream); normally the narrative simply says "Jahwe spoke," without our knowing where and how He was seen; Rebecca "went to consult the Lord" (25:22), but the narrative does not know how He can be found. Even in the tableau scenes God shuns observation in a peculiar way: Jacob's nightly adversary says, "Why dost thou ask my name?"; only as a result of his might does Jacob understand who He is, and calls the place "the face of God" (32:30). This blurred, nocturnal deity is characteristic of the entire tradition of Israel, the only difference being that He otherwise does not have as much external personality as in the vision. The God of the ancestors does not visibly interfere with the plot; one sees His work only in that which wins victory: He speaks the words of His covenant; He gives His promise and His blessing; His "angels" bring His message, e.g., the two who come to Sodom, but it is not they who physically cause the rain of brimstone over the town.

In this way, the religious extends beyond the simple effect of causation, which is the usual character of folk tradition. It is like a parenthesis within the progress of the plot. It adds a large number of speeches and thoughts; it imparts a new causal relation to everything and an insight into the inner life of the characters, deeper and more conscious than otherwise in oral narrative composition. This is what raises Israeli heroic poetry above the ordinary level, a step further toward what we call literary art, as a manifestation not of individual production but rather of the general view of the people.

There is another important characteristic of Israeli heroic poetry, falling not outside but inside the usual domain of oral narrative: the extraordinary role of localization. In the names of the tribes and in their idiosyncrasies, in altars, wells, and many other names of localities, or in their simple existence, the narrator sees the traces of past events. On every page in the history of the patriarchs, one will find some or many features of this kind, and it is rare to find an episode that lacks them. A few stories do not expressly mention that the item still existed, but, according to its nature, it must have endured through time, as, e.g., in both the wasteland of Sodom and Lot's wife as the pillar of salt, or in Abraham's sacrifice on Mount Moriah as the predecessor of the consecration of the large temple of Israel on Mount Moriah in Jerusalem. If one distinguishes between narratives with localization and [narratives] without localization, the indisputable examples of the latter group are few.

One could attempt to distinguish between straightforward origin legends, which interpret only the origin of a thing, and those in which an original motif is woven into a more comprehensive, self-sustained story. But again it will turn out that even the more fully executed narratives most often are artistically shaped origin legends.

Example 1. *Jacob's death* (49–50, mixed sources): "And he charged them, saying: I am going to be gathered to my people: bury me with my fathers in the double cave, which is in the field of Ephron the Hittite, over against Mambre in the land of Canaan, which Abraham bought together with the field of Ephron the Hittite for a possession to bury in ... there also Leah doth lie buried. And when he had ended the commandments, wherewith he instructed his sons, he drew up his feet upon the bed, and died: and he was gathered to his people. And when Joseph saw this, he fell upon his father's face, weeping and kissing him. And he commanded his servants the physicians to embalm his father. And while they were fulfilling his commands, there passed forty days: for this was the manner with bodies that were embalmed, and Egypt mourned him seventy days. And the time of the mourning being expired, Joseph spoke to the family of Pharaoh: If I have found favour in your sight, speak in the ears of Pharaoh: For my father made me swear to him, saying: Behold I die: thou shalt bury me in my sepulchre which I have digged for myself in the land of Canaan. So I will go up and bury my father and return. And Pharaoh said to him: Go up and bury thy father according as he made thee swear. So he went up, and there went with him all the ancients of Pharaoh's house, and all the elders of the land of Egypt. And the house of Joseph and his brethren. . . . He had also in his train chariots and horsemen: and it was a great company. And they came to the threshingfloor of Atad, which is situated beyond the Jordan: where celebrating the exequies with a great and vehement lamentation, they spent full seven days. And when the inhabitants of Canaan saw this, they said: This is a great mourning to the Egyptians. And therefore the name of that place was called The Mourning of Egypt [*Abel-Misraim*]. So the sons of Jacob did as he had commanded them. . . . "

The name *Abel-Misraim* means "the meadow of Egypt," but must for a Jew evoke an echo of *Ebel-Misraim,* "the mourning of Egypt."[4] This naturally gave rise to the idea that the Egyptians had been present in the meadow and celebrated the funeral ceremony there. The other point of departure is that Jacob is thought to be buried in the cave of his fathers; and since he was the one for whom one could best imagine the Egyptians celebrating a funeral ceremony in grand style in his home country, the two ideas naturally had to find each other, and the account (which gives the Egyptians such a conspicuous part in the funeral procession!) came into existence.

Example 2. *Jacob blesses Ephraim* (48, J and E). Joseph comes to Jacob's death bed with his two sons Manassa and Ephraim. Jacob strengthens himself and sits on his bed. Whom are you bringing? he asks, for his eyes are dim because of his old age. And when he hears it is Joseph's sons: Bring them to me, so that I can bless them. "And he set Ephraim [the younger] on his right hand, that is, towards the left hand of Israel, but Manassa [the elder] on his left hand, to wit, towards his father's right hand, and brought them near to him. [But he stretching forth his right hand, put it upon the head of Ephraim the younger brother; and the left upon the head of Manassa who was the elder,] changing his hands." But when Joseph saw that he was about to put his right hand on Ephraim's head, he said to his father: "It should not be so, my father: for this is the firstborn, put thy right hand upon his head." But he, refusing, said: "I know, my son, I know: and this also shall become peoples, and shall be multiplied: *but this younger brother shall be greater than he: and his seed shall grow into nations.* And he blessed them at that time. . . . "

The purpose of the narrative is thus to explain that Ephraim's tribe became much mightier than Manassa's, and that they both received a place among the tribes of Israel: "So thy two sons who were born to thee in the land of Egypt before I came hither to thee, shall be mine: Ephraim and Manassa shall be reputed to me as Ruben and Simeon" (P 48:5).

There are stories that in themselves appear as narratives of a rather special category, e.g., Lot's two daughters, who get their father drunk and trick him into fornication. But the origin legend also shows forth here.

Example 3. "So the two daughters of Lot were with child by their father. And the elder bore a son, and she called his name Moab [smallness]:[5] he is the father of the Moabites [the tribe] unto this day. The younger also bore a son, and she called his name Ammon, that is, the son of my people: he is the father of the Ammonites unto this day" (19:36-38). Already here the name elicits the notion that she gave birth to a child by one from her close family. The Israelites' hatred of the Moabites and Ammonites, along with the immorality of the Sodomites living around Lot, prompted the growth of the motif into a narrative.

The story about Jacob's youth is the fullest and most artistic of the patriarchal stories. One is not inclined to look for puns and the like in the features of this both poetically and religiously poignant account. Closer examination, however, reveals that it is by no means free of such devices: Esau's entire relationship to Jacob is foreshadowed in a lyrical strophe. During pregnancy, Rebecca feels the children struggle in her womb, and she goes to consult Jahwe, who says: "Two nations are in thy womb, and two peoples shall be divided out of thy womb. And one people shall overcome the other, and the elder shall serve the younger" (25:23). The main content of the narrative thus appears as a foreshadowing of the later relationship between Israel and Edom; a present reality is personified—literally and correctly with regard to names—as an ancient narrative.

The narrative continues: "And when her time was come to be delivered, behold twins were found in her womb. He that came forth was red, and hairy like a skin: and his name was called Esau. Immediately the other coming forth, held his brother's foot in his hand, and therefore he was called Jacob." The account of the birth is based on the names Jacob ("heel") and admoni ("red"), which was felt to be related to Edom (the name of a tribe, and in the narrative = Esau). But in this we find the embryo of the captivating account of Jacob who, with the skins over his neck, receives the blessing meant for Esau (27).

The same name motif is used immediately afterwards to explain Esau's selling of his birthright: Esau comes home from the field: "Give me of this red pottage, for I am exceeding faint. For which reason his name was called Edom." This deception also corresponds to an interpretation of Jacob's name: Esau later says: "Rightly is his name called Jacob; for he hath supplanted me to this second time: my birthright he took away before, and now this second time he hath stolen away my blessing" (*jaqob,* "a person who covets, a person who deceives").[6]

The narrative describes their different personalities: "And when they were grown up, Esau became a skillful hunter, and a husbandman but Jacob a plain man dwelt in tents." It is evidently the life of two tribes that is being characterized, the nomadic and predatory Edomites versus the settled and wealthier Israelites. The tribal characteristic comes forth even more strongly in Isaac's blessing: "In the fat of the earth, and in the dew of heaven from above, shall thy blessing be. Thou shalt live by the sword and shalt serve thy brother: and the time shall come, when thou shalt shake off and loose his yoke from thy neck" (27:39–40).

It is said about their childhood that "Isaac loved Esau because he ate of his hunting: and Rebecca loved Jacob." This continuation, which develops their characters and roles in more detail, has evidently borrowed from the great story about Jacob, who changes the blessing, and evidently must be a preparation for it. The contrast is carried out in more detail; Esau marries wives from Canaan (26:34), and Jacob is sent by Isaac to find a bride among his old relatives.

The vision in which he sees the heavens open up and hears Jahwe speak to him appears clearly with localization: "And trembling he said: How terrible is this place! This is no other but the house of God, and the gate of heaven. And Jacob, arising in the morning, took the stone, which he had laid under his head, and set it up for a title, pouring oil upon the top of it. And he called the name of the city, Bethel ['God's House'], which before was called Luza" (28:17–19).

Linguistic schematizing appears everywhere. The same expressions used in an address are often used in a reply; and pronouncements are repeated verbatim to a third person (thus until the last chapter [50], where Joseph repeats Jacob's decision about his burial in the cave of his ancestors). A peculiar kind of schematizing is the frequent repetition of Jahwe's promise to give them the land.[7] It is not so much an epic formula as a religious one; it is addressed more to the people of Israel in later times than to the plot of the narrative.

There is, however, only a small amount of narrative schematizing. The dream about God (the heavenly ladder) begins his journey to the foreign land, as another dream about God (the wrestle with God) precedes the meeting with Esau. From the standpoint of an Israelite, these two episodes must be of major importance: they establish Jacob's relationship to God, and the following plot is a fulfillment of this covenant.

In spite of the overall similarity in style, there is such a difference in composition and presentation from one story to the other that it is worthwhile to examine them separately.

(1) The story of Abraham has a unity of plot: its point of departure is God's promise to give him a land and make his descendants an entire people. The suspense of the plot is that the expected offspring fails to appear until God reveals Himself in person and promises him the birth of his son. The climax of this suspense occurs when God Himself orders him to sacrifice his son, to whom the promise applies. The point of closure occurs when Isaac goes to meet his bride; at that point, the plot moves unencumbered toward the realization of God's promise (the Law of Closing).

Abraham's story is interwoven with that of his nephew Lot. The story of Lot has an external claim to this juxtaposition, because his story gives the origin of some of the peoples living near the Israelites.[8] But there is also an inner coherence. Lot's life and to a certain degree his character (agreeing with the Law of Contrast) are offered as counterparts to Abraham's: his moroseness as opposed to Abraham's harmony and his effort at keeping the family together; the immodesty, the contemptible offspring with the hostile mind, and the poor fate of wandering in the desert. Therefore, these sections concerning Lot belong to an "ideal" unity of plot that has Abraham as its main character. But still the single-strandedness of the story is retained: the visit of the three men to Abraham drifts, inadvertently as it were, into the revelation of the condemnation of Sodom; Abraham's prayer for the town brings the two events even closer together (and also serves to reveal his compassionate disposition). When his prayer accomplishes nothing (with regard to the plot it is a wasted feature), it indicates that this well-composed single-strandedness in the story is not original but the fruit of an artistic presentation.

Another counterpart to the main story is the birth and fate

of Ishmael, told with greater sympathy for the wild sons of the desert than the one about the origin of the Ammonites and Moabites in Lot's incest. Moreover, they are regarded as Abraham's family, like the Israelites themselves, albeit as the children of the slave woman. The Law of Contrast also asserts itself here, but to a lesser degree. Ishmael's life is set against that of a subordinate character, Isaac, not against the main figure of the story itself. The slave woman, Agar, is viewed with sympathy, as is revealed by the fact that the angel of God saves her life in the desert (21:17).

The palpability of the story of Abraham is strong. Individual characters are everywhere the bearers of the action; even the deity reveals itself in an external form (by Abraham's tent and in Sodom), which is not common in the religious part of the Israeli narratives. Only the Sodomites form an exception to this palpability, both in their general description and when they try to seduce the messengers of the Lord, as well as in their punishment (19). Otherwise, the folk tradition has a preference for the crime and punishment of an individual character, as, for example, in the numerous legends about a farm that sinks into the ground as punishment for its owner's depravity.[9] But here in the patriarchal narratives, a local narrative survival about the town of Sodom must have been too strong, or the general description of the townspeople was strong enough to break with the strict personification of the narrative tradition. (Gunkel[10] is hardly unjustified in seeing a later expansion of the story of Lot by a narrative in which Lot is almost only a subordinate character and which is remote from the settlements of the desert tribes.)[11]

The Law of Contrast is strong throughout, not only for the main character; all figures oppose each other as paired contrasts, either simply by virtue of their difference, or expressly through their interplay: Abraham's and Lot's herdsmen quarrel (13:7), Agar taunts the childless Sarah (16), Ishmael plays with the younger Isaac (21:9).

The Laws of Numbers in folklore are found, but not at the

most decisive points in the composition: the three men who come to Abraham in Mambre (18); Abraham sees Mount Moriah on the third day and sends the young men back (22). The number three for sacrificial animals (15) is in reality contingent upon cultic, not epic, reasons. The number three plays a more important role in the genealogical tables: the trinity of the patriarchs (Abraham, Isaac, Jacob) is purely genealogical and does not bear any relation to the plot. When the story of Abraham is introduced with the three sons of Thrare and their offspring (11:27), they have different epic roles: Abraham himself as the main character, his one brother as the father of Lot, and his other brother as the father of the people from whom the patriarchs take their wives. The number three is therefore present, but more to give a certain narrative-like color than to serve as a structural basis for the composition.

The Law of Twins is very conspicuous: the two men who speak as the messengers of God in Sodom (19) (precisely their duality prevents us from taking an independent interest in their fate); the two servants who accompany Abraham on his way to Mount Moriah (22). Lot's two daughters, who seduce their father (19:30), belong to the Law of Twins in a broader sense; i.e., each acts in her own way, but they are identical in character; the interest must be directed away from them and focused on their offspring, the Moabites and Ammonites.

The Law of Final Stress is found insofar as the interest focuses on the younger brother Isaac, not on the older Ishmael. Among Thrare's three sons (11:end), Abraham is, however, in the position of initial stress, just as in the patriarchal series Abraham is always in the position of initial stress in these stories and in Judaism generally. But this is a hierarchy of genealogical tables and does not appear to concern the epic material.

Schematizing occurs less often than we normally find in folklore; it is obviously kept in check by full and vivid description. One will hardly find a more pertinent example than that of Abraham's servant who, in his prayer to God, gives an exact description of Rebecca's reception of him and his camels, which is soon realized (24:12). (This can be compared with the Icelandic saga style, the realism of which prevents a schematizing of the material.)

The Law of Two to a Scene is obeyed throughout. A borderline case, however, is the scene where Sarah laughs while Abraham and the man speak together. But the line is not transgressed: she herself does not appear speaking, but her laughter is heard by the guest, who continues to address his words to Abraham just as he had previously done.

The smooth progress of the plot (its single-strandedness) is noticeable. The man's visit with Abraham leads the dialogue to Lot and Sodom; Abraham prays for the condemned city, and he accompanies the men on their way to it, thus functioning as an external intermediary link.

The story about Abraham has its introduction, quiet and lingering in the first part, the Thrare genealogical table (11). It is set in motion by the next part concerning God's revelation about the land He will give him; but in the episode itself, it is still lingering. The events on the road (the division of land with Lot [13]) are still quiet in comparison with the more personal struggles that soon fill the plot. And the Law of Closing reveals itself in the scope in which concluding episodes are depicted, especially the courtship scene with Rebecca; the interest moves from Abraham to the posterity he has founded.

In certain respects, the story of Abraham stands highest among the patriarchal stories. The individual episodes are well-rounded and often have a tableau, which is only rarely reached in other narratives. The story seems to be pieced together from smaller narratives. In order to create a unity out of this scattered material, it has been necessary to place the character of the protagonist strongly in the foreground along with a recurrent theme, namely, the land and the posterity. These general notions receive fullness exactly by being associated with the various narrative motifs. A peculiar dignity is bestowed upon Abraham as the bearer of the promise; a noble consideration separates him from the other patriarchal figures, and his submission to

God's will is far deeper than that of any of his descendants. To these technical and aesthetic peculiarities must also be added the simple forms of external life (as depicted in the story), which emphasize the weighty simplicity of the episodes.

General heroic features are only faintly found in Abraham. He never carries out any great personal deed, but he is victorious over King Chodorlahomor with the help of his tribe (14). The emphasis lies not on the battle, but on the generous righteousness with which he refuses payment but considers a reimbursement of his own expenses to be sufficient, and on the blessing which Melchisedech gives him and in which the heavenly reward is expressed.[12] Throughout this saga of Abraham, he is without the personal ingenuity that is characteristic of his grandson Jacob; instead, he possesses a peace-loving and upright dignity. Throughout the entire story, his great age forms part of the explanation (thus an epic reason); but even more, it is a simple, human, yet unheroic view of life that creates this ancestor of the people of Israel.[13]

A single story distinguishes itself completely from the other adventures with Abraham, and has nothing in common with them except for the personal unity. It is the story about Abraham when he passes off Sarah as his sister in a foreign land. External evidence shows that it has been transmitted independently in three versions:

(A) Abraham in Egypt (12 J)

(B) Abraham with King Abimelech (20 E)

(C) Isaac with the Philistine King Abimelech (26 J)

Version A is the best: During a famine, Abraham travels with his wife to Egypt. To avoid being killed by those who desire Sarah because of her beauty, he arranges to pass her off as his sister. Pharaoh's princes see her, and she is brought into the house of Pharaoh; Abraham receives great wealth from him, but God punishes Pharaoh with severe plagues. Pharaoh then reproaches Abraham for having passed off his wife as his sister and for having subjected him [Pharaoh] to God's anger by marrying another man's wife. And he commands Abraham to leave with his wife and all his belongings.

I will mention a couple of the differences in the other presentations. God reveals himself to Abimelech in a dream and says: "Lo, thou shalt die for the woman thou hast taken: for she hath a husband." But Abimelech had not yet touched her, and he said: "Lord, wilt thou slay a nation, that is ignorant and just? Did not he say to me: She is my sister." But God answered him in his dream: "And I know that thou didst it with a sincere heart: and therefore I withheld thee from sinning against me, and I suffered thee not to touch her. Now therefore restore the man his wife: for he is a prophet. And he shall pray for thee, and thou shalt live." In the morning, Abimelech called his servants, and they were very afraid when they heard what had happened. Next he summoned Abraham and asked why he had committed such a crime. Abraham answered that he had done it to save himself in this strange and ungodly land. Then Abimelech took sheep and oxen, servants and handmaidens, and gave them to Abraham, and he also gave Sarah back to him; to Sarah he said: "Behold I have given thy brother[14] a thousand pieces of silver: this shall serve thee for a covering of thy eyes to all that are with thee, and whithersoever thou shalt go: and remember thou wast taken." Then Abraham interceded with the Lord, and the Lord healed Abimelech, his wife, and his handmaidens so that they again could bear children (B). Variant C: Isaac takes refuge with Gerara in the land of the Philistines, and because he fears the inhabitants of the land, he passes off Rebecca as his sister. On one occasion, King Abimelech sees "from the window" that he caresses her, and calls to Isaac: How easily could you not have brought blame on us! and he commanded that anyone touching [him or] her would be put to death.

The plot is obviously the best in A, the weakest in C, where no single character appears who will take possession of the wife of the patriarch. In B, the conversations are between God and the king and not especially between humans. In itself, the plot is well-rounded and powerful. But contrary to the practice of this narrative cycle, it is peculiar that Abraham's ingenuity forms the main motif; in this it shows a similarity to the following story about Jacob. God's appearance as the one who punishes crimes (without regard for the main character, and who punishes an entire people or royal house, even though only a single one is guilty) also moves outside the mentality that is otherwise associated with the ancestor.

The plot is simple, and reminiscent of the structure of the folk narrative, where a single trick so often is the decisive factor. In its structure, the Law of Two to a Scene is conspicuous; the plot moves forward through a series of episodes, and especially dialogues *tête-à-tête:* the patriarch and his spouse, the foreign servants and their master, the king and the patriarch. In B (with its Elohistic[15] preference for God and for priests), Abimelech's visionary conversation with God is the decisive factor, and the other motifs are suppressed in relation to it; it also creates an additional episode in having Abraham, because he is a prophet, prevail upon God to put an end to his affliction. With this additional feature, a hybrid is formed, and although it obeys the Law of Two to a Scene, it is confusing because of its multiplicity of roles. C is the weakest, because the king is not really the acting character; only the wife is threatened by the possibility of abduction. It is so much weaker because in this way one character of the narrative is erased. However, it has a striking palpability; from his window, the king sees the patriarch caressing his wife and suspects the connection. The same theme as in the other versions lurks behind what is extant; i.e., it is the king who intends to marry the wife.

Finally, we also have the Law of Closing and the Law of Opening in very pronounced forms. The law of Opening can be seen in the famine that forces the starving Israelites to go down to Goshen, which is abounding in water, and only then the more intricate narrative thread commences relating Abraham's fear for his life in the strange land. The Law of Closing can be observed when not only the wife is handed over, but also a large number of cattle are added as a gift; a further point of closure is the designation of the place where the patriarch now settles (13:1 and 26:17).

The entire narrative is a typical collection of the pecularities of folk tradition, but arranged in such a way that in three versions we have a declining value in the quality of these motifs.[16]

(2) Jacob versus Esau.

(3) The story of Joseph forms a very pronounced unity of plot: the point of departure is when the jealous brothers sell him to Egypt. The content consists of his gradual rise in the new surroundings. The point of suspense is his imprisonment, the danger of which is emphasized by the misfortune of the baker and the butler under the same conditions, and by Pharaoh's mercy on him. The point of conclusion is his revelation of his true identity to the brothers; and the actual Law of Closing is satisfied by the transfer of Jacob and the brothers to Egypt.

There is a fairytale quality to the story, although it cannot be assigned to any single type. Here, the younger brother is cast off by his older siblings and sent away to perish; yet he advances to a highly respected position in the foreign court, and finally stands before his humiliated brothers as the fortunate one. Here is the story about Potiphar's wife, which must be regarded as a current epic motif.[17] But the story has finer nuances than the fairytales: consider the oldest brother, Ruben, who is comparatively compassionate, and the youngest, Benjamin, who is dearest to him, and whom he tricks into his power in such a way that the brothers' remorse is immediately awakened (42f.). The fact that the plot lacks the schematizing of folktales corresponds to this sense of modifying features.[18] The Law of Three combined with final stress is found only in the fates of the imprisoned characters (the baker, the butler, and Joseph), and additionally in the three days before each of them experiences his fate. The tale-like impression, however, is strengthened by the use of certain numbers to express non-individualized numbers (the 12 brothers, the 7 fat and 7 lean cows).

One is more strongly reminded of tales here than in any other patriarchal narrative, because the fate of the hero is at the center of attention: it is his personal misfortune and success that are the subjects of the story. The focus in this story is quite different from the tribal prophecy in the Abraham and Jacob stories. Yet behind this the fate of the people also lurks, namely, how Israel came to Goshen in Egypt. But the motif is not directly expressed, and it is unnecessary in order to sympathize fully with the fate of the hero.

The palpability of the narrative is present, but within certain limits. The main character himself is never in a direct tableau situation. The dreams are richest in this effect: the eleven sheaves and the eleven stars that bow down, the seven fat and the seven lean cows, the baskets of meal out of which the birds eat on the way (40). There are additional tableaux scenes, such as when Jacob receives his lost son's coat (37); but the purely naive tableaux, in which the protagonist usually looms large, is somewhat reduced by the number and multiplicity of motifs.

In all, the story can be designated as a kind of tale or folk novella devoid of the local tradition and origin legends that play such an important role in the patriarchal stories proper; for this and other reasons it forms a rather closed unity. It does not correspond very well to the impression of coherent legendary motifs found in the other stories of the patriarchs of Israel, but rather indicates an independent product of an author, and which perhaps has no more in the way of historical elements than what serves to explain how the tribe of Israel settled in Egypt. The account about the Israelite who raises himself up to a respected position at a foreign court can be compared with the much younger composition about the success of Esther and Mordocai at the court of the Persians; in both instances, the foreign and suppressed tribe is compensated for suffering by having one of their own advance to the most distinguished position in the royal house.[19]

(4) Narratives about the sons of Jacob. A series of short stories about Jacob and his sons are not connected with the important story about Joseph, which has a purely Canaanite horizon, and their passionate, violent, and tragic events differ from the happy ending of the story of Joseph. To this series belong the rape of Dinah and the violent revenge of Simeon and Levi (34), Ruben, who slept with his father's concubine

(35:22, the rest of the story deliberately left out),[20] and Judah, who is seduced by his childless daughter-in-law (38). Another, yet related small group comprises Jacob's blessing of Joseph's two sons (48) and, above all, his death poem (49) about the destiny of his sons and their tribes, which, among other things, contains full allusions to the narratives just mentioned.

One will naturally find relatively few of the more elaborate epic laws in these short origin narratives; but there is present a certain fullness in the description that at times approaches the tableau scenes: Themar sits at the roadside veiled as a prostitute, and tempts her father-in-law in order to give birth to the child that has been denied her (38); Joseph leads his two sons to the dying Jacob, one at his right hand and one at his left hand, but the old man crosses his hands so that he gives the younger one the actual blessing. A certain inner connection with the story of Joseph has given this episode life and fullness. But most often a detailed description is given only of the plot as a whole (to create the decisive event), or reveals itself only in conversations (Sichem's courtship after the rape of Dinah). It is therefore with some caution that we mention individual laws as applying here: Simeon and Levi as Dinah's avengers or in their later fates reflect the Law of Twins; Ephraim's being preferred to his older brother Manassa reflects the Law of Contrast and Final Stress.

Jacob's death poem (48) (only in P?) forms a recapitulation of all these stories, but it removes itself from the direct folk epic. It does not so much contain the history of the individual sons as the later history of the tribes, but is a lyrical recapitulation of the general conditions of later times.[21] It deliberately deviates from what one would expect. The reason Ruben has lost his seniority among the sons, and why Judah has become the leader instead, is expressly given; the strong final stress is on Joseph, to whom all the blessings of heaven and the eternal mountains are given, not on Benjamin, to whom only a few words are allotted about his warrior ferocity. Throughout, one realizes that tribal legends and a sense of tribal conditions determine the loosely connected narratives about the sons of Jacob.

## B. CONCLUSION: A DEFENSE OF THE FINNISH-DANISH METHOD

Finally, there is von der Leyen (1916), who offers a general survey of "the tasks of folktale research," first of the extensive investigations of a more recent date and the possibilities of still increasing the material, especially by a systematic collection of Asiatic folk tradition (the many millions from China), and second, of what has been achieved up to now: a firmly coherent (i.e., poetically composed) original form of the tales. And, with partiality, von der Leyen emphasizes how much the more recent research has asserted India as the specific place of origin. Because of the incompleteness of the material, he is doubtful about the historical-geographical method, which has been cultivated most strongly in Northern Europe: "Those unavoidable deficiencies in the material of folktale research are too easily overlooked by the Axel Olrik School."[22] The comment involuntarily invites contradiction. There is no "Axel Olrik School"—as far as I know—and I myself have not created it, but have learned the method from Grundtvig.[23] The method could more correctly be called the "Finnish method," because it was most accurately developed there and passed on from scholar to scholar.[24] But, of course, the content is more important. It is, therefore, the incompleteness of the material that prevented oral narrative research from reaching the same methodological stage as philology and other established branches of scholarship. But do not the established branches of scholarship have incomplete material? Has not one breviary of a monastery been preserved while another (or many others) has been lost? Does one not have a Frankish law from the era of the Great Migration,[25] but not a Saxon law? How complete is the linguistic material of the Goths, e.g., from the time of Christ or from the era of the Great Migration? Or how complete is the lexical material from the Middle Ages in Denmark?[26] Is it any guideline at all with regard to scholarly investigation that the material is complete or almost complete? How many remains[27] do we possess of the vanished plant or animal world? Is it not rather the case that it is the method that makes an investigation scholarly or not, that it is the reliable procedure that recognizes the incompleteness of the material and knows what means the scholar has available to overcome it? This is the method that has taught research to work not with two or twenty variants of a tale, but with two hundred.[28] This is the method that teaches us to look for what is positively contained in the sources, and only from very strongly negative evidence to declare that something did not exist (or, more accurately, has not existed with a lasting importance).

# INFORMATION AND REFERENCES

## A. ABOUT THIS EDITION

As editor, I have naturally followed Axel Olrik's manuscript closely. I have, however, made corrections that I assume Olrik would have made himself if he personally could have seen his work to the press and proofread it. I have therefore corrected all obvious errors, rectified dates, titles of books, and quotations, continued the paragraph divisions from chapter IV onwards, ordered the cross-references, etc. I have placed in square brackets the sections that I have added to the manuscript, without being certain that Olrik would have accepted them. This applies especially to the conclusion of §78, example 1, and to §179, where Olrik's manuscript unfortunately ends abruptly in the middle of a sentence. I have naturally not regarded myself as entitled to try and expand the sections where material is completely missing; I list the titles of these missing sections only as a guide to scholars. At the beginning of the notes to each paragraph, I have throughout listed all the non-obvious corrections that have been made in the manuscript. In these notes, I have been exceedingly careful to specify the sources of Olrik's references (e.g., §§6, 7) and to mention parallels in Olrik's other works where he discusses the same question. In addition, I have gone through Olrik's preliminary works and notes concerning *Principles for Oral Narrative Research* and mentioned in the notes what appeared to me to be valuable for the elucidation of the content of the given text. In the notes, I have also called attention to the examples that Olrik gave his pupils in lectures and seminars on "Principles" according to Miss Ruth Gerner Lund's and my own recordings (1912 and 1915–1916), even though Olrik did not use them in the manuscript printed here. These notes are marked (S). In a few instances, I have used my own examples to illustrate the text (e.g. §99, n. 2). Such notes are marked (Hans Ellekilde).

For the benefit of those who wish to study beyond Olrik's text, I have, as far as folk belief, legends, and tales are concerned, referred to such main works as Feilberg (1886–1914), DS, BP, and of course DgF. In quotations from and references to Saxo, I have referred to *Sakses Danesaga,* and for quotations from the *Elder Edda* I have referred to *Den ældre Edda.*

Previous to the notes and the corrections in the individual chapters and paragraphs, I have collected what I am able to say about the origin of the chapter or the paragraph; all of this is written as concisely as possible like the other notes. As an introduction to this, I now give a brief survey of the origin of *Principles for Oral Narrative Research.*

## B. THE ORIGIN OF THE WORK

The first disposition, or rather draft, of *Principles for Oral Narrative Research* dates from 17 March 1905. Here we find the first five current chapters planned out and indicated, but not the last two, VI and the Appendix. Olrik had not yet made a division between the later subsections A, B and C. The main difference between this first outline and the work published here is that "The Epic Laws" is still not an independent chapter but is closely connected to chapter IV, "The Life of the Narrative." From this it gradually disengages itself, first as a subsection, (3) "The Logic of the Narrative—and the Breach of It," and then as a specially demarcated chapter entitled "?Epic Laws." No wonder that among the later well-known epic laws we find a series of laws such as "Poetic Justice," "the Happy Ending," "the Law of Approximation," which since then have found their rightful place in IV, "The Life of the Narrative" (cf. §§97, 99–100). In chapter IV, the current section C, "Survival," comes immediately after the subsection (1) "The Life and Death of the Narratives," (2) "Transformations," (3) "Disintegration," which corresponds to current section IV A. Below (4) "Survival" a more recent hand has written "localization," and above it an even more recent hand has written "horizon." Localization (or "localizing" as it was first called) was first placed in III, "The Relationship between the Versions" ( = current chapter V, "The Original Form and Development of the Narrative"). The distinction between sections C and D, "Views on the Structure and Transmission of the Narrative" and "Views on Narrative Material," is maintained, even though the material in these sections overlaps in the same way as current chapters III and IV. In chapter II, references to C, "Traditions of a Literary Origin," are missing.

In the next undated disposition, "a preliminary draft," probably from the early summer of 1906 (presumably written after Olrik had written I, II A and B, and was about to begin II C), we rapidly approach the final arrangement of the manuscript. Current chapters III and V remain reversed, but V, "Epic Laws," is now finally separated from IV and III; "The Original Form and Development of the Narrative" is divided into the same subsections A, B, C, and D as now, but without traces of the section that I have called V "Introduction." Chapter IV B, "Horizon and Localization," has broken the former close connection between "Survival" and IV A, "The Life and Transformation of the Narrative," which was at that time divided into two sections: (A) "The Life and Death of the Narrative," (B) "Expansion and Change" ( = current §§89–118), which we have observed in the first disposition. Olrik doubts where to place the subsection "Survival": in a corner he writes in pencil: "Survival! Where?" Also, as far as chapter II C is concerned, he doubts whether it is in the right place. Finally there are traces of chapter VI, which is called "Oral Narrative and History." This chapter has the same name in the third disposition of 17 February 1912, which, as far as the first five chapters are concerned, presents the final arrangement of the material as it is found in this work. As of 6 June 1915, Olrik accepted this disposition, except for chapter VI. He now calls it "Concerning the Individual Genres of Folklore," and plans a division of this chapter: A "Tales," B "Heroic Poetry," C "Folk Legends," and D "Oral Narrative and History," which I have adopted in this work. But even at this late date, one and a half years before Olrik's death, there still is not the smallest trace of the disposition of "Appendix: From the Domain of the Epic Laws," which was planned in the early summer of 1916.

This was Olrik's plan for the work. We can now turn to the realization of this plan. It can most clearly and with most certainty be observed in chapter I. There is a version of this chapter from the spring of 1906, finished for Mrs. Sophie Olrik's birthday 28 March, and probably hectographed and placed in the institute of the university for use by the students at the same time. The present manuscript is marked "Revision 1912. Print-MS," and below a more recent hand has written "(completed 1915)." What was added in 1915 is, however, quite unimportant and easy to pick out (the section about religious legends and §6 comment 2, a bibliographical reference, and a single sentence at the end of §9 comment), and therefore is in all probability essentially Olrik's revision from the spring of 1912 that is now at the press. A comparison of the new manuscript of 1912 with the former one of 1906 shows that the main difference between the two is that in 1912 a section on language in §3 has been added and a long comment on the theories regarding the origin of the ballad in §9. Also, the revisions are almost everywhere of a formal character. This chapter was written, in its final form, in 1906; the material was also at that time formally arranged in the same twelve paragraphs as now.

There is also a hectographed manuscript of "The Epic Laws" written in 1906. Unlike the manuscript of chapter I, which was laid out in detail ready to be printed, it is a brief schematic outline for use in seminars in the philological institute (fall 1906), with very few, incomplete examples. A comparison of this outline with the thorough revision in Olrik (1908b) reveals that Olrik here closely follows the outline written in 1906, except that he still, in 1906, has not formulated "the Law of Initial Stress." From his postscript to 1908b, p. 89, we know that this law is a result of the keen observation of his pupil Dr. Gudmund Schütte (cf. here p. 41). Olrik's earliest draft of the epic laws (from the early summer of 1905?) shows that he is aware of the peculiar exception to "the Law of Final Stress" which is "the Law of Intitial Stress" (see §75, fn.). But Dr. Schütte has the honor of having defined the reason for this: the most distinguished person in the group is mentioned first, the dearest last. A close examination of the present manuscript shows that §78ff. is new, from the spring of 1916, but that the rest of the manuscript, except §57 and §§61–63, is a quite moderate revision of a manuscript which, like the outline of 1906, does not contain "the Law of Initial Stress." Therefore, it must have been written before Olrik adopted the law formulated by Schütte in his seminars in the fall of 1906 (not the fall of 1905, as stated in Olrik [1908b], p. 89). Now we also understand the close relationship between this manuscript and the outline of 1906; the outline of 1906 is probably based on the manuscript of 1906. Concerning chapter III, we then arrive at the same result as for chapter I: the main thoughts and much of the formal revision go back to 1906, even though Olrik's later famous investigations of the epic laws in 1908–1909, especially as they appear in Olrik (1908f) and (1909a), have left stronger traces in the final draft of 1915–1916 than the revision of 1912 and 1915 of chapter I.

An analysis of the outline of 1906, aided by Olrik's earliest revisions, leads further back into the history of the development of the epic laws and to interesting conclusions concerning the development of this major scholarly discovery. It turns out that the outline of 1906 is an expansion of an older outline, probably from April 1906 (BO 1906 I), where only twelve epic laws have been formulated, not seventeen as in BO 1906 II (in "Epic Laws" in Olrik [1908b] 17 + "initial stress"). The following five laws are missing in BO 1906 I: "the Unity of Plot," "the Epic and the Ideal Unity of Plot," "the Single-strandedness of the Plot," "the Law of Centralization," "Two Main Characters" ( = Olrik [1908b], nos. 6–10, here §§66–70); therefore, these must have been added in the summer of 1906. The last of the twelve former laws, "Poetic Justice," a remnant of the original connection between "The Life of the Narrative" and "Epic Laws," is deleted in BO 1906 II (see §97, fn.); the first of these twelve laws is divided into two: (1) the clarity of the narrative and (2) the schematizing of the narrative (§58 and §60). Within the twelve former laws, those concerning narrative structure, which are associated with numbers, constitute the nucleus of the "Epic Laws." In the earliest draft from the summer of 1905 (?), we find these laws of numbers in the following order: (1) "the Law of Three" and "the Law of Final Stress" (cf. §§74–75), then (2) "the Law of Contrast" or "the Law of Two to a Scene" (cf. §§71–72), (3) "The Law of Doubles" ( = "the Law of Twins," §73), and (4) "Multitude" (cf. §74 under "the Law of Three"). Judging from the handwriting, the revision of "the Law of Opening" and "the Law of Closing" (cp. §§76–77) are from the same time; on the basis of internal evidence "Epic Justice" must also be from the same time. In the drafting of outline I (April 1906?), Olrik conflates "the Law of Multitude" with "the Law of Three," but does not otherwise alter the order of these laws: they receive the numbers 5–12. Preceding them, Olrik places the following laws: (1) "the Clarity of the Narrative," (2) "Few Characters," (3) "the Tableau of the Narrative," and (4) "the Logic of the Narrative" (§58 and §60, §59, §64, §65). As mentioned above, five new laws are added in the revision of BO 1906 II; one of them, "the Law of Centralization," is, however, already indicated in the draft of 17 March 1905. In the composition of Olrik (1908b) at the end of 1907 or the beginning of 1908, "the Law of Initial Stress" is added. The laws formulated in §§61–63, "the Law of Repetition," "the Law of Progressive Ascent," and "the Plot Constraints of the Narrative," are found in Olrik (1908b), but not as independent discussions: the first two are connected to "the Law of Three," the last one to "the Tableau of the Narrative." On the other hand, they do receive independent status in the next revision of the epic laws, in Olrik's lecture at the Historical Congress in Berlin in 1908 (cf. here p. 41), and especially in the expanded version of this lecture as it appears in Olrik (1909a).

In the reworking of MS 1906 in the spring of 1916 and in the works printed in 1908–1909, no new laws are added, even though their number is hardly exhausted. Let me mention as an example "the Law of Dramatic Suspense": the decisive event in the progress of the plot, the rescue of the hero, the redemption of the heroine, or the like, takes place at the very last moment. Instead, Olrik chose to give samples of the occurrence of the epic laws in different categories of sources, especially the ones bordering on oral narrative composition and literary composition: *Hrólfs saga kraka,* the stories of the patriarchs, etc. In the early summer of 1916, he altered this plan: he made a special appendix, "From the Domain of the Epic Laws," where he planned to place (1) The Literature on the Epic Laws, (2) The Stories of the Patriarchs, and (3) The Lives of Danish Saints; instead of the former §78 with the examination of *Hrólfs saga kraka,* he added in his table of contents to I-III the new §§78–81 (the current §§79–82), of which he managed to compose only a part of the paragraph "Epic Laws and Literary Works." Presumably he would have completely left out the current §78, examples 1–2, *Hrólfs saga kraka,* and Krohn's extract about numbers in Finnish composition if he had carried out this last plan of 1916, but I have not considered myself justified to make such alterations in this edition.

For the other main chapters, we have largely retained the former manuscript of 1906 in the present book. In the manuscript, there are traces of chapter IV, not only of the division of section A into two subsections, A "The Life and Death of the Narrative" and B "Persistence and Change," as in outline II, but also of the still-older connection between current sections A and C "Survival," which we observed in the disposition of 17 March 1905. The former paragraphs in IV A are marked with roman numerals I-XX, and C "Survival" continues with roman numerals XXI-XXVII, while the paragraphs of current section B are unmarked. The former manuscript of IV A was reviewed in 1916 after Olrik's thorough study of Moe (1914) and (1915), but after that he revised only two of the twenty former paragraphs, nos. XV and XIX, the current §§97–104. In the others, he simply added a quotation, an example, or a comment, and made a few stylistic improvements here and there, something he also did before 1916, but to a very limited degree. With the aid of a copy from 1915, which Olrik gave me, I can assess which changes in the original are older and which are younger (1916). The subsection "Horizon" in IV B presupposes that "the Law of Approximation" (§114) belongs in a following chapter, "Epic Laws," as in the disposition of 17 March 1905, for which reason it must have been written at a very early date: in none of the former drafts of the epic laws do we otherwise find the smallest trace of this law. It is written on a page inserted later. It is in keeping with this that at the bottom of the first page of the manuscript the following note is found: "This is in effect a section of 'The Life of the Narrative'; for practical reasons it appears independently" (cf. the disposition of 17 March 1905). The last paragraph (§118) was also added later, although at a much later date than "the Law of Approximation"; it is found in the copy of 1915 and therefore is not due to the revision of 1916, which we observed in IV A and which also asserts itself in a single paragraph of "Localization" (§127). We do not have decisive evidence of the early origin of this section as we do of the section "Horizon," but that it existed early in 1907 is indicated in a letter to Feilberg of 12 February 1907: "Now I have the beginning of the lectures or rather of the seminars. I find the methodology of oral narrative research I use with my clever group of students very interesting. On Friday [i.e., 15 February], we discuss horizon and localization, then 'survival.'" A letter of 15 March 1907 suggests that he intended to discuss "survival" with his group on Friday 8 March (on this, see Olrik [1908b], p. 89). The pagination of the manuscript also indicates that "localization" was written in direct connection with "horizon." In chapter V, the original manuscript is preserved in A, B, §163 and §178 in C. A and B were never revised, even though references in pencil show that Olrik intended to do so. It is different with C. First, he added a number of paragraphs (§§173–177) about the local distribution of the versions in the former uncompleted manuscript. This presumably took place early in 1908, when he became acquainted with the work of von Sydow (1907 and 1908). After that, he revised the other paragraphs (usually just formally) and rearranged the various views so that the manuscript was generally in the same state as we have it now by the time of his seminar in the spring of 1912. Later (but before 1916), he incorporated view D, "the most natural" ( + §179, comment, about the history of the development of this method), from Krohn (1910) on the Finnish folkloristic method, but neglected to include the new view in §161, which is like a table of contents for V C and V D. It cannot be ascertained with certainty when the small rudiment of this last chapter was composed. I presume that in 1906, when Olrik was fatigued by the investigation and the composition of the various views on the structure of the narrative, he suddenly leapt to the next chapter without getting beyond the first view, "the mythical view"; from my notes, it is clear that Olrik, when he was about to discuss the other views on the material of the narrative, the cultural–historical, etc., jumped to IV C, "Survival." Notes from the seminar in the spring of 1912 show that when he had reviewed the first two paragraphs of V, "Introduction," Olrik immediately moved to V C. It is uncertain whether this section was written before 1912 or in connection with the revision of V C, which presumably took place in 1912. Sadly, Olrik did not manage the thorough revision of chapter V which he must have intended for the section that I have called V, "Introduction." In the spring of 1916, he managed only to make a very small addition to this section (§144, comment). The other paragraphs seem to be older than 1916 but younger than 1912.

Concerning chapter II, we have generally retained what was in the manuscript written in 1906, as in chapters IV and V A and B. In Olrik's drafts, a shorter revision of chapter II A with a somewhat different arrangement and paragraph numbering is found, but it does not represent a 1906 revision in contrast to a final 1912 revision as in I or V C; it represents a 1906[I] revision in contrast to a 1906[II] revision, as with III, "Epic Laws." A letter dated 21 June 1907 from Professor Erslev, whom Olrik had asked to review chapter II A, "Narrative and Recording," shows that the manuscript was at that time divided into paragraphs as in the present manuscript, but that the paragraphs were then numbered one higher than now. This is because Olrik still considered incorporating a §13, dealing with the relationship between oral narrative composition and literary composition, into the manuscript of chapter I. But only six words from this section are preserved in the draft: "When a poem or a narrative." The same peculiarity in the paragraph numbering is found in II B, which presumably indicates a revision in connection with A. Since the manuscript and the preliminary work show that not only the examples to §44, 4 and 5, which quote Olrik (1912), but also the example to §44, 1, which quotes Olrik (1907b), p. 175, are later additions, and since it is evident from a letter to Feilberg of 6 February 1907 that Olrik had just then become familiar with the story about the straw-doll Bovi mentioned in the example to §44, 1, then this likewise supports the view that II B (and A) was composed in 1906. Judging from the manuscript, the last paragraph (§46) was written later than the rest of II B, but still at a time when the former paragraph numbering prevailed. This also agrees with disposition II, where we find A containing §§14–42, B §§43–46, and C beginning with §47. However, the current first paragraph (§47) in C does not carry this designation. It is missing in both the older, shorter and the younger, fuller composition of C, both of which begin with current §48. In the older revision, the paragraph is not numbered; in the younger, which constitutes the nucleus of the present manuscript, it is numbered 47. The current §47 was written in two stages, the first two parts at the same time, to which was added the last paragraph in B; but the third part was written at the beginning of 1912 on a receipt dated 20 February 1912. Here we have evidence that all of chapter II, like chapter I, was reviewed early in 1912 for Olrik's seminar on principles for oral narrative research (cf. that disposition III is from 17 February 1912). In his review, Olrik inserted additions and made minor corrections here and there, least in A, more in B (the *Danske Studier* quotations from the beginning of 1912 in §44, 1, 4, and 5), and most in C, where especially §51 and examples 1–2 in §53 are later insertions. These additions, however, did not alter the original character and features of the chapter, especially not in comparison with chapter I, where a thorough revision was made, although it was decidedly of a more formal nature. In chapter VI, "Oral Narrative and History," as it was first called, the completely unfinished section, "Heroic Poetry," probably dates from 1915, when Olrik, on 6 October, planned the expansion of the former chapter, "Oral Narrative and History," with three new sections: A "Tales," B "Heroic Poetry," and C "Folk Legends." It is possibly older, i.e., from the time when Olrik received Chadwick (1912). The current section D, "Oral Narrative and History," presumably dates from 1912, although it was planned in 1906 (disposition II), because in contrast to the earlier chapters it contains references to "the Epic Laws" and "The Life of the Narrative" in the younger order (disposition III), not in the older order (compare §25 with §§187, 191). The close connection with V "Introduction" (cf. §§144–145 and §190) might indicate that the two chapters were composed at the same time; but the original date of the composition of this chapter is uncertain.

The general result of this investigation is that the nucleus of the work, with all the main ideas and including in large part the five former chapters along with the original formal elaboration, dates from 1906 (with outlines going back to 1905, when the first disposition was written). By this time, Olrik had gained a reputation and rich experience in all of the most important areas of his folkloristic research. He felt a need to present the research method common to all these areas that he himself had worked out, and he then wrote this work, which he first discussed with his students, "his clever group," in the institute of the university in the spring and fall of 1906 and part of the spring of 1907. But instead of rushing his work to the press as soon as possible so that he could transfer the success from his research in individual areas into this larger study, which nine out of ten scholars would have done in his place, he calmly shelved the manuscript to allow it to mature for later publication: "Far from everything is suitable for presentation to the public, but a sample will probably be of interest," he wrote in July 1908 (Olrik [1919a], p. 177). Before the publication of the various essays concerning epic laws (first Olrik [1907e], p. 193), Olrik published his essay ([1906b], especially pp. 175ff.). Thus, before the final publication of the complete principles, he felt a need to present his principles for a single area of research—the ballads. If Olrik underlined the contrast to his teacher Grundtvig here, then he stressed his unshakeable student relationship to him in the commemoration of Sophus Bugge after the latter's death in July 1907 (Olrik [1907d]), pp. 180ff.), as he did ten years later in his response to von der Leyen (see p. 134). After the publication of the various essays on epic laws (in 1908), Olrik lost his strong interest in the theory of oral narrative research for some years in order to reap new laurels in the practice of oral narrative research: Olrik (1903–1910) II, Olrik (1911c). In the first new series of lectures after his wife's death (31 October 1911), he took up the former work in order to complete it: here he had profited from her cooperation to a particularly high degree (cf. Olrik [1908b], p. 89), but he was unsuccessful; in the spring of 1912, he managed to prepare the manuscripts of I and II for print, to revise V C, and to write VI, but he came to a complete stop without getting any further with III and IV, V A and B. Three years after the publication of Olrik (1902–1914) II, after Moe's death in December 1913 and the appearance of the latter's "Episke grundlove," Olrik began for the third time in preparation for the fall seminar in 1915 and especially for the spring seminar in 1916. He then went through and revised III (after having reviewed I and II) and thereby came to write about "The Patriarchal History of Israel." Next, he revised a part of IV A and B and V "Introduction" and returned again to III and to its new "Appendix." But then, in June 1916, he finally came to a complete halt in the three or four difficult paragraphs treating the psychological and historical reasons for the epic laws that he wanted to add to chapter III; he did not get further in his lifetime. Unfortunately, he did not manage to revise V A and B, or to write VI A and C, which would have presented no difficulty to a man such as Olrik. Therefore, his work now stands incomplete, neither finished nor flawless as he, the son of an artist, intended his works to appear. Nevertheless, this work will be of great use in the study of oral narrative composition in honor both of the man who wrote these "principles" and, at the same time, of the profoundly human and profoundly national discipline whose faithful servant he was throughout his life.

## C. NOTES TO THE INDIVIDUAL CHAPTERS

### I. Introduction: The Narrative as Folklore

See p. 138. In the outline of 17 March 1905, the following is found about I: Folklore. Narrative. Oral narrative composition—personal authorship. In MS 1906, this chapter is called "Introduction: Narrative and Folklore." In Olrik's papers, there is an even older draft, but it is quite close to MS 1906 and hardly deviates from it, except in the spelling. When there are no special remarks to the paragraphs, they are almost or completely identical to MS 1906.

§2. 1. Hallfreðr's *Ólásfdrápa* vv. 20–25, see *Skjaldedigtning* I B, p. 154; *Heimskringla* I, p. 455.

2. *Saga Olafs konungs ens Helga,* p. 70 (cf. p. 62 and *Fornmanna sögur* X, p. 370); Jónsson (1894–1902) I, p. 464 note; II, p. 398.

§3. See p. 138. Literature incorporated by the editor from MS 1906, probably forgotten by Olrik. Formal revision especially in the comments, and the following lines from MS 1906 deleted in part 1 of the conclusion: "and correspond to the educational level of these classes with regard to perception and horizon."

1. "Tools, dwellings, dress, etc., are best classified under ethnoarcheology (in Sweden called 'folklife research'). The English word 'folklore,' i.e., the knowledge of the people (not the knowledge about the people), designates the entire material (of folklore)."

2. We can, furthermore, refer to von Sydow (1919).

§4. Part 2 expanded a little; last sentence missing in MS 1906.

1. See, e.g., Erslev (1902-1904), p. 145, the death of the dragoon Niels Kjeldsen, 28 February 1864.

§5. Formal changes here and there, especially in comments 2-4; example 1 in comment 5 missing in MS 1906. Here "village" is corrected to "fishing hamlet," "Hellebæk" to "Hornbæk."

1. The word "lay" is preferable to the word "song," which implies a lyrical element.

2. See DgF 324 with Mr. Palle's long contemplation of his stone house, which has no impact on the plot.

3. E.g., Valdemar Everday, when he lapses into thought with his foot in the stirrups (see, e.g., Danmarks Folkesagn I, p. 42). Or Frederik VII, who hits Martensen in his belly: How's the health, bishop; or Christian IV and the peasant (S).

4. "The animal fable about why the bear's tail is short is close to the origin legend." (See §88 n. 1.)

5. See Herodotus II, chap. 121; Feilberg (1886-1914), s.v. skatkammer and stejle.

6. "Svenska Folksagor" means Swedish folktales. (Cf. §53 n. 3.) "In Danish, something like 'lively story'; the actual meaning of 'saga' is that which is said or told."

7. Jónsson (1894-1902) II, p. 386

8. Olrik (1903-1910) I, p. 46; poems such as Vafþrúðnismál, Skírnismál, Fáfnismál (Den ældre Edda, pp. 36, 49, 174).

9. I have not been able to find Olrik's source; cf. Olrik (1911a), p. 13; DS III D types 9-12 "Old Forest."

10. From DFS 1906/23: 23 (from 1908), cf. DS II G type 15.

11. See DS II G type 14; Feilberg (1920), pp. 97ff., cf. §194 n. 1. "A narrative can be transferred into the future, e.g., there is a serpent inside the mound or under the church; a bull will kill it once it comes out" (see DS II E 82; Olrik [1902], p. 254).

§6. Cf. p. 138; comment 4 has been expanded; Schück (1904) (fn. 7) is explicitly mentioned in MS 1906. In comment 3, the word "hardly" in MS 1906 has been changed to "not" (2nd occurrence) by Olrik.

1. Thuren (1910), pp. 45f.; DS II A type 15 (the charcoal-burner, not the elf-woman, is the protagonist).

2. The humorous story about the man from Funen who was created from horse manure (see, e.g., Skg I, p. 222; DS II, p. 260) is thus not a legend, whereas the tales of the three green twigs (BP III 463) or the roses growing out of the stone table (Lyriske digte, p. 198) are legends.

3. DS II G 75; *Natursagen* II, 221.
4. See, e.g., Feilberg (1915), pp. 69f. Väinämöinen, among the Finns, is a creator-hero.
5. Olrik (1903–1910) I, pp. 223f.
6. Thus in Jacobsen (1913).
7. In Schück (1904) I, p. 20, the word "myth" is used for "origin legend" (with a connotation of religious value), the word "legend" for tales about gods that are, in his view, without religious significance.
§7. The conclusion is expanded a little.
1. "The entire Irish heroic literature is saga; lays do not appear until the Middle Ages" (see A. Bugge [1904–1906] I, p. 127).
2. E.g., the conception of the sword of Ogier the Dane (DS II G 319–320).
3. Thus the heroes associated with Dietrich; in Greek and French heroic narratives, there is a grouping into a succession of generations (cf. §67 n. 4, §185).
§8. 1. The tale of Herodotus (chap. V, 35) about Histiaios, who is staying with Darius in Suza, and who sends a message to his friends in Asia Minor by tattooing the request on the head of a faithful slave telling them to rebel, is a historical narrative, created to explain how the Ionic rebellion came about. The narrative about Luther's inkspot at Wartburg (*Deutsche Sagen* II, p. 346) is a local narrative attached to a historical personage. It is also a local narrative when the people in Brandsø tell about a stone table in a garden, and that the Swedish king ate here when he crossed the Belts (S).
§9. Cf. p. 138, also part 4 missing in MS 1906. The conclusion in part 2 is presented directly in MS 1906, not in the form of a question. Examples (to 3 and to 5) have been reversed by the editor.
1. "Therefore, it is the individuality of the people as a group, not the individual character, that we must consider as the author of folk poetry" (Grundtvig's statement in his preface to Warrens' translation, cf. Petersen [1905], p. 74).
2. The ballad originated "nicht von einem nebulosen Dichteraggregat, Volk gennant," but "von einem dichtenden Subject," the German ballad scholar Ferdinand Wolff claims in his preface to *Schwedische Volkslieder,* p. XV; cf. *Old English Ballads,* pp. XXXV and LX (with additional literature); *English and Scottish Popular Ballads,* p. XVIII.
3. "The Finnish school speaks of the author of a folktale *urform*"; cf. Aarne (1913a), p. 12.
4. The *Marsk Stig ballad,* the *Finderup ballad,* and the *Ballad of Axel and Valborg* (DgF 145 A, F, and G; DgF 475) are so consistent in their structure that they must be regarded as the works of individual poets.
5. Especially the Faroese satirical ballads (*Færøiske Quæder,* p. 14).
6. DgF 486, p. 463; *English and Scottish Popular Ballads,* p. XXI.
7. "here a new interest in the young man who sees life slip away"
8. Olrik (1906b), p. 204; cf. here p. 143.

§10. Ll.7-9 added, comment not separated from the text in MS 1906.

§11. "Example" and "other examples" are part of the text between parts 1 and 2 in MS 1906; the example is somewhat expanded, and 2 more revised than usual in MS 1912.

1. *Den ældre Edda,* pp. 73 and 76. The giant sister is missing in DgF 1, *Tord of Havsgard,* either because she has been thrown overboard, or because she was missing from the beginning.

2. *Den ældre Edda,* pp. 134 and 150; Ussing (1910), pp. 22f.; cf. here §18 example 2.

3. *Den ældre Edda,* pp. 238 and 235 (the incitement of Guðrún to seek revenge); Ussing (1910), p. 160; Olrik (1907a), p. 45.

4. *Den ældre Edda,* p. 11; Olrik (1907a), p. 65.

5. *Den ældre Edda,* p. 36.

6. *Den ældre Edda,* pp. 77, 145.

7. Olrik (1907a), p. 75; Olrik (1917b), p. 81.

8. E.g., the *Iliad* and the *Odyssey* (§48 example) among the Greeks, the *Mahabharata* of the Indians (§162), the Old French *Song of Roland* (cf. §77 nn. 4 and 10). The contrasts between hero and traitor and the repetition of Roland's blowing the horn reflect oral narrative composition, but it is literary composition when new characters are constantly presented to the reader.

9. E.g., the *Arabian Nights,* which is, however, "more novella than oral narrative composition, more moral than folktale."

§12. The example is a little more expanded from MS 1906, with changes especially in parts 1 and 3. In the example "Fiot" is corrected to "Fjort."

1. *Hervarar saga,* chap. 11, cf. Feilberg (1898), p. 21; Heusler (1901), pp. 117f.

2. *Sturlunga saga* (1906-1911) I, p. 344, cf. 398 (Kålund's translation I, pp. 309, 358); *Færøiske Ordsprog,* p. 308; Feilberg (1904) p. 163.

3. See DS II G nos. 277-284; *Danmarks Trylleformler* (1917) I, p. 477; Köhler (1898-1900) III, pp. 320-351 (Little Credo); *Flateyjarbók* II, pp. 400ff., cf. Fritzner (1886-1896) II, p. 342; Paasche (1914), p. 39.

4. Ohrt (1916), p. 189. Olrik (1925).

5. The chapbooks have suffered the same fate (see, e.g., *Danske folkebøger* VII, p. XXV, *Magelone and the Silver Key*).

6. In the second century A.D.; see *Apuleius's Amor og Psyche,* p. 27; retold in *Poetiske Skrifter* I, p. 503. Cf. BP II, p. 266; Olrik (1892-1894) II, pp. 236f.; here §178 example, cf. §107.

## II A. Narrative and Recording

In the outline of 17 March 1905, Olrik had made the following disposition for chapter II: The Individual Account: Its Genuineness. Its Unity. Its Home. Its Age. Its Kind. When he started his first draft of II in 1905 or the beginning of 1906, he proceeded according to this plan: (1) the relationship between narrative and recording, (2) evaluation of literary sources, and (3) evaluation of oral sources. The paragraphs of this elaboration are marked with the letters a–g (cf. the Greek letters in V, the roman numerals in IV A and C), and they often correspond closely to the following current paragraphs: §§13–15, 22–24 (the last one designated §e comment 1), §§37–38 (40) (§e comment 2), (40) + §§30 and 31 (§e comment 3), and after that §§25–26 (§f and §g). To the old §e belonged a comment 4, which formed the basis for most of those paragraphs missing in the first draft, without its specific content being incorporated into the later MS. Therefore, it is given here in full: "It is frequently the case that a literary work is based partly on older works, partly on narratives. Many historical works in particular contain narratives scattered here and there. The written work is then the primary source for the narratives, but the rest of the content is derivative (e.g., the account of ancient times given in the *Ryd Chronicle,* composed on the basis of Saxo, the *Lejre Chronicle,* the *Runic Chronicle,* and a small number of folktales). Literature: Erslev (1892), especially §§12–21." During Olrik's revision of the earlier comments into independent paragraphs, which are placed after g (i.e., current §26) and designated with the paragraph numbers 22–29 (a–g had become §§14–21, cf. p. 142), comment 4 evolves into three new paragraphs, §§27–29, corresponding to current §19 comment, §34, 1 and §§36 and 35. These paragraphs, in turn, give rise to new paragraphs, the first one current §16, the last one current §33, 1 and §27, which, like §35, developed from Olrik's work on the Bald stories in Saxo and the study by Kauffmann (1902). These last new paragraphs are placed in the MS extant at that time, current §16 in its final position, §27 separate from §26 through current §33, 1. §16 is linked with the substantial old §31, or rather §§31–34 evolved from the old §§31–34 and §35 as well, and they are thus assigned their final position as current §§17–21. Inserted in their former positions at the end of the MS, we now find those paragraphs evolved from §e comment 2, current §§37–38 and §40. Current §33, 1 first is linked with §§34 and 35, after which this entire complex is placed after those paragraphs originating in §e comment 3, current §§30 and 31. After this comprehensive exchange, the MS of 1906 is in its final form, although new transitional paragraphs are added here and there (especially §29, most of §§32 and 36, and the concluding §41). On the other hand, the MS remained stable after 1906 (cf. p. 142). The most important changes were made in §25 comment 2 and §37 as a result of Professor Erslev's criticism in his letter of 21 June 1907. In his drafted reply, Olrik reveals the origin of the entire chapter: "In all essentials I have used your work (i.e., Erslev [1892]) as a model for this chapter. But the different nature of the material has necessitated some deviations, especially because *monument* and *account* are the two contrasts in your work, *tradition* and *author's work* in mine. Note also that I use *first-hand recording* and *derived recording* (current §37), which represents neither 'witness' nor 'account' in your work." Later, smaller additions are mentioned for the individual paragraphs, and whether they are extant in ED (i.e., older draft, §§a–g = §§14–21 and §§22–29), or whether they are extant in REV (i.e., the revision and the expansion of the older MS). Unless noted, the current paragraphs correspond essentially to the oldest draft in ED or REV. MS designates the manuscript as it appeared in 1906 without its later expansions. "Literature: Reference to Erslev" (1911) inserted in 1912.

§13. ED §a comment 1 younger than MS, comment 2 probably from 1912.

§14. ED §b Hartland (1891) quoted in English.

§15. Comment 11. 1–2 missing in ED. §c "Præsteberetninger" (also in ED) in 1. 10 of the edition corrected to "Præsteindberetninger."

1. Præsteindberetninger, pp. 1ff., cf. the register DS VII, p. 526.

2. See, e.g., DgF III, p. 410 fn. 3.

§16. Earlier stages of this paragraph missing, as explained above.

1. Cf. Schütte (1907), p. 198, and here §75 comment 2 and n. 10.

§17. REV §31, beginning.

§18. Missing in REV §31.

1. Saxonis Grammatici Historia Danica I, p. 250; see Sakses Danesaga I, p. 270; cf. Olrik (1892–1894) II, p. 39; Olrik (1919a), p. 57 and here §166 example.

2. Örvar-Oddr means Arrow Odd; cf. Olrik (1898), p. 80 fn.

3. Sakses Danesaga II, p. 71; cf. Olrik (1894a), pp. 232, 250.

4. I.e., the deeds of the Danes.

5. Cf. §11 n. 2.

§19. Part 1 and example 1 revised from REV §31, 2, where example 2 is indicated in connection with §20 example. On the other hand, part 2 is missing, and comment revised from ED §27 (>REV §29), see current §§32, 34, 39.

1. Sakses Danesaga I, p. 157f.

2. Snæbjörn the Skald (see Skjaldedigtning I B, p. 201; Jónsson [1894–1902] I, p. 530).

3. Sakses Danesaga I, pp. 152.

§20. See §19, Rydberg and Gollancz not mentioned in REV. Main text merely indicated in REV §31 comment 1.

1. Cf. Olrik (1899), p. 361.

§21. Earlier REV §35.

§22. Last 5 words missing in ED §d.

§23. Parentheses missing ED §e; in fn. 2 Olrik changed "recreate" in ED to "establish" in MS.

§24. =ED §e comment 1.

1. Translated in Krøniker fra Valdermarstiden, pp. 9–22 (cf. J. Olrik [1899–1900], pp. 222ff.; Olrik [1892–1894] I, p. 98; II, p. 296).

§25. In ED §f, comment 1 is part of the main text and slightly revised; references to Erslev (1911) added later. Remaining from comment 2 are only the words "'Learned narratives' are no narratives at all." Before Erslev's criticism in his letter of 21 June 1907, the comment said "'Learned narratives' are not narratives in the folkloristic sense of that word; but according to common usage the expression signifies an incorrect theory of history prevalent during a certain period." On 25 June 1907, Olrik replies: "I have now changed the use of the expression 'learned narratives.' It was used only provisionally." This change is presumably current comment 2.

1. The tradition about Harald Blue-tooth, who has the people drag a big stone, is thus a variant of the narratives of the strong giant who drags the big rock on an iron sled (see, e.g., *Segner fraa Bygdom* I, p. 8), and it represents a later rationalistic transformation of this narrative (S). (Cf. Olrik [1890–1892b], pp. 143–148.)

2. "It lacks point and figurative episodes, and presupposes knowledge from elsewhere."

3. See DS III D type 16, naive explanation of place names.

§26. Last line in example 1 and the last two lines in example 2 missing in ED §g. However, the references to "the unity of plot" and "the logic of the narrative" in part 1 are fuller than in MS.

1. *Sakses Danesaga* I, pp. 29, 36.

2. *Sakses Danesaga* I, pp. 89, 91; cf. §154 comment.

§27. Example 2 missing in REV §24, but probably still dates from 1906. The words "or one of his contemporaries" in example 1 are later than MS.

1. *Sakses Danesaga* I, p. 127, and III, p. 51; cf. Erslev (1911), §57.

2. Olrik calls it a "Romantic description of Sigersted parish."

3. Beyer (1791), pp. 37 and 39.

4. DS II C no. 116; Beyer (1791), pp. 37 and 36; cf. Severinsen (1917), p. 17.

5. Cf. DS IV A type 2, *Petty Kings and their Treasures.*

§28. Revision of REV §25; here no reference to section B.

§29. Missing in REV.

§30. In ED §e comment 3, only the first 3 lines are found. In the first revision ED §24 (later REV §28), current last line missing in the example. Comment is probably from 1906; reference to Heusler in the last line seems to have been added later.

1. Olrik probably alludes to Salin (1903), pp. 133f.; cf. Heusler (1908), pp. 97f.; Ambrosiani (1907), p. 6.

2. The theory that the gods originally lived like people (kings or sorcerers), but were elevated to divine status through their meritorious acts (or through their deceitful practices). The theory derives its name from a Greek travel writer, Euhemerus (from about 300 B.C.), who founded this theory in his work *The Holy Story* (cf. Olrik [1895], p. 47 and [1892–1894] I, p. 37). In section I, 2 in Olrik and Ellekilde (1926–1951), "Forskningens historie," Olrik discusses this question extensively.

§31. Last line missing both in ED §e comment 3 and in REV §25.

1. "One must be able to prove that the account is based on a narrative, that it is a narrative or is not a narrative, and one also has to prove that the written text is really from that period" (S).

§32. In REV §29, we find part 1 + §34, 1 + current §19 comment, but the rest of the paragraph is missing. Comment perhaps younger than MS 1906; reference to Erslev (1911) added later.

1. "Historians are worse than poets when it comes to changing the narrative arbitrarily."

2. Olrik is thinking especially of historians such as Paulus Diaconus, whose Longobard narrative he retold in Olrik (1908e), p. 426. Cf. also §24 example.

3. See, e.g., Aarne (1914a), pp. 12, 15f.

§33. In REV §23, the first and third parts and comment to §33, 1 are missing.

1. *Sakses Danesaga* I, pp. 118ff.; II, pp. 13ff.; cf. here §35 example and §155 n. 4.

2. Adam of Bremen: *Gesta Hammaburgensis Ecclesiae Pontificum,* I, 37: "In 'Hystoria Francorum' it is told that Sigafrid and his brother Halpdan ruled jointly. . . . There were also other Danish and Norwegian kings who ravaged France through piracy at that time. Foremost among them were tyrants such as Horich, Orwig, Gotafrid, Rudolf, and Ingvar. The most gruesome of them all was Ingvar, the son of Lodbrok, who everywhere tortured the Christians to death."

3. *The Lund Chronicle* (in *Scriptores Rerum Danicarum Medii Ævi*): In those days the *sons of Lodbrok,* who ravaged France with piracy, were the wildest and most gruesome Danish princes. The foremost among them were Horwic, etc. The most gruesome were *Ivar* and Ingvar, the sons of Lodbrok, who tortured the Christians to death everywhere." In MS, Olrik crossed out after this: (cf. §34, examples to 1, 2, and 5). "One will notice that the names not known in Adam (1) appear in a Scandinavian linguistic form, (2) correspond to known legendary characters: the sons of Lodbrok, Björn Ironside, Ivar the Legless, and Ubbe (Ulf otherwise unknown); Sigafrid has been included in this list perhaps because the author regarded him as Sigurd Worm-in-Eye."

§34. In the outline of ED §28 (cf. §36), one finds only (1) without example (+ §19 comment), but not (2) to (5). In REV §28, which presupposes current §33, 2 and is much closer to MS than ED, (3) to (5) are missing, and §34, 1 and §19 comment are now separated from each other (cf. §32).

1. See §33 n. 3, conclusion. Olrik (1892–1894) II, pp. 112–113. *Sakses Danesaga* II, pp. 160f., 167f.; Steenstrup (1876–1882) I, pp. 112f.

2. Cf. Olrik (1907a), pp. 40f.; Ussing (1910), pp. 97f. (see §11 n. 2). The names mean "fragment" (cf. §38 n. 1) and "the longer lay about Sigurðr."

§35. ED §29 rather different outline. Examples only indicated.

1. See Olrik (1903a), pp. 181f. (cf. §155, example 3 and §33, 1).

§36. Indicated in comment to ED §28 (see current §34): "A special variant form of plot structure is that the story contains 'doublets,' i.e., sections whose content is similar." This is perhaps the seed not only of §36 (and §35), but also of V B, "Variant and Doublet."

1. In *Flateyjarbók,* it is called *þáttr Hálfdanar svarta* (i.e., the section on Hálfdan the Black).
2. *Ágrip,* p. 96; *Heimskringla* I, p. 95.
3. See Olrik (1892–1894) I, p. 40; the attack on Olrik in Jónsson (1899), p. 262; Bugge (1900), p. 1; Moe (1906), pp. 581ff.; Jónsson (1894–1902) II, p. 776; cf. §155 example 1.

§37. The main text written in June 1907 after Erslev's criticism. Example goes back to ED §e comment 2 (at that time briefer) except for the last 3 lines. The comment was written in 1912, but the first 6 lines are based on a manuscript from June 1907; the second half is based on Erslev (1911). Before Erslev's criticism, the main text was as follows: "Up to now we have treated cases where the author's work is based directly on a narrative, i.e., it is a first-hand recording (the 'primary sources' of the historians). It becomes more complicated if the work is based on a written work and the latter is, in its turn, based on narrative. This is the origin of derived recordings ('secondary sources')." Olrik agreed with Erslev when he criticized the identification of first-hand recordings with "primary sources" and derived recordings with "secondary sources"; but unlike the historians, he refused to restrict the meaning of the word "derived" to "secondary": "A word that is common and comprehensible to all should not be removed from its natural meaning. . . . (I would like to dispense with everything called 'secondary sources,' because they are not sources)" (draft for the letter of 25 June 1907).

1. See Olrik (1894b), especially p. 138 and pp. 152ff. (cf. Jónsson [1894–1902] II, p. 665).
2. The saga about Knud the Great's successors; see Jónsson (1894–1902) II, p. 780; cf. §125 example 1.
3. *Ynglinga saga,* chapter 29; *Edda Snorra Sturlusonar,* pp. 106f.; cf. Olrik (1894b), p. 154.

§38. The last 3 lines missing in ED §e comment 2, but are found in the revision of ED §25, which is close to MS.

1. As Olrik did in his essay (1894a). A revision of this essay is found in DFS 1917/46, Harald Wartooth. *Sögubrot* means "saga fragment"; see Jónsson (1894–1902) II, p. 836.

§39. Missing in ED §e comment 2 or 3; like REV §30, composed together with current §32 part 1 + §34, 1 and §19 comment.

§40. Example missing in ED §e comment 3.

1. *Sakses Danesaga* II, pp. 143f.
2. *Den danske Rimkrønike,* p. 80.

§41. Missing in REV.

## II B. The Inner Character of the Tradition

See p. 142 cf. pp. 147–148; current §42 first sounded like this: While the value or lack of value as a source is determined by the genuineness of the tradition as folklore, this value is graded according to its inner character. This especially concerns (1) its time and place, (2) its inner poetic structure, and (3) its connection with other contemporary traditions.

§44. See p. 143. Also the last 5 lines in (1) comment part 1, the last 2 lines in part 2, and (2) example 2, missing in MS 1906 but included in REV 1912, which has also affected comment to (1), parts (2) and (3), but not the main text of (1), (4), (5), and (6). Example to (6) was inserted later but probably before 1912.

1. See also Olrik (1903–1910) II, p. 256; Schütte (1919), p. 113.

2. Olrik must be referring to Saxo's preface: Quorum thesauros historicarum rerum pignoribus refertos curiosius consulens, haud parvam præsentis operis partem ex eorum relationis imitatione contexui (*Saxonis Grammatici Historia Danica,* p. 8; cf. Notæ uberiores LXII).

3. Olrik (1919a), p. 87.

4. *Sakses Danesaga* I, p. 114; II, p. 37.

5. *Saga Olafs konungs ens Helga,* p. 71; see §2 n. 2.

6. I.e., the lay (*ríma*) came from Iceland, written down in a book so broad (i.e., elaborate). Olrik is thinking of *The Troll in Hornaland* (*Færøiske Kvæder* II, p. 120; DFS 133–148 III, pp. 417f.), which is a variant of the famous ballad *St. Olaf's Sail Race* (DgF 50, see DgF IV, p. 879), which probably came from Denmark, certainly not from Iceland. See also *Færøsk anthologi,* introduction, p. 47. Concerning the dissemination of the formula in Faroese lays—which is not very great—see DFS 133–168 XVI, Appendix I, p. 31.

7. "I have heard it told in tales of yore" (the Eddic poem *Oddrúnargrátr,* v. 1, cf. *Den ældre Edda,* p. 213).

8. *Sakses Danesaga* I, p. 15; Olrik (1892–1894) II, p. 310.

9. Olrik (1892–1894) I, pp. 79f.; cf. Steenstrup (1897), pp. 134f.; Olrik (1898), pp. 76f.

10. See Olrik (1892–1894) I, p. 31.

11. Feilberg (1886–1914) s.v. *torden* and *trommespil; Edda Snorra Sturlusonar,* chapter 20; Olrik (1905), pp. 132f. On a draft sheet, "Djævelen i Vitskøl kloster endnu engang," Olrik refers to JFm 6, p. 78 no. 116, which he believes to be a variant of the same narrative despite considerable deviation.

12. See Feilberg (1886–1914), s.v. *konebarsel.*

13. See Feilberg (1904) II, pp. 229f.

14. *Sakses Danesaga* I, p. 178; *Sven Aggesøns værker,* p. 37; Olrik (1892–1894) II, p. 182.

15. I.e., "Enumeration of Ancestors"; cf. *Sakses Danesaga* I, p. 194; Olrik (1892–1894) I, p. 114; Olrik (1919a), p. 88.

§45. 1. *Sakses Danesaga* II, p. 9.

2. See §78 example 1.

3. Olrik (1906a), p. 40, and Olrik (1906b), p. 175; see above p. 143.

4. See Olrik (1903–1910) I, p. 115 and §157 example.

5. Gr + 3 B, BP I, p. 549; cf. here §§60–62 example.

§46. Younger paragraph; see p. 142.

1. Especially in Aarne (1914b), p. 69; cf. §171 n. 2.

## II C. Traditions of a Literary Origin

Olrik's outline for this chapter argued polemically against those who expressed the superficial opinion that folklorists could do something more useful than collecting and scrutinizing old folk stories: "it is just pure repetitive rubbish, stories from old almanacs and the like, which 'the people' advertently or inadvertently push on gullible folklorists." But he dropped this polemical argument; he had often enough argued against those who were "sufficiently convinced of their own infallibility" to put these kinds of loose, unfounded ideas into print (see, e.g., Olrik [1904a]). He preferred to present his concepts in a purely scientific manner as elsewhere in "Principles." In order to solve the problem "Can narratives recorded in books make the transition into folklore?" he first narrowed the question down as follows: Can narratives that have been orally transmitted and then written down pass from the written record back into folklore? As an example, he selected the current Danish transmission of folk ballads, comparing them to the old printed editions and broadside prints (cf. §§47, 54) and the current European transmission of the Polyphemus tale, which he compared with Homer. But this takes him back to the first question, "Can narratives recorded in books make the transition into folklore?" and he tried to answer this question first. He then wrote the older, shorter 1906 draft: Folklore originating from books? (OED), that comes very close to current §§48–50, 52 + 56, comment part 1. In the younger draft (YED), he also attempts to answer the second more limited question pertaining to the vitality of literary folklore, in §§53–55. See further p. 142, especially concerning §47.

§47. 1. *English and Scottish Popular Ballads* I-X; cf. §9 comment, pp. 7–9.

2. See Ellekilde (1919), pp. 172f. with references.

3. See Grundtvig's postscript to JFm I, p. 372; cf. Petersen (1905), pp. 82 and 72, and here §54.

§48. Part 2 in §49 belonged in OED to this paragraph and was placed in front of the example.

1. Homer's *Odyssey,* Book 9.

2. Richter (1889), p. 87.

3. *Dolopathos,* composed by the monk John from Haute Selve in Lorraine in 1185.

4. Lindholm (1884), p. 110 (cf. Wiklund [1908], p. 164).

5. Cf. §55 comment 2.

§49. In OED, which here is more formally revised than §48, the example was at the end, and the quotation from Wehrhan (1908) was naturally missing.

1. "The best proof of the genuineness of a narrative is in the final analysis the attitude of the people themselves, whether they accept it or reject it."

§50. Examples 1–2 only indicated in OED; otherwise only insignificant formal changes.
1. See *Danske folkebøger* III, p. XVII; cf. *Svenska Folkböcker* I, p. 140.
2. Cf. A. Christensen (1917), pp. 52f.; Bédier (1895) in his introduction discusses this question in particular.
3. See DgF IV, p. 781; Nyrop's introduction to *Holger Danske;* see Nyrop (1883), p. 169.
§51. Missing in YED, cf. pp. 142–143.
1. See Jónsson (1907), p. 409.
§52. = OED.
§53. Examples 1 and 2 missing in YED, cf. p. 144. A draft exists for the main text, perhaps belonging to OED.
1. In 1697, he published *Contes de ma mère l'Oye;* here some of the most well known fairytales: *Cinderella, Puss'n Boots, Little Red Riding Hood,* and *Bluebeard.*
2. Especially Countess d'Aulnoy and Count Caylus (see Aarne [1914a], p. 15).
3. On the basis of this, they published the best collection of Swedish fairytales in 1844: *Svenska folk-sagor och äfventyr;* see §5 n. 6.
4. See *Svenska Folkböcker* II, appendix.
5. Grimm nos. 47, 52, 110.
6. E.g., *Historiegubbar,* pp. 37, 41, 103, 319, 326.
7. Aarne (1913a), cf. Liestöl (1918), pp. 90f.
§54. Belongs to YED.
1. Cf. *Danske Folkeviser* I, pp. 88f.; it is DgF 467 that existed as a broadside print in 1572.
2. "Part of the Hammerum tradition is closer to the tradition of the nobility than is otherwise the case with peasant folklore, but it is unlikely that it would be based on written sources or on the versions of the nobility for that reason." (S)
3. E.g., the *Svejdal ballad* (DgF no. 70).
4. DgF no. 120 III, p. 908, cf. DgF no. 325 C b and V 2, p. 117.
5. Cf. §166.
§55. Belongs to YED.
1. Ellekilde (1917), p. 219.
2. *Danske folkeæventyr* II, no. 17 (cf. Skg III, p. 170).
3. No. 28, p. 177, *Von der Tochter der Sonne.*
§56. General text and comment part 2 missing in OED; comment part 1 here closely connected with current §52 as the last part.
1. A close examination usually reveals that the oral tradition changes the form of a subject from the more simple to the more complex, where the literary forms function as fringe elements, not as constituent elements, often containing peculiar changes that cannot be found elsewhere (OED); cf. the "No one" of the Polyphemus narrative in Homer to the "Self" of the popular forms (§48, n. 4).
2. See Weston (1900); BP II, p. 261.

3. See GldM I, pp. 110, 232. In a Norwegian fairytale of the same type (Gr + 10) in *Norkse Folkeeventyr*, p. 11, the horse is named Bucephalus, after Alexander the Great's horse; cf. Moe [1914], p. 246); BP III, 18f.

4. See *Danske folkeæventyr* II, no. 7, cf. §67 n. 1 and §70 n. 1; DgF VII 408; BP II 519; Köhler (1898–1900) I, pp. 161f. I do not know where the name originated.

5. See DgF VIII, p. 32; §147 n. 4.

## III. The Structure of the Narrative: The Epic Laws

See above pp. 137, 138–139. The various phases in the development of this section are as follows: D = disposition of 17 March 1905, O = outline of 1905, BO I = basic outline of 1906 I, BO II = basic outline of 1906 II, MS = manuscript of 1906 II; E = Olrik (1908b); F = Olrik (1919a), printed from Olrik (1908f); Z = Olrik (1909a). MS 1916 (or 1915) indicates that part of the manuscript that stems from MS 1916. No. refers to the number of the law in the various unprinted and printed editions. Literature: MS 1916; 11. 1–12 and 20 to the end written earlier, presumably from 1912.

1. Professor Hermann Gunkel wrote to Olrik on 1 March 1910: "I recently read your essay in *Zeitschrift* and I was pleasantly surprised to find an almost uncanny affinity between your research and mine, which I have presented especially in my Genesis commentary (first edition published in 1901). My Genesis commentary will appear in its third edition at Easter; I have been able to include some references to your essay at the last minute [in the introduction]." Cf. Appendix A, pp. 128f. from 1915–1916.

2. See p. 138, cf. §75 n. 1.

3. About the narrative technique in the individual tales by Herodotus.

§57. MS 1916, cf. E. p. 69, F p. 177, Z p. 1; however, missing in BO introduction.

1. Cf. §11.

§58. MS 1916 = BO II no. 1, but not = E p. 70. In BO I and MS 1906 this paragraph also included current §60.

1. Gr + 25 A *Born of a Fish:* horse, dog, and sword are selected as the hero's military equipment (S). Cf. BP I 544.

§59. MS 1916 (or 1915) for the main text and example 1, MS 1906 for example 2 and comment. BO no. 2, E 70, F 181, Z p. 5.

1. Concerning this tale (Gr + 35), see BP I 99 and here §63, §139 example 1. Olrik here relates from memory, which is why his reproduction resembles the normal type of the Danish fairytale more than the actual text in JFm V no. 16.

2. *Völsunga saga* chapters 14–20; see von Sydow (1918).

3. As Odin does it here.

4. *Brot* vv. 6–12, *Den ældre Edda,* pp. 185f., cf. §34, n. 2.

5. An exception is DgF 127, where King Valdemar, his niece, and

the queen are on stage at the same time, exchanging replies almost as in a modern drama. (Heusler [1902b], p. 235.)

§60. Example and comment originally belonged to MS 1906 I §1 (cf. §58, p. 139); main text is an edited copy of MS 1906 II. Cf. E 71, F 183, Z 8. In D the Law of Simplification.

1. Cf. §45 examples, §§61 and 62, retold DSÆ I, 34.

2. Cf. Olrik (1919a), p. 144, DSÆ I, 28; "shed a shift" is not part of everyday speech.

3. Cf. Olrik (1908b), p. 72; Olrik quotes from memory; it says (GldM I no. 248) "Yes, I'm coming two more times"; "Yes, I'm coming one more time"; "I'm never coming again" (cf. DSÆ II, pp. 28f.); about the tale itself (Gr + 52), see BP I 116.

4. The dialogue is unsuited to this tale; I assume it is borrowed from tale type 35, *The Little Duck* (see §59, 1), where the duck's statement, "Now I'm coming two more times," etc., has its necessary epic function in the plot (Hans Ellekilde).

§61. MS 1916, cf. p. 139; literature is older; see F 179, Z 3, cf. E 83.

1. The difference between schematizing means incorporating similar expressions. Repetition is a poetic effect, but a poor imagination forces the poet to schematize (S).

2. Repetition, not embellishment, is the language of a primitive or simple sensibility; and the ballads that are poor in embellishment are rich in repetition. Actually, a kind of progressive repetition is the major characteristic of the ballad style found in the tradition discussed in the present work (cf. §9 comment).

§62. MS 1916, cf. p. 139; see F 179, Z 4, cf. E 83.

§63. MS 1916, cf. p. 139; see F 183, Z 8 note, cf. E 72. Part 2 of the main text belongs to MS 1906.

1. This feature cannot be found in JFm V no. 16 (cf. §59 n. 1), but is known from other versions of the same tale (e.g., see DFS 1929/43, no. 7); cf. Feilberg (1886–1914), s.v. *perle;* BP I, p. 100 fn.; it is far more frequent for the heroine to comb gold and silver out of her hair.

2. In Z 8 fn., it says: "In this manner misfortune, goodness, and beauty are made into the three stages of the plot."

3. §12 n. 6, §74, §178.

4. Cf. Olrik (1919a), p. 104.

5. Olrik is thinking of Gjellerup's description of Sigurðr and Brynhildr when Sigurðr placed the sword between himself and her at Hindarfjall (*Brynhild,* pp. 154f.).

§64. MS is closer to BO I no. 3, where part 5 is not found and part 1 is only indicated. BO II no. 4, E 72, Z 9, indicated in F 183.

1. The small number of characters is not the only peculiarity, but also the simple yet expressive attitude of the characters (S).

2. Cf. §59 example 2, Sigurðr and Grani; *Sakses Danesaga* I, p. 27; *Edda Snorra Sturlusonar,* chapter 47; Olrik (1903–1910) I, 59 (*Bjarkamál* v. 34); *Völsunga saga,* chapter 10.

3. See §59 example 2; GldM II, p. 31, or JFm V, p. 40; GldM I, p. 168, cf. DSÆ I, 65; *Danske folkeæventyr* II, p. 32 (*The Swan Maiden* tale, see Ellekilde [1919], p. 167).

§65. BO I §4, BO II §5, E 73, F 183, Z 9. MS part I = ED and BO part 1; MS part 2 differs considerably, however; see fn. 2. Reference to Moe added later.

1. Everything that is brought onto the stage must be used; if a magical implement, e.g., an invisibility hat, is given to the hero without his using it at some point in the plot, then something is wrong with the narrative. As an example of this kind of faulty logic, we can mention the Faroese lay *Lokkatáttur* (cf. GldM I no. 2 and p. 227), where the troll discovers the hero's hideout three times, so that the troll seems to be the victor, but still dies the last time in a way that seems rather too fortuitous compared to the nature of the test (from ED, where it was originally written as a comment to the Law of Final Stress, see §75). Cf. DgF II, p. VI; Olrik (1911c), pp. 552, 576.

2. This does not hold in all cases. There are always some narrators who manage the material less skillfully, and a few nationalities display a similar lack of skill. The transition to saga or epic form is, furthermore, often accompanied by a growth in volume that weakens and sometimes even counteracts the close connection between the parts. But such special forms will die out again, simply because they cannot be remembered. The longer a piece of narrative material has existed as folklore, the more closely it will retain this connection (ED part 2, BO a little shorter).

3. See DgF II, p. VI and 208; Moe (1909), pp. 1f.

4. Cf. Olrik (1904b), p. 16. Olrik (1919a), pp. 157, 160f.

§66. BO II no. 6 ( = MS part 1); E 74, F 183, Z 9. MS has revised ED in previous paragraph fn. 2, and has been developed from it; cf. p. 139.

1. The logic of the narrative and its demand for clarity creates the unity of plot. This unity, more than anything else, holds the narrative together as it is orally transmitted for centuries (ED §6).

2. In the *Hagbard ballad* (DgF 20), H's sewing and the derision of the maidens belong outside the usual tradition of oral narrative composition (S). (Cf. Olrik [1919a], p. 102.)

§67. BO II §7 ( = MS main text), E 74, F 183, Z 10.

1. Cf. §70 n. 1, §56 n. 4.

2. I.e., to ride through the flames; Sigurðr does this (see §59 example 2 and comment) in the guise of Gunnarr, whom she marries (cf. §73 example; Olrik [1907a], p. 42).

3. §73 n. 1, *Sakses Danesaga* I, pp. 177, 190, cf. Olrik (1919a), pp. 76f.

4. Cf. §§7, 185.

§68. BO II §8 ( = MS main text parts 1 and 3; MS part 2 deviates; most examples indicated here, but literature that is added later is missing). E 75, F 183, Z 8 and 11.

1. The main action cannot have happened before the beginning of

the narrative, as is the case in Sophocles: *Oedipus Rex,* and as Ibsen often does in his dramas. (An exception is the Eddic poem *Hamðismál* [*Den ældre Edda,* p. 238], the main plot of which presupposes the murder of Svanhildr, and which abruptly begins the plot. But this poem also violates the Law of Twins [§73].)

2. From the royalist ballad DgF 145 F and G (cf. §9 n. 4), *Danske Folkeviser* I, 55, 181, and 174 v. 2.

3. *Völsunga saga,* chapter 14, *Den ældre Edda* 169; cf. §59 example 2.

4. §78 example 1, §45 n. 4.

5. *Sturlunga saga* (1878); cf. *Sturlunga saga* (1904) I, p. 30. §69. Mentioned in D; cf. p. BO II §9 = MS (minus example), E 76, F 184, Z 10.

1. Same tale as in §146 n. 1.

2. *Danske folkeæventyr* III, fn. 1, BP I 22.

3. *Sakses Danesaga* II, p. 143, Olrik (1892–1894) II, pp. 163f.

§70. BO II §10; MS expanded a little, especially comment, E 76, F 184, Z10.

1. §56 n. 4, §67 n. 1, von Löwis (1912), p. 2.

2. Olrik (1892–1894) II, pp. 131f.

§71. In D, MS's main idea is indicated: the Law of Two to a Scene, good and evil, strong and weak (cunning). ED §3 is very close to MS, and has all examples except the one about Gunnarr and Högni, but emphasizes the contrast sympathetic-unsympathetic more. BO I §7 quite brief. BO II §11, E 77, F 181, Z 6.

1. Not yet published in DgF, see JFm XI, 186.

2. JFm V no. 44; Gr + 149; see Feilberg (1886–1914) II, 476a s.v. *lykke;* Olrik (1919a), p. 181 fn. 6 is wrong.

3. §59 comment, *Völsunga saga,* chapter 31, *Guðrúnarkviða* II; especially in the *Niebelungenlied* (cf. §108 n. 4) this contrast is characteristic.

4. Gr + 54, Aarne (1910), p. 43, BP III 333.

5. See Olrik (1911c), p. 551.

§72. In D, the main content of MS is indicated: the weak descendant of the great king, also the fall of the hero owing to deceit. ED corresponds to the main text in MS part 3f., cf. fn. 4. BO I no. 8 assumes, as in §71, an intermediate position = BO II no. 12. E 77, F 181, Z 6.

1. Olrik (1903–1910) I, 29, pp. 179f.; §59 example 2.

2. *Hervarar saga,* chapter 4.

3. *Atlakviða,* vv. 22–25, *Völsunga saga,* chapter 39.

4. The bad assassin and the deceitful death belong together. If the hero is slain in an open fight, the contest is one of equals; the defeat of a hero by an adversary detracts from his greatness. Example: In German and some Scandinavian sources, Sigurðr Fáfnisbani is killed by Högni by being struck from behind. The killing receives greater emphasis in common Scandinavian sources, where he is killed in his sleep by the young Guttormr. Hrólfr killed by Hjörvarðr; Helgi Hundingsbani by Dagr; the Persian Rustem by his evil brother. Weaker:

Achilles hit by an arrow; Roland and Emperor Charles's rear guard conquered by treason.

§73. In D: the Law of Doubles, two against one always weaker (Haddings); Kete and Vige; Högni and Gunnarr against Sigurðr. Subordinate: Geri Freki, Huginn Muninn, Byggvir Beyla, Þjálfi Röskva, Hrist and Mist [valkyries], Göndul and Skögul, the Dioscures. ED = MS (minus the period in 11.5-7, which is added later). Also in ED and BO I §9 the law is called the Law of Doubles; besides quite brief. BO II §13 the Law of Twins, E 78, F 182, Z 6f.

1. §67 n. 3.
2. E 79. Olrik (1903-1910) I, 14.
3. §159 example 2.
4. *Grímnismál* vv. 19-20, *Edda Snorra Sturlusonar,* chapter 37.
5. *Edda Snorra Sturlusonar,* chapter 43.
6. Olrik (1903-1910) II, 256: Skírnir asks for the giantess Gerðr's hand in marriage on behalf of Freyr (in *Skírnismál, Den ældre Edda,* p. 49).
7. Jónsson (1894-1902) I, pp. 455f; *Skjaldedigtning* I B 57; the two valkyries are sent by Odin to choose Hákon Aðalsteinsfóstri.
8. See further E 87, F 184. On violations of the Law of Twins, see §68 n. 2. The reason for this is either a historical survival, or that Hamðir and Sörli are felt to be "twins" compared to Jörmunrekkr (cf. Ussing [1910], p. 165).

§74. Part 1 is close to ED §1, BO I §5 ( = BO II §14). Part 2 probably corresponds to the paragraph Multiple Numbers, indicated in ED; cf. E 82, D: Multiple Numbers, (the number seven), the number twelve: companions, nine very (?) holy ones. Example 1 adopted in 1916 from E 81, example 2 probably added in 1912. F 179, Z 4.

1. Note how often Indian and Asian tradition in general has four identical characters acting together where others have three: four brahmins find the dead lion (the fourth will stop the others); or similarly four brothers (all perished); *Tales of the Punjab,* pp. 391f.; cf. E 82, F 180. In North American Indian tradition, one finds the Law of Four among the Shushwap Indians (Boas [1895]), but Spinden (1908), pp. 13f., says of the Nez Percé Indians: "Five is very strongly evident as the sacred number as opposed to four on the Plains." Among the Musquakie Indians, however, Olrik finds more threes than fours in their short tales (Owen [1904], cf. Lund [1908], p. 179). See further §78 n. 8 with other excerpts from Olrik's recordings concerning numbers. The editor (Hans Ellekilde) calls attention to the number 4 as emphasized in the proverb about unsuccessful attempts: "All good times three, but number four it will be," and to the fact that Gr + 37, *The Girls in the Well* (BP I 207), seems composed around 4 not 3.

2. Thus in Gr + 9, *The Strange Companions,* and its variants (see BP II 86); cf. the cumulative tale *The Fat Cat* (DSÆ I, 9), with its 5 birds in a flock, 7 maidens in a dance.

3. E.g., Hrólfr kraki and his 12 berserks (Olrik [1903-1910] I, 201). About the number 12 in Homer, see Weiske (1842), p. 327.

4. This sequence of numbers is, however, rare; it is common to have dragons with either 1, 2, or 3 heads or 3, 6, or 9 heads (cf. Feilberg [1886–1914], s.v. *hoved*). The opposite numerical sequence, trolls with 3, 2, and 1 leg(s), can be found in, e.g., the narrative type "altar cups stolen from the mounds" (see DS I, types 48–50); see here *Sønderjydske folkesagn,* p. 19; cf. §78 example 2 (Hans Ellekilde).

5. §178 example, §12 n. 6, E 81.

6. In Hallström (1912).

§75. See p. 138. MS 1916 except comment 2, which is older, may be from 1912; if Olrik had finished his book, it would probably have been placed in the appendix. It has been inserted into chapter III by the editor, Hans Ellekilde. MS 1916 is based on MS 1906 which, as mentioned above, does not discuss the Law of Initial Stress. Comment 1 sounds like this in MS 1906 (= ED, shortened a little): "Even apparent exceptions fall under the law: Odin, Hœnir, Loki (the last acting character, even though Odin is theologically the most powerful). Real exceptions are a few mythological groups where the second and third characters are split off from the first character, or are presented as subservient to him: Odin, Vili, Vé. On the whole, 'Final Stress' does not pertain to divine worship, but to epic narration. (When Odin, Just-as-high, and Third are introduced into a story—as in Snorri's *Gylfaginning*—then Third is the most clever.)." Except for the question of "Initial Stress" (main text part 2, example parts 2 and 4), MS 1916, ED, and especially MS 1906 are extremely close, not least in the examples used. BO I §6 = BO II §15 quite brief; cf. p. E 83f., F 182, Z 7.

1. Cf. pp. 41, 138. Schütte (1920), p. 2, claims to be the author of the Law of Final Stress, and his claim may be proven right by Olrik's remark under comment in ED (see above) where he writes "Literature: Schütte...," i.e., he knows that Schütte is working on the question in his doctoral dissertation (published February 1907), but he does not know its exact title.

2. Cf. Gravlund (1916), p.13; it is especially in Gr + 15, *Esben and the Cat* (BP II 33), that this sequence of names appears; see, e.g., JFm XIII no. 30 (Hans Ellekilde).

3. *Edda Snorra Sturlusonar,* chapter 2f.

4. See further E 84 fn. 2.

5. "They say that in the old days Humli ruled the Huns, Gizurr the Gauts, Angantýr the Goths" (*Eddica Minora,* p. 105).

6. *Edda Snorra Sturlusonar,* chapter 5; *Völuspá* v. 18 (*Den ældre Edda,* p. 18).

7. *Sakses Danesaga* I, p. 270, *Hyndluljóð* v. 22 (*Den ældre Edda,* p. 91); cf. *Örvar-Odds saga,* chapter 26; *Hervarar saga,* chapter 2.

8. Cf. §73 example 11.1–3.

9. *Sakses Danesaga* I, pp. 282f.

10. See §16 example 2; cf. Olrik (1903–1910) I, 11.

11. *Die deutsche Heldensage* (1897), p. 292.

12. "Phol and Odin went into the forest"; see further §12 n. 4.

13. Cf. *Danske Folkeviser* I, 162; also DgF 33, 73, 124, 125 b.
14. DgF 40, *Danske Folkeviser* I, 128 and 67, cf. DgF 54 B, C; 58 A, 126 A, F.
15. Also DgF 20, 37 a, 50 and 76.
16. Offa ruled over the Angles; see Olrik (1919a) I, 75.

§76. MS 1916; (3) missing in BO I §10 ( = BO II §16) and in MS 1906 (presumably = ED, cf. p. ). The first 4 lines in the examples = MS 1906; in MS 1916, Olrik left a page for the Spanish quote; the editor (Hans Ellekilde) has made 8 lines of it suffice. Cf. E 84, F 178, Z 2.

1. See §77 n. 1.
2. See DgF 186, *The Shield-maiden* (dialogue), DgF 240, *The Wendish King's Abduction of Virgins,* and DgF 90, *Aage and Else* (women at their handiwork).
3. Especially characteristic in a Norwegian variant (*Norske folkeviser*, p. 22) of DgF 44; cf. DgF 258.
4. I.e., *The Avenging Child.*
5. "Look at him, look at him! There he comes, the avenging child, riding with short stirrups on a speeding horse; his face has changed color, and he holds a sharp spear in his right hand." The poem continues with a detailed description of the spear, which, in the judgment of the editor, fully serves according to the Law of Opening to introduce the main action of the poem, which is that the avenging child throws the spear at the assassin, hits the emperor, but is saved by his daughter. (See Olrik's summary [1889] of the ballad, DgF 2, p. 117, cf. E 85, where he trusts his memory too much and repeats the plot incorrectly).

§77. MS 1916; in MS 1906 ( = ED? see p. 139) missing (example 4) and (example mixed); MS 1906 (also comment) is slightly revised: the same examples can be found, only in a different order. BO I §11, BO II § 17, E 85, F 178, Z 2.

1. §76, 1, §103 example 1, *Danske Folkeviser* I, 248 and 34f.
2. *Danske Folkeviser* I, 173.
3. *Danske Folkeviser* I, 128, cf. II, 23.
4. *Rolandskvadet,* p.148.
5. *Danske Folkeviser* I, 176.
6. *Danske Folkeviser* I, 104, cf. §96 example.
7. Cf. §122 comment.
8. *Danske Folkeviser* II, 13.
9. Olrik (1906b), p. 178.
10. *Rolandskvadet,* pp. 122ff.

§78. See pp. 140, 143–44, note to Appendix A, Patriarchal History of Israel. Example 1 was probably written in the spring of 1916; example 2 was copied from older recordings, presumably from 1908–1909.

1. Cf. Olrik (1903–1910) I, pp. 175f., *Helge* (1814). About the saga, published by Jónsson in 1904, see Jónsson (1894–1902) II, p. 829. *Die Geschichte von Hrolf Kraki.*
2. See §138 example, §139 example 2.
3. Cf. E 79.
4. Olrik (1903–1910) I, 145, 219, 215, and 115; §157 example.

5. Olrik (1903–1910) I, 215.
6. Olrik (1903–1910) I, 219.
7. Chapter 26, Olrik (1903–1910) I, 205; cf. here p. 136.
8. Olrik's studies on numerical relationships (cf. §74 nn. 1–4) are especially concerned with the presumed sacredness of the number 3 and the number 9 among the Aryan race, as evidenced in works such as Diels (1897), with many references; cf. Diels (1902), p. 8, Weinhold (1897); cf. also Weinhold (1894). By contrast, the number 7 is, according to Diels, the Semitic sacred number, but it entered Greek fairly early and is also found in Orphic worship. On the number 13, see Bergström (1905), Østrup (1888). See also Feilberg (1892–1894b); Meyer (1906c).

§79. Cf. pp. 144–145. Here I add the titles of the works Olrik had either studied or was planning to study for the composition of this paragraph. Under "Psychology concerning the Epic Laws" he cites Fechner (1876); Wundt (1908–1912); Lehmann (1914) (however, he discards Ziegler [1893], "many reprints, poor!"); Dessoir (1906). Under "Epic Laws, Psychological," Olrik cites Larsson (1914), and he has also familiarized himself with Larsson (1912) (cf. Hjelholt [1917], p. 156). Under "Epic Laws, Psychological Aesthetic," Olrik cites references to Scherer (1888) (concerning "Vormythologische Novellenschemata"), from Meyer (1906a), pp. 166f., 172f.; Meyer (1906b), p. 11; and Meyer (1906c).

§80. E 88.

§81. MS 1916, cf. p. 140.

1. However, there is no Law of Opening; the poem begins in the middle of the battle with a vertical effect, not with a preparation for battle or such (cf. §76).

2. See also Bertram (1915), p. 101.

3. German literary historian and mythologist, born 1860 in Berlin. See introduction to chapters III and V, §79 n.

4. Separation of primary and secondary concept (process of centralization).

5. The moral, aesthetic group formation.

6. The Law of Symmetry.

7. The well-known story about Heracles at the crossroad; Sigurðr between Brynhildr and Guðrún (cf. §67 n. 2).

8. Concentration on the theme almost inevitably leads to a continuation of the composition, and may even lead to the formation of a whole cycle of compositions (as when Goethe takes the story of Dr. Faust as the subject for his drama).

9. "The law about the formation of poetic works of the same kind," especially "approximation to (extant) works of the same kind"; more specifically, "the Law of Convergence, which is based on the formation of close analogies." As is also apparent from the note, Meyer believes in the peculiar uniformity that appears in the compositions of certain eras and nationalities: "We may say: a certain degree of stylization is given *a priori* for any literary work. But stylization is nothing but an approximation of the poet's personal impression of the products of

earlier artists. . . . This stylization produces the universal, whereas the presentation of the unique personal impression produces a specific; and without the union of both these elements no art work can be created. . . . But this suffices to cause *compulsive use of literary forms* that are universally valid, i.e., independent of historical, national, or individual conditions. By 'compulsive use,' we mean the phenomenon that a certain set of conditions is, by necessity, derived from another." 10. Cf. especially §§98, 101.

§82. Cf. E 86–89, Z 11–12.

## IV A. The Life and Transformation of the Narrative

See pp. 137, 140. MS designates the manuscript of 1906 with no later additions. A = my copy of 1915, *older than* A with additions. Where no comment is given, except concerning the old paragraph designation and its content (from §89f.), MS = A = T (the current text), except for quite insignificant formal changes from MS to A, or from A to T. *Literature* 11.2–3 = MS; reference to Aarne and Krohn younger than A.

1. Olrik did not, of course, know the last part of "Episke grundlove" (from 1917). Concerning the relationship between Moe's Basic Epic Laws and Olrik's Epic Laws + The Life of the Narrative, see Olrik (1915a), p. 36; Olrik (1915b), p. 51 (cf. here p. 137). From this, it is clear that Olrik has sent Moe a basic sketch of III, but strangely enough not IV A, and he is not really able to explain the reason for this. Axel Olrik's behavior toward Erslev, his teacher in the evaluation of sources, is quite different; see p. 148, introduction to II A, "An Evaluation of Narrative Sources."

§83. MS §I.

§84. MS §II, I part 2, conclusion, revision earlier than A.

§85. MS §III.

1. Also by inciting the indignation of the audience. The learned historian Hans Gram was morally offended by the folk ballad about Valdemar and Tove and therefore remembered it (DgF III 34).

2. "Since the tales are used as a means of entertainment, it is natural that the humorous tales, which attract a larger audience, disseminate faster than the dry, boring ones. The tale *The Musicians of Bremen* has apparently become popular in European countries because of its humorous tone, while the related tale about 'the traveling domestic utensils' [which must be its source] has had to be satisfied with a much more limited dissemination." (Concerning these tales, see Grimm nos. 27, 10, and 41, BP I 237f., 75f., 375.)

§86. MS §IV; comment younger than A, 11.8–9 older than A.

1. I.e., beforehand.

2. Olrik writes F. v. Holten in unclear pencil.

§87. MS §V.

1. Zealand is better suited to being a cultural center than the distant, sparsely inhabited Jämtland (S).

2. Cf. §§94, 98; Grundtvig's introduction to this ballad is recommended to all who wish to study narratives; it is one of the most brilliant in DgF.

3. See Nutt (1899) and Weston (1899). Cf. §56 nn. 2, 4, and 5.

§88. MS §VI; example younger than A. The word "possibly" (end of para. 2) younger than A. Here the old chapter IV A in D II, "The Life and Death of the Narrative," ends; cf. p. 137.

1. "Animal fables" written in pencil above. Olrik was thinking of the fable about why the bear's tail is short: it was frozen in the ice when the bear started fishing with it upon the advice of the fox. This animal fable is best preserved in its northern place of origin, but has been distorted during its dissemination southward to areas where people are unfamiliar with the freezing of lakes. Cf. §5 n. 4, §179 n. 2, BP II 111.

2. See Olrik (1913), especially pp. 3–140.

§89. Here chapter IV B begins in D II, "Addition and Change," which takes up the rest of current IV A (cf. p. 137). MS §VII ("The Continuous Transformation of the Narrative"); example older than A.

1. "A person who sings a ballad twice will sing different, even completely different, variants: two siblings who have learned the same ballad from their mother sing it differently" (S).

2. See Feilberg (1886–1914) s.v. *Sand-sage, Lemmike, Æmter;* the last word is the popular pronunciation of *æventyr.*

3. Concerning this tale, see Gr + 97, BP III 214f., Kristensen (1907), p. 145, Anderson (1923).

4. Related by former teacher Kierckebye in Anst. Concerning similar divisions in Indian oral narrative composition, see Barbeau (1915) (narrative considered as true or invented); cf. §100 comment.

§90. MS VIII (The comparative durability of the plot).

1. Cf. §48 example.

2. Plutarch *Moralia* III 93; see Mannhardt (1875–1877), p. 133; Moe (1915), p. 91.

3. DS I type 23 *Atis and Watis.*

4. See also Grundtvig (1881), p. 1; cf. *Danske Folkeviser* I, pp. 69, 126; II, p. 20.

5. Grundtvig is thinking of DgF 47 G and Q: "these arose by restriction, compared to the wonderful one (A) in Karen Brahe that gives us expansion, depiction." Cf. §91 example 2, §108 n. 1.

§91. MS IX (Reduction and Expansion). Comment and example 2 younger than A.

1. Moe is thinking of the Finnish term meaning "the old hag current," i.e., a countercurrent in a river, a name stemming from this tale (see *Norske Folkeeventyr* [1871] no. 4; Köhler [1898–1900] I, 506).

2. Cf. Moe's introduction to *Lappiske eventyr og folkesagn,* p. VI. In Wiklund's opinion, the Lapp epic about the sons of the sun is a product of pastor Fjellner (Wiklund [1906], p. 248, and [1908], p. 165).

§92. MS §X (Changes).

§93. MS §XI (Conscious or Unconscious). The quote from Moe is younger than A.

1. Moe (1914), p. 9; Moe continues: "he very rarely makes a conscious change."

§94. MS §XII (Gradual).

1. The earlier stage of the narrative; being whipped to death is more recent (von der Recke [1906], p. 155).

2. Here we see a development from being non-existent in the ballad to being the main character in the ballad; cf. §87 example 1, §98 example, DgF III 73, 78–79, 911f., GldM III, p. 239.

§95. MS §XIII (A *half-forgotten* narrative changes significantly). Example 2 part 2 older than A.

1. Cf. §45 comment 2, Olrik (1912), p. 149.

2. See *English and Scottish Popular Ballads* V, pp. 3f.

3. *Danske Folkeviser* I 29, 211.

4. JFm X, 70 B, DgF 325 C b.

§96. MS XIV (The Free Ends of the Narrative); already indicated in D of 17 March 1905, "The Free Ends."

1. Cf. §98 example, §108 n. 2, §153, *Danske Folkeviser* I 42, 156f., 154f.

§97. MS 1916, cf. pp. 142–143. In D of 17 March 1905, the following reasons for transformations are indicated: "External reasons: a change in place—in time and culture. Internal reasons: epic necessity." In the old index §XV, the following reasons for changes are cited: (1) in the narrative, (2) with the narrator, (3) other narrative material, and (4) external reality; the very same as here in T. In MS 1906 (= A 1915), the following parts are missing: 1 b and 1 d; 2 b (cf. §100), 4 a. MS part 3 = T, but part 2 sounds like this in MS: "*In the mind of the narrator:* a need to express his sympathy or moral opinion regarding persons and events."

1. See p. 140, originally §12 in part III G I, where it sounds as follows: "Besides the more formal laws for the material, there is one that unconditionally concerns the plot. A certain justice must be done, especially retribution for transgressions, and vindication for suffering." Olrik gives his students this assignment: "Make a closer examination of poetic *justice*. Does the narrative have its characters pronounce judgment themselves, or is this implied in the plot? Does the narrative show compassion for the offender?"

§98. Main text and comment new, but comment is written on older paper than the main text (cf. §100). Examples = MS (and A XV example to 1).

1. See Feilberg (1915), pp. 83f., 86. *Natursagen* I, p. 69.

§99. Main text and comment new; examples are close to MS and A XV example to 2, except that they are in a different order.

1. Cf. the change in Ibsen's *A Doll House* in Germany, so that it ends in Helmer's and Nora's reconciliation.

2. In a North Zealand version of DgF 241, *Skipper and Maiden*. Here the beautiful maiden perishes in the wild blue waves; in the other

Danish and foreign versions, she is rescued; the sad ending was felt to be more poetic (Hans Ellekilde).

3. E.g., a modern change of the *Agnete ballad,* DgF 38 K: they divide the children between them. "He had two and she had two, the fifth one was to pass back and forth between them" (DgF IV 808).

4. Quartered by horses, thus in A, a contemporary version from Bråby near Sorø. This ending forms a characteristic contrast to the bourgeois inclination to have all end well. See DgF 362, *The Indulgent Husband.*

5. Olrik (1919a), p. 155; Olrik (1889), p. 260.

6. Olrik (1919a), p. 109, *Danske Folkeviser* I, 69, 136f.

§100. Missing in MS and A. Main text except for the quote from Moe and example (a), except for the last three lines, written on the same paper as §98 comment, and presumably they form an earlier stage in the revision.

1. *Völuspá* v. 46, cf. vv. 27–28; *Sigrdrífumál* v. 14 (*Den ældre Edda,* pp. 12, 14, 182); cf. *Edda Snorra Sturlusonar,* chapter 14.

2. *Grottasöngr* (*Den ældre Edda,* p. 101); Olrik (1903–1910), pp. 280f.; cf. here §20 example.

3. See §37 n. 1; cf. Olrik (1894b), pp. 106f., 85. Another striking example of rationalism occurs when the Roman historian Livy says that a shepherdess named Lupo (she-wolf) nursed Romulus and Remus (Livy I, chapter 4).

4. Cf. Moe (1914), pp. 14–15.

5. The mousy, mousy grey.

6. See Olrik (1903–1910), §38, *Tribal Ancestor and Grainwright.*

7. I.e., rationalistic and pedestrian changes.

8. In blue pencil, Olrik has written under example 3: *The Little Duck* "tale 35."

§101. Main text from 1916; example almost identical to MS and A (example to 3).

§102. Missing in MS and A.

1. In this manner, the concept of the hero as Ash-boy was disseminated by analogy to large portions of fairytale material, while the Ash-boy type initially may have belonged to only a single or very few fairytale types; I assume Gr + 15, see §75 n. 2 (Hans Ellekilde).

§103. Main text and comment from 1916; example 1 almost identical to MS (and A) §XV (example to 4); example 2 revision of deleted §XIX example 2; see §108.

1. *Danske Folkeviser* I, 78; II, 75.

2. *Danske Folkeviser* I, 76; DgF I 351. In Olrik's opinion, the penance scene in the ballad of Ebbe Skammelsen was borrowed from this ballad (DgF VI 218f.); cf. §77 n. 1.

§104. In 1916, Olrik combined the last part of §XV and the last part of §XIX example 1 from the latter; cf. §108.

§105. MS §XVI Shift, Glide. This and following paragraphs indicated in D of 17 March 1905: "Development in glide and in leap. Interpenetration."

§106. §XVII Loan, Contamination; Interpenetration.
1. See §122 n. 4.
2. See §128 example, §168 example 2, Olrik (1919a), p. 107, Olrik (1889), p. 249.
§107. MS XVIII Change through *leap.*
§108. MS §XX (The aesthetic value of changes). The preceding §XIX (Change of culture, change of location) was omitted by Olrik in the 1916 revision, but is partly used in §§105 and 104. The main text is as follows: "The steady continuation of narrative transmission will primarily depend upon whether the receiving group of narrators has the same world view as their predecessors. *Change of culture* or *the transference of the narrative to another country* will always make it likely that the narrative will be either forgotten or transformed (i.e., receives a great number of changes or additions)." (Cf. §§88, 125.)
1. Cf. §91 example 2; Faroese ballads are also characterized by verbosity. Cf. Olrik (1915a), p. 3. DgF V, 2 preface, cf. pp. 90, 120, 256.
2. See §96, n. 1. In Danish, we have the ballad in its flourishing form.
3. *Danske Folkeviser* I, pp. 54, 56, 181f., and 195f.
4. *Niebelungenlied.*
5. Olrik is thinking about the ballad *Elfshot;* cf. §90 example 2.

### IV B. Horizon and Localization

See pp. 137, 140–141, 144, 164; the same designations as in IV A. Copy 1915 goes as far as §129 inclusive; the following order of paragraphs is uncertain, as the manuscript consists of loose, unnumbered pages, but they have been put in order according to the prescription in §129.
§109. Cf. §115; Schiern (1840); see further Moe (1908b), p. 502.
§110. 1. Cf. Gravlund (1917), with a special examination of home and routes of communication.
§112. 1. Cf. Olrik (1907a), p. 79; Olrik (1892–1894) I, pp. 7f. In *Atlakviða (Den ældre Edda,* p. 217), we have likewise preserved the central European horizon of the Burgundians from the final period of the Great Migration. Gnita Heath or Gnitaheiðr (probably Sieben-bürgen's countries rich in gold) appears in a historical connection here, in *Reginsmál (Den ældre Edda,* p. 171), however, in a fantastic connection.
§113. Cf. p. 141.
1. Cf. §76 n. 1, DgF VI 207.
2. DgF IV 866f., *Le romancéro populaire,* p. 84, *Le roi Renaud;* cf. Nyrop (1901), p. 211.
§114. Younger than MS; cf. p. 141.
1. Such a Law of Approximation is applicable when the wild hunts-man shoots the elf-maiden with his gun (!) (cf. Olrik [1901], p. 144; DS II D 80, 86, 88, 90, 93). Or cf. *Oddrúnargrátr (Den ældre Edda,*

p. 216), where the Hun princess, Oddrún, on *Læsø* hears about Gunnarr's death in the snake pit.

§115. 1. See Olrik (1903–1910) I, pp. 214f.; II, p. 196; Olrik (1919a), p. 49.

2. Especially in the 37th and 35th songs of *Niebelungenlied* (cf. *Die deutsche Heldensage* [1913], pp. 115f.); Symons (1900); Schütte (1917), p. 240.

§116. = A 1915.

1. See Olrik (1917a); Symons (1900), p. 690; *Die deutsche Heldensage,* p. 150.

§117. 1. *Hervarar saga,* chapter 2, conclusion; *Örvar-Odds saga,* chapter 27 (cf. §75 n. 7, §18 example 1, and Olrik [1919a], p. 57).

2. Hellquist (1903–1906).

§118. Younger than MS; cf. p. 141.

1. Cf. Olrik (1903–1910) I, pp. 11f.; Olrik (1919a), p. 14; therefore Jutes ("Geats") and Danes play the leading role in *Beowulf.*

2. See *Eskimoiske Eventyr og Sagn* I, pp. 4, 198–209; II, pp. 206f.; cf. *Grönlandske sagn,* p. 14.

3. See Olrik (1914), p. 12.

4. Bugge (1907), p. 9. < Zimmer (1891), pp. 1f.; cf. A. Bugge (1904–1906) I, p. 129.

§119. Cf. pp. 140–141.

1. *Fagrskinna* (1847); cf. *Fagrskinna* (1902–1903), pp. 243, 248.

2. See *Folkesagn og Folketro i Ods Herred,* nos. 11–13; cf. §132 comment and §175 comment.

3. Directed at Steenstrup's criticism of Olrik (1892–1894) II.

§120. 1. Cf. §131 n. 1.

§121. MS main text and comment slightly revised, but before 1915.

1. See *Norröne skrifter* I, p. 67; cf. Olrik (1903–1910) II, 163, 124, 215. It probably was the tooth of a mammoth.

2. Vv. 196, 198; see *Rímnasafn* I, 30, and *Carmina Scaldica,* p. 124; Jónsson (1894–1902) III, pp. 45f.; Fáfnir's tooth weighs about 5 kilos.

3. Cf. JFm V, p. 83; JFm XIII, p. 159; §77 mixed example; Petsch (1900), pp. 70f.

§122. In comment, "ugly" corrected to "ridiculous."

1. §77 n. 8; *St. Olaf and the Trolls;* see *Danske Folkeviser* 131.

2. *Den ældre Edda,* p. 147.

3. §125 example 2; §96 example, Nyrop (1907), p. 23.

4. §106 n. 1.

§123. 1. See DS III A type 6f. From Schiødte (1908), pp. 97ff.; cf. §129 example 2.

2. *Edda Snorra Sturlusonar,* chapter 49; Olrik (1911c), p. 559.

§124. 1. See DS III B type 22, the troll Finn; cf. here §171 n. 3, §174 example n. 1.

2. *Sakses Danesaga* I, p. 287 (cf. DS IV nos. 41f., *Danmarks Folkesagn* I 13, 374).

3. The conclusion of the tale about the mill explaining why the ocean turned salty is an essential but weak localization because it lacks precise determination (S) (cf. §174 example).
4. *Sakses Danesaga* I, p. 267; cf. Olrik (1892–1894) II, p. 282; Olrik (1919a), p. 89.

§125. 1. Chapter 92 (see §37, n. 2).
2. See H. Olrik (1888), pp. 241f., with reference. *Sakses Danesaga* III, p. 130. DS III 1103.
3. See, e.g., *Flateyjarbók* II, p. 435; *Biskupa sögur* I, p. 674; *Landnámabók,* chapter 63 end.
4. In the record mentioned by Syv (E 122), the king says: "For never shall you have the pleasure of stepping over her with your steed." See Løffler (1876a), p. 40; cf. §133 n. 1.

§126. 1. Cf. Olrik (1892–1894) I, p. 10; all characters appear in *Hrómundar saga Gripssonar* (Jónsson [1894–1902] II, p. 808).

§127. Revised 1916 (cf. p. 141). T and the main text of MS are essentially identical; but the example is much more elaborate in T than in MS, where it was example 2. Olrik does not indicate what the content of example 1 should be.
1. Havbyrd and Sigersted (*Sakses Danesaga* II, p. 37).
2. Hærvig and Skedevad, Helkær, Valbrønde, Hakehøj (see §155 example 2); see Olrik (1892–1894) II, pp. 248–249.
3. §63 n. 4, §27 example 2.

§128. Last line in main text younger than A.
1. §168 example 2, DgF VIII 156.
2. The *Adelbrand ballad* (the head in the attic at the Drenderup manor, DgF V 2, 106, DgF IV 715f.); the *Norntoft narrative* from Ty (DS IV 882, DgF VI 212).

§129. See Olrik (1890–1892b), p. 148.
2. §123 n. 1.
3. DgF I 259f., III 791, IV 755, GldM I no. 238; cf. §27 n. 2.
4. §134 example, §196.

§130. About the order of this and the following paragraphs, see notes to IV B. Above, Olrik has written "to be revised" in pencil, and below, "the scientific importance of localization"; but the planned revision was not completed (cf. p. 144).
1. Especially §196. After "role," Olrik has deleted: "in any case, for the tableaux, perhaps less where insignificant and ephemeral remnants are concerned" (cf. §5, p. 3).

§131. 1. Cf. Dähnhardt's distinction (*Natursagen* I, p. X) between genuine origin legends and arbitrary ones; by the latter he means those that do not have an explanation of natural phenomena as their main content, but merely end with an arbitrary etiological motif. Cf. §123 example.
2. *Voyage of Bran* I, p. 147; cf. d'Arbois de Jubainville (1883–1902) V, pp. 385f.

§133. 1. §125 example 2, DgF III 88 fn. 2; Aagaard (1802), p. 148.
2. In Sogn in western Norway, DgF I 264; *Danmarks Folkesagn* I, 191 (the church at Højby).

§134. 1. The handmaiden stones in Hviding (GldM I, p. 193, DgF I 267). The cave of the goatsucker in Sigersted (DS II C no. 116; cf. §27, example 2 and DgF I 266 from Viken in southern Norway). The soul of the evil handmaiden who is buried appears in the shape of a bird. Cf. Skg III, p. 79.

### IV C. Survival

See pp. 137, 141–142. I have no copy of this from 1915, as I have for IV A and B. The old paragraph indications in MS are written in pencil.

§135. MS §XXI.

1. Olrik has written "Literature" above, but has not cited any; he is thinking of works such as Tylor (1871) I (chapter 3, "Survival in Culture"); Lang (1885), p. 11, "The Method of Folklore"; cf. Cox (1895), introduction, pp. 50, 176; Müller (1892–1894), especially p. 236; Feilberg (1914), pp. 15, 109; see Olrik (1919b) and Ellekilde (1923).

2. Olrik has this information from Feilberg, but we have no information about which church it is. In Olrik (1919b), he informs us that it is the church at Ørsted, but this is incorrect. Further information will be gratefully received by the Danish Folklore Archives. An examination by O. Andrup on 17 August 1907 at the church in Skævinge in North Zealand produced a negative result.

§136. MS §XXII.

1. See further Moe (1908b), pp. 458–460. The actual reason is to prevent a person from being put under a spell by whoever possesses that person's cut-off nails. Cf. Ellekilde (1923).

§138. MS §XXIV.

1. See §78 n. 2.

2. Olrik (1894b), pp. 87, 112, 160f.; §139 n. 3.

§139. MS §XXV.

1. It is actually the boon granted her by the third witch of the well: "if she was ever shipwrecked she would not drown, but would float on the water like a small wild duck"; cf. §§59, 63.

2. In terms of mythic consciousness, drowning signifies transformation into a creature of the sea (seal, small duck, etc.); therefore tale 67 B, *Overboard* [where the hero is saved on the ocean by the dead helper, cf. §149 n.1], is influenced by rationalism (cf. §100 comment, example 3).

3. *Völsunga saga,* chapter 8, in turn has borrowed from the heroic narrative about Hagbard and Signe, where we have a natural, unartificial unity: Signe does not want to survive the death of her lover, but wants to follow him in death (Olrik [1919a], p. 100; cf. Olrik [1903–1910] I, p. 155).

§141. MS §XXVII.

§142. Not marked, cf. p. 141.

1. III B, chapter XVIII, "The Rescue of Andromeda: Its Relations to Human Sacrifices"; cf. §177 example.

§143. Not marked; presumably from 1908.

1. Survival is a hypothesis that often can be neither proven nor

disproven. Does the Hildebrand narrative, for example, have its origin in a period when matriarchy was predominant, and the son therefore was raised by his mother's family without knowing his father? (See Potter [1902], pp. 107f.)

2. In *Untersuchungen und Quellen zur germanischen und romanischen Philologie Johann von Kelle dargebracht von seinen Kollegen und Schülern*. Prager deutsche Studien VIII–IX. Prague, 1908; see further Olrik (1913), pp. 93f.

3. Here §144, n. 2; Olrik (1919a), p. 45.

### V. The Original Form and Development of the Narrative

See pp. 137, 141–143, 144. The oldest name of the chapter is III. "The Relationship between the Recordings," but this is corrected to "The Methods to Determine the Original Form and Development of the Narrative"; and here the first four words are erased, and the chapter has its present title in Disposition II, tentative leaf. See also the introduction to V B and V C. MS designates the manuscript of 1906, T the text published here. Literature younger than the rest of the manuscript, from 1912 onwards. V introduction.

§144. See p. 143. Comment 1916 inserted into the manuscript. There is an older draft (1908?) for this and the following paragraph, which corresponds fairly well to the main text part 1 and then jumps to §145 part 1.

1. This conceptual element may be clear and conscious (re-creation) or dying (thus §143 example 3). A third precondition is not mentioned here: the purely personal-psychological (the author of the narrative and his view of his material).

2. Cf. Olrik's criticism of Müllenhoff's original form of the Starkad material in Olrik (1903–1910) II, pp. 142f., and Olrik (1919a), p. 43.

§145. See previous paragraph. D corresponds to part 1, but not to parts 2 and 3.

1. Cf. here §179; cf. e.g., the methodology in Olrik (1904b) or Olrik (1913).

2. Under this, Olrik has written in pencil: "Lit. Sydow, review of Panzer, *Beowulf, Zeitschrift für deutsches Altertum* (1911)"; see next paragraph.

§146. Cf. p. 141. The location of this and the next paragraph is not certain in Olrik's unnumbered manuscript. I assume this paragraph was written first as a completion of the reference in the previous paragraph (possibly in the fall of 1913, when von Sydow held a seminar with Olrik on *Beowulf* in Copenhagen).

1. Gr + 5 A, BP II 316; cf. Panzer (1910–1912); cf. §150 n. 1, part 2.

§147. See §146. the order of parts 3, 4, 5 (and 6) is not certain in the manuscript.

1. There is a typological similarity between the Babylonian and the

Jewish myth of the deluge, but only individual features are similar in the Babylonian and Jewish creation myths. The Babylonian creation myth may have occasioned the formation of the Jewish myth, but it could not have been the basis for the narrative (Feilberg [1915], pp. 161f., 87f.; *Genesis* III, especially pp. 67ff., 127f.).
2. Thus vv. 887, 2553, 2744. Olrik is referring to Bugge (1890–1892); cf. Olrik's postscript, p. 240.
3. See Olrik (1891), p. 87.
4. §56 n. 5, DgF 470.
5. Cf. von Löwis (1912), pp. 15f. (§70 n. 1).
6. Thus in *Norske Folkeeventyr* (1852) no. 14 (Gr + 8, BP III 94, Moe [1906], pp. 604f.); cf. e.g., *Popular Tales of the West Highlands* I, pp. 244, 330, II; pp. 232, 307, etc.

## V A. The Relationship between Narrative Traditions

See pp. 137, 141, and V B introduction. The chapter indicated in D, 17 March 1905: "The Connected Traditions." In the MS, the paragraphs are marked $\alpha$–$\epsilon$.
§148. MS §$\alpha$.
1. "A much too common expression which cannot be avoided, it does not convey an impression of the real situation."
§149. MS §$\beta$. Last line younger than MS.
1. After this, Olrik has written in pencil: "Ex. *The Dead Helper,* Aarne 505–07, 'The Grateful Dead' (Folklore Society)." Olrik is referring to Gerould (1908), which is about 505–507 in Aarne (1910), p. 22, corresponding to Gr + 67 *The Help of the Dead.* (About this, see BP III 490ff., Ellekilde [1919], pp. 164f.) Among the various tales with the grateful dead as helper (cf. §139 n. 2), the type of the "snake-maiden" exists in most of Europe, especially in the east, but not in Scandinavia; the type of the "traveling companion" (after Hans Christian Andersen's tale of this name) exists only in Scandinavia, the British Isles, and Germany; the type of "the poor corpse" (Gr + 67 A, see GldM I nos. 81, 108) occurs only in Denmark, where it was probably created. Cf. §174 conclusion.
§150. MS §$\gamma$.
1. After this, Olrik crossed out the following example: "The notion of tied-up or imprisoned beasts of prey, whose liberation leads to the end of the world, is common to Scandinavians and Estonians. Its occurrence only among peoples who have been connected historically goes against the opinion that this notion arose independently in several locations" (Olrik [1902], pp. 238ff.). Cf. chapter III, "The Tied-up Beast of Prey," in Olrik (1913), especially p. 164. Between the main text and this crossed-out example, Olrik has written in pencil: "Grendel and the Irish." Here he is referring to the notion of his student von Sydow that the fight of Grendel in *Beowulf* arose under the influence of Irish fairytales (cf. §146 n. 1).
§151. MS §$\delta$. The last two lines in the example younger than MS

(presumably from 1908). In the first sentence, Olrik initially wrote: "cannot be related."

1. On the cover of his draft, Olrik refers to Dähnhardt's statement in *Natursagen* III, p. V, as follows: "Experience has taught me that it is easier to prove the migration of a tale than its independent origin. [The scholar must count on the possibility of migration as a basic rule in all cases, and he will not always be able to ascertain whether it is a case of migration or independent development] . . . Similarity in several motifs is probably always a sign of migration."

2. Olrik wrote in pencil in the margin: "Thor's goats and the butchered beaver (DSt 1910)." See p. 79, where von Sydow demonstrates a striking similarity between the story about Thor's butchered goats and the creation myth of the Omaha Indians about the butchered beaver.

3. Olrik thought that Tylor also treated "tribal ancestor" or "cultural-heroic" myths of this kind in his famous work (see Olrik [1911c], pp. 572ff.), but this is not the case (cf. Tylor [1891] I, pp. 353, 394; II, pp. 274f., 311).

4. Von der Leyen (1902); (cf. von der Leyen [1899], p. 53); Feilberg (1915), pp. 52f.; Feilberg (1899), pp. 41f.

5. Especially the tale about the swan-maidens (Gr + 1; Holmström [1919]; cf. Ellekilde [1919], p. 169, BP II 318, I 21 and §178 n. 2).

6. About such "colliding rocks," see Tylor (1891), I, pp. 347–350; Rohde (1876), p. 184 fn. "Hnitbjörg" in *Edda Snorra Sturlusonar,* pp. 72f., are such colliding rocks.

§152. MS §ε. Example younger than MS, presumably from 1908, at the same time as the expansion of §151 example.

1. Von der Leyen (1902), p. 150; BP I 513, II 394. Olrik's lecture on "The Mead of the Skalds" (from 1908).

### V B. Variant and Doublet

See pp. 137, 141, note to §36. The pages of the manuscript now marked 6–12 were marked α–θ in the beginning, and this means that this chapter is the earliest part of section V, which was originally called III. "The Relationship between the Versions." The original title of the chapter has been erased. "B. Variant and Doublet" is a younger title. After the addition of A, the paragraphs have been marked ζ–ν, i.e., the continuation of A's §§α–ε.

§153. MS §ζ.

1. In *Den ældre Edda,* p. 188; the lay in question is *Brot;* see §34 n. 2.

2. §§96, 98 examples.

§154. MS §γ.

1. *Sakses Danesaga* II, pp. 65–66.

2. Here Norwegian; see Olrik (1892–1894) II, p. 91; cf. §26 examples 1–2.

§155. MS §θ example 1.

1. §36 n. 3.

2. I.e., with the nickname "the Proud."

3. After this, Olrik crossed out the following in the manuscript: "Hakehøj, situated close to those places named after Sigar and Hagbard, was probably meant to be Haki Hámundsson's hill, and only younger doublet forms have made its owner into a doublet of Haki the Viking; also the third Haki. . . . " Olrik explains the first two Hakis as being geographical variants of each other. In the first, he advances through the countryside (§127, the wandering forest); in the second, he sails up the Suså in order to destroy Sigersted (cf. Olrik [1892–1894] II, pp. 248f.).

4. *Sakses Danesaga* I, p. 126 fn.; Kauffmann was the first to demonstrate this, cf. §35 example, §33 example, Olrik (1892–1894) II, pp. 19f.

§156. MS § ι.

1. *Sakses Danesaga* I, pp. 125f.; Olrik (1892–1894) II, p. 23; cf. *Edda Snorra Sturlusonar,* chapter 48.

§157. MS §κ.

1. *Sakses Danesaga* I, p. 97; *Bjarkarímur,* see pp. 64f., pp. 138f.

2. §78 n. 4, *Bjarkarímur,* pp. 71f.; Olrik (1903–1910) I, p. 115.

3. *Bjarkarímur,* pp. 36f., 44ff. Olrik (1903–1910) I, p. 220.

§158. MS §λ.

§159. MS §μ. An older draft for this and the following paragraph with the page number θ exists, on which Olrik has written "not good enough" in pencil. Here the main text is: "The doublet may also have arisen in remote times, even though the double nature in that case is less conspicuous. It flourishes especially in the heroic narrative with its fluid outline and episodic style." The examples are exactly the same.

1. See *Den ældre Edda,* pp. 179f., p. 187; *Völsunga saga,* chapters 21, 29; cf. Ussing (1910), pp. 85ff.

2. *Den ældre Edda,* pp. 204, 221; cf. p. 239; Ussing (1910), pp. 166ff.

§160. MS §ν. ED is identical to this in content but not in form.

### V C. Views on the Structure and Transmission of the Narrative

See pp. 137, 141. In D, 17 March 1905, we find the following "principles of content": the mythic, the simplest narrative, the best narrative (later insertion), the historical [corrected to specified in time (?)], the geographical [corrected to the localized], and the cultural-historical. After V A and V B came into existence with the §§α–ν, and after Olrik wrote the first two paragraphs of C, ο and π, he then arranged the various views of the separate sections C and D in a "temporary draft." With regard to C, he decided on the following order: "The most complete narrative." "The simplest narrative." "What is common to narratives." "The most perfect narrative." "Placement in time." "Typologization." "Arrangement by place." "Arrangement by type and place." "Cultural type." He also followed this system in the first edition of the paragraphs of MS 1906, where he stops at "typologization," as mentioned on p. 141. The most important change in the later 1912 revision is that the views change places: "the most perfect narrative" is inserted between "the most complete narrative" and "the simplest narrative"; "typologization" and "arrangement by place" have also exchanged places. Later, the new Finnish view D, "the most natural narrative," is added; unfortunately, Olrik dropped the final view, "cultural type"; it is not indicated in the new key §161 from 1912 (cf. p. 141).

§161. View D is also missing in this index, but the enumeration of the view in V D corresponds exactly to the disposition "temporary draft" (from 1906): Mythic. Cultural–Historical. Historical. Linguistic.

§162. MS §*o*. Here part 1 is the main text, the rest comment; same items as in T, but in a different order.

   1. See A. Bugge (1904–1906) I, p. 6 (§118 n. 4). < Zimmer (1888), pp. 232f.; (1891), pp. 42f.

   2. *Kalevala* (1907) II, pp. 62ff.

   3. Olrik (1906b), p. 178; cf. §68 and §108.

§163. T = §*π*.

   1. Especially §§84, 91, 95.

   2. §54.

§164. Parts 1 and 2 almost identical to MS §*τ*, parts 3 and 4 a little more expanded and revised.

   1. E.g., about the power of fate (Gr + 68; BP I 276; Ellekilde [1919], p. 174, with reference).

   2. As is the opinion of the British anthropological school; cf. §135, n. 1.

   3. In MS (younger addition), it says: We are more justified in presuming that *the simplest and also the most aesthetically perfect form of a narrative* is the original one (cf. §166, formerly §*ρ*).

§165. Missing in MS.

§166. T revised from MS §*ρ*; there is no example here, and the text after the example is only indicated.

   1. §54 example 2; §56 comment.

§167. Completely new; §161 from 1912 missing; cf. pp. 141–142.

   1. "The view: 'the most natural narrative,' includes the view 'the most perfect narrative' and 'the simplest narrative'" (S 1916); cf. §164 n. 3.

   2. Ibid., p. 41.

   3. Cf. Aarne (1913a), p. 46, pp. 79f.

§168. The examples are missing in the first edition of MS §*σ*; in the second edition the examples are found in §*σ*$^1$: example 2 is identical with T, example 1 is slightly revised in T. Part 2 is missing in *σ*$^1$, and part 3 is considerably expanded in T.

   1. *Danske Folkeviser* 45, 164.

   2. Swedish A; see *Svenska Fornsånger* II, no. 153, p. 346; cf. DgF III, 222.

   3. Olrik crossed out the following: "e.g., that many recordings

from *different regions* agree in this"; cf. example 2.
4. §106 n. 2; cf. §128 example, DgF VIII 57f.
5. The following statement comes after §σ¹ (originally attached to example (1), which Olrik possibly forgot: "The proof of the correctness of the thesis is not only derived from the general genealogical fact that a quality distinguishing the later generations probably goes back to a common tribal ancestor. The versions also testify that these motifs are especially enduring; and one is thus able to deduce that the most enduring is also the oldest."
§169. MS §σ², example missing here.
§170. Younger than MS.
§171. MS §*v*, which also corresponds to §172 part 1. Part 3 about the tale is a comment. After the text, the publisher omitted: "Ex. of incorrect conclusion": see n. 3.
  1. Aarne (1914a), beginning.
  2. §46 n. 1.
  3. Olrik has written "Finn" in pencil above the missing "ex. of incorrect conclusion." Olrik is referring to the Scanian historian Lauritz Weibull, who mocks von Sydow in his article "Den lundensiska Finnsägnen," *Fataburen* (1908): 28–41, because the latter in his "Studier i Finnsägnen och besläktade byggmästarsägner," *Fataburen* (1907): 65–78, 199–218, *Fataburen* (1908): 19–27, claims that the oldest recording of the Finn narrative (in Jens Lauritsøn Wolff's *Encomion Regni Daniæ* [Copenhagen, 1654], pp. 568f.) is further removed from the original form of the narrative than some quite modern narrative records from 1906, which, like the Danish versions (§124, n. 1), omit Finn's and his wife's turning into stone that we know of from Poul Møller's poem (*St. Lawrence*). Olrik agrees with von Sydow: the three modern versions manifest their genuineness in their style and content; Wolff is hesitant in his reproduction of the narrative; the Finn verse especially (Believe me, Finn, I give thee no wages before the church is finished) is essentially not genuine (cf. Olrik [1908a], p. 61). And in an unpublished review of von Sydow's works, Olrik writes the following about Weibull's study: "It contains a couple of most interesting older recordings of the Finn narrative, but—'from a folkloristic point of view'—it is completely naive. The author thinks that he can fully evaluate the recordings from Lund without using all the other recordings of the narrative; he uses the genuineness of one version to prove the spuriousness of another; he believes that a rhymed dialogue in a fairytale is 'a recreated ballad,' that the 'economy' of the narrative can exist only in its lost original form, etc. It is not enough to be an excellent historian; you also have to recognize the character of the material you examine, i.e., possess the *special* method required for its evaluation."
§172. See §171; part 2 is a revision of an edition younger than MS §*v*. After text, "comment" is omitted (see n. 1).
  1. Olrik has written in pencil "heroic poetry, development ≠ chronology [?]," and under that "Herules: Bugge"; here he is referring

to Bugge (1896), pp. 159f.; cf. Olrik (1903–1910) I, pp. 18f., 22.

§173. See p. 141; only slight indication of MS §χ.

1. Therefore, the fairytale type "the poor corpse" (see §149 n. 1), which exists only in Denmark, must be relatively young.

§174. 1. Cf. §171 n. 3, §124 n. 1. In the following paragraph, which is crossed out, Olrik writes: "In many cases, this can be corroborated by the fact that precisely in this area one finds all these natural conditions, cultural conditions, and notions presupposed in the narrative. Ex. The Finn narrative presupposes two narratives, the cheated giant and the discovery of the troll's name; both of these narratives are well known in Northern Europe, and are probably restricted to this area."

2. Olrik continues: Ex. 1 (!) The fairytale about the princess in the mound is exclusively Scandinavian; it presupposes a simpler narrative about the princess [who is hidden in the mound with her sisters so as not to fall into the hands of evil suitors; see *Danmarks Folkesagn* I, p. 9; cf. DS IV no. 1256 and no. 30]; cf. Olrik (1892-1894) II, p. 247, with references; BP III, pp. 445f.

3. Olrik has written: "Moltke Moe: 'Norges Land og Folk' *Nordland* II. . . . " After this, Olrik has written "Aarne," perhaps implying 505, i.e., the type of the dead helper, "the poor corpse," extant only in Denmark (see §149 n. 1).

§175. 1. BP II 439; cf. §100 n. 2.

2. §132 example; §119 example 2; DS II E type 5.

§177. See p. 141.

1. Especially III, p. 148, conclusion; cf. §142 example.

2. I.e., the sword, which had been stuck into a particular tree (or similar token), shows the brother, who stayed at home, that the hero is alive; if it is rusty, for example, the hero is in mortal danger (cf. BP I 545).

§178. MS §φ; cf. p. 142; the genealogical table of fairytales is younger in its present form.

1. See §74 example 1; cf. §63 n. 3, §12 n. 6; BP II 245f., 266ff.

2. Olrik (1892-1894) II, pp. 236ff. Olrik assumes that the ancient taboo still found in Negro tribes, that bride and bridegroom are not allowed to see each other but can meet only at night, lies behind the origin of this fairytale (cf. §12 example; §151 n. 5).

§ 179. Cf. pp. 136, 141. Part 3 and the location of the comment uncertain in the manuscript (loose pages) are inserted by the editor.

1. Krohn (1910), pp. 35f., cf. §167; *Kalevala* (1907–1908) II, pp. 75f.

2. Cf. §88, n. 1; Krohn (1888).

3. The history of the lays in the *Kalevala;* cf. Olrik (1908a), pp. 62f.

4. Cf. Olrik (1907b), p. 62; (1907c), p. 141; (1908c), p. 240; and (1911b), p. 39.

## V D. Views on Narrative Material

See pp. 137, 141; cf. §161 and n.

§181. 1. Cf., e.g., Odin in the Sigurðr narrative; he is at the periphery of the plot, not in the middle of it. See §59 n. 3.

## VI. Concerning the Individual
## Genres of Folklore

### VI A. Tales

See Olrik (1919b), pp. 370–372, Olrik (1904b), p. 1 (= 1919a, pp. 140f.), and idem, p. 41, "Nordisk æventyrliteratur fra de sidste år." 'Lidt om Æventyrene' (DSÆ I, p. 63; cf. II, p. 63; Olrik [1892], pp. 117f.). See especially §5, §46, II C, III, V C, and Appendix B.

### VI B. Heroic Poetry

See pp. 137, 143; this incomplete section has been marked "April 1912" on the cover. In Literature, Chadwick (1912) was later added in the manuscript. A couple of references to Serbian heroic poetry on a special page, partly from Chadwick's book, have been omitted by the editor. The last three words in the section are unclear.

§185. 1. Cf. §7, §67 comment, §195, Olrik (1903–1910) I, introduction, and §56; Olrik (1903–1910) II, §46 Heroic poetry and social sense; Olrik (1909b); Olrik (1919b), p. 370.

2. As is the case in *Beowulf,* where the Anglo-Saxon poet praises Danish, Geatish (Jutish or Gothic), and Swedish heroes (cf. §118 n. 1).

3. See *Kalevala* (1907–1908) II, pp. 82ff.; Olrik (1913), pp. 140 and 200, with references.

4. I.e., the lay of the "widely wandering" singer (Olrik [1903–1910] I, p. 11); cf. §16 example 2; §75 n. 10 and comment 2.

5. Nyrop (1883), pp. 292ff.; Vogt (1876); Olrik (1886).

6. *Kalevala* (1907–1908) II, pp. 101f.

### VI C. Folk Legends

See Olrik (1919b), p. 368, and Olrik (1890–1892b); here especially §5 and IV B, §119f. Localization.

### VI D. Legend and History

See pp. 137, 143. In Literature, Neckel (1910) was added later in the manuscript. §§187–192 are indicated by the nos. 1–6 in the manuscript; §§193–196 are not indicated at all, and for the last three paragraphs the paragraph symbol has been added by the editor.

1. This article addresses Olrik (1890–1892b), pp. 136f., particularly the section on the Tislund stone. In Olrik's papers, one finds a rather sharp reply to Nielsen, which he never printed; it contains a draft of Olrik's principles for oral narrative research from his youth ca. 1893 (cf. Olrik [1890–1892b], p. 153).

§190. 1. See Gravlund (1911–1914), p. 33.

2. Cf. DS VI A types 6–8.

§192. 1. Olrik has written in pencil below: "Gamalt fraa Sætesdal III . . . the sons in the boat," and again below: "the fire at Rurup Nørregård." Olrik refers to Skar (1903-1907) (most likely I, p. 110) and to Fausbøll (1909), pp. 42f.

§193. 1. In 1019, he appears at the end of the list of the king's Scandinavian thanes; in 1032, he appears at the beginning.

2. Cf. Olrik (1903b).

§194. 1. See Feilberg (1920), pp. 105 and 115, with references; Olrik and Ellekilde (1922).

2. The youthful experience on the Orkney Islands has nothing to do with the Danish Earl Sivard (d. 1055); it has presumably been transferred from Earl Sigurðr the Fat on the Orkney Islands, who fell in the great battle at Clontarf in 1014 (Olrik [1903b], p. 214).

§195. 1. Cf. Schütte (1907), p. 198; *Widsith,* p. 48 (§75 comment 2).

2. Cf. §185, beginning.

3. After his campaign in Scotland.

§ 196. 1. Cf. §109, the William Tell legend; §129, example 3 (and §134), the Hagbard and Signe legend.

## Appendix: From the Domain of The Epic Laws

See pp. 138, 140, 144; §75 n. In the early summer of 1916, Olrik intended to divide this section into three parts: I. "The Literature on the Epic Laws," II. "The Patriarchal History of Israel," III. "The Lives of Danish Saints." Under I, the following was found in his papers: "Comments to Gudmund Schütte's doctoral dissertation of 21 March 1907." But in my opinion, there is no reason to print these after the appearance of Olrik (1907e), p. 193. Instead, I have included Olrik's reply to von der Leyen of August 1916, which was actually intended for *Danske Studier,* but I have placed it after the patriarchal history, not before, in order to conclude Olrik's book. The third section is missing, but Olrik incorporated the results of his study in his large, unprinted literary history of the Middle Ages.

### A. The Patriarchal History of Israel

After an examination of Miss Ruth Gerner Lund's paper from November 1915, it was initially Olrik's plan to describe the stories of the patriarchs of Israel *in their entirety* in order to characterize their relationship to the epic laws, emphasizing those factors that distinguish Hebrew narrative poetry from other narrative poetry: the strong religious content and the immense importance of localization. During the editing, Olrik abandoned this plan in favor of another, that of characterizing the major sections: (1) the stories of Abraham, (2) the stories of Jacob, (3) the story of Joseph, and (4) the story of the sons of Jacob, by viewing them in the light of the epic laws. This plan was not carried out either; (in the fall of 1915?) he wrote section 1, 3, and 4, but did not wish to complete section 2, since he had used examples from the story of Jacob in particular in plan I. In this edition, I have chosen to combine the two plans. I print Olrik's general description first (plan I from p. 118, l. 5 to p. 124, l. 5), and then add the description of the major individual sections (plan II, p. 124 l. 8 to p. 133 l. 37). In this way, I believe the material is shown to its best advantage, or, at any rate, better than if I had restricted myself to the younger plan alone. For the sake of coherence, I have included a small section (p. 118 l. 5 to p. 118 l. 28), which Olrik had discarded because it did not fit his new plan II. On the other hand, the following lines have been omitted in the beginning of plan II because they would disrupt the composition of plan I + plan II: "Common to all traditions is the smooth narrative prose, which now and then expands into a certain descriptive fullness, especially at the climax of the plot; in exceptional cases, verses have been used in especially strong statements in which fates are decided." [Continuation p. 124 l. 3.] The immediately preceding section about linguistic schematizing (p. 123 l. 33), without page numbers, is probably a draft for plan II part 2, the story of Jacob; but for the sake of coherence I have placed it at the end of plan I, immediately after the Jacob section that should have been rewritten for plan II, as mentioned above.

1. Cf. §36 and V B, §155f. Cf. III Literature n. 1.

2. P, see 25:8, cf. *Genesis,* pp. 247, 257, 278.

3. Here and in the following, the present translators have used the English Douai-Rheims translation for Olrik's quotes from Genesis.

4. Cf. *Genesis,* p. 489; the real meaning of the name is a reminder of the earlier rule of the Egyptians in the country.

5. There is also a pun on the Hebrew word *me'ab,* i.e., from the father (*Genesis,* p. 219).

6. In the Jacob narratives, there are survivals of a narrative form that made him into a Samson-like giant (the struggle with God, the stone that is erected at the well). The Israelites cultivate strength increasingly less over time; seen from an ethno-psychological point of view, they emphasize cunning instead. (Cf. here pp. 128f., *Genesis,* pp. 359f.).

7. See 12:7; 13:15; 15:7; 17:8; 24:7; 26:3; 28:13; 35:12; 48:4 (*Genesis,* p. 166).

8. Moabites and Ammonites; cf. pp. 121, 126.

9. See, e.g., DS III D types 1–3; cf. *Genesis,* pp. 214f.

10. P. 216.

11. Cf. Feilberg (1915), pp. 138f.: "Furthermore, there are many stories about sunken castles and strongholds, towns and cities, where the scheme is repeated: an ungodly people, who are warned, but persist in their wickedness, or who arrogantly deny shelter and food to poor people or to angels and gods transformed into human beings. A single person among the residents, usually a poor family, kindly opens the door to the guests and is saved, while the castle and the town sink, and all people perish, and a big lake is created.... The well-known ancient narrative about Philemon and Baucis, with whom Zeus and

Hermes found shelter when all other doors were closed to them, belongs to this group. The flood of water broke out from the earth, engulfing everything, while the couple's hut rose like a magnificent temple on pillars, where the two people became priest and priestess until their death (Ovid, *Metamorphoses*, VIII, v. 625); and I almost believe that the account in the Bible about the destruction of Sodom and Gomorrah might belong to the same group. The motif is continuously repeated. In the mountain valleys of the Alps, it is the torrent, the avalanche, or the glacier that suddenly plunges forward, destroying lives and possessions and turning rich and fertile areas into wasteland." Lot, who receives the two wandering angels, is then the personal content of the plot; the strong emphasis on the Sodomites' unchastity (they even want to seduce Lot's guests) is a younger moralistic reflection. But the question raised by Gunkel remains: What were the ancestors of the tribes living in the desert really doing at the mouth of the Jordan?

12. According to *Genesis*, p. 288, this is a very late piece of poetry, far removed from legend tradition.

13. Under this, Olrik has written in blue pencil, "Abraham buys a grave." This story (23) originates from P (see *Genesis*, pp. 273f.) and is "extremely funny and oriental": the purchase of the family grave is meant to be experienced as a significant event.

14. The variant explains that it is not quite untrue that Abraham is Sarah's brother; they are in fact half-siblings (!).

15. Cf. p. 116.

16. See especially *Genesis*, pp. 225–226.

17. See *Genesis*, p. 421, with references.

18. Frequently, the story has a certain broad palpability; when they had cast Joseph into the well, they sat down "to eat bread" (so little did they care about their brother's fate!), and looking up "they saw some Ishmaelites on their way coming from Galaad, with their camels, carrying spices and balm, and myrrh to Egypt." (Concerning the items that were used especially for embalming, see *Genesis*, p. 408.) And Judah said to his brethren: "What will it profit us to kill, brother," etc. (J); distinguishing features are that one of the brothers (Ruben) intends to pull him out of the well secretly, and another (Judah) advises them to sell him; it is, after all, more considerate than killing him. But to actual folk tradition proper, such a waste of motifs is alien. (Cf., e.g., Gr + 13, where the jealous brothers cast the hero into a well in a number of versions; cf. BP I 514; *Genesis* pp. 399, 407, with references.)

19. The Book of Esther (2).

20. Cf. 49:3 and *Genesis*, p. 383.

21. Cf. *Genesis*, p. 477.

## B. Conclusion

Cf. p. 180. Von der Leyen had sent an offprint of his paper to Olrik 29 June 1916; Olrik's reply is contained in a draft of a letter dated 14

August 1916. It is possible that Olrik did not finish the manuscript. Its title has been added by the editor (Hans Ellekilde).

22. Diese unvermeidlichen und inhärenten mängel im material der märchenforschung werden zu leicht von der schule Axel Olriks und auch vom meister selbst übersehen (p. 405).
23. Cf. p. 144.
24. V C, §179 comment.
25. The Law of the Salian Franks.
26. Cf. Dahlerup (1896), pp. 27 and 39.
27. I.e., survivals, remnants.
28. Aarne (1913a).

# D. BIBLIOGRAPHY

Manuscript material in the Danish Folklore Archives (DFS):
DFS 7
  Evald Tang Kristensen's folktales, index.
DFS 9
  Svend Grundtvig's catalogue of folktales I–II. Manuscript. Copenhagen, 1856–1861.
DFS 1906/23
  Original records of legends and folk belief.
DFS 1917/46, 47–48
  Axel Olrik. Danmarks heltedigtning III–IV. Manuscript.
DFS 133–148
  Svend Grundtvig & Jørgen Bloch. Føroyakvæði. Corpus Carminum Færoensium I–XVI. Manuscript. Copenhagen, 1872–1888.

Editions and Translations:
Ágrip
  Dahlerup, Verner, ed. Ágrip af Noregs konunga sögum. Samfund til udgivelse af gammel nordisk litteratur 2. Copenhagen: Møller, 1880.
Ambales saga
  Gollancz, Israel, ed. Hamlet in Iceland being the Icelandic Romantic Ambales Saga. London: Nutt, 1898.
Apuleius's Amor og Psyche
  Nutzhorn, Frederik, trans. Apuleius's Amor og Psyche. Copenhagen: Reitzel, 1867.
Fra Bindestue og Kølle
  Tang Kristensen, Evald, ed. Fra Bindestue og Kølle. Jyske folkeæventyr. 2 vols. Copenhagen: Rom, 1896–1897.

*Biskupa sögur*
Hið íslenzka bókmentafélag, ed. *Biskupa sögur.* 2 vols. Copenhagen: Möller, 1856–1878.

*Bjarkarímur*
Finnur Jónsson, ed. *Hrólfs saga kraka og Bjarkarímur.* Samfund til udgivelse af gammel nordisk litteratur 32. Copenhagen: Møller, 1904.

*Voyage of Bran*
Nutt, Alfred, and K. Meyer, eds. *The Voyage of Bran, Son of Febal, to the Land of the Living.* 2 vols. London: Nutt, 1895–1897.

*Brynhild*
Gjellerup, Karl A., ed. *Brynhild. En tragedie.* Copenhagen: Schou, 1884.

*Carmina Scaldica*
Finnur Jónsson, ed. *Carmina Scaldica. Udvalg af norske og islandske skjaldekvad.* Copenhagen: Gad, 1913.

*DgF*
Grundtvig, Svend, et. al. eds. *Danmarks gamle Folkeviser.* 12 vols. Copenhagen, 1853–1976.

*Danmarks Folkesagn*
Thiele, J. M., ed. *Danmarks Folkesagn.* 3 vols. Copenhagen: Reitzel, 1843–1860.

*Danmarks Trylleformler*
Ohrt, Ferdinand C. P., ed. *Danmarks Trylleformler.* 2 vols. Copenhagen and Kristiania [Oslo]: Gyldendal, 1917–1921.

*Danske folkebøger*
Jacobsen, J. P., R. Paulli, and Jørgen Olrik, eds. *Danske folkebøger fra 16. og 17. Aarhundrede.* 14 vols. Copenhagen: Gyldendal, 1915–1936.

*Danske Folkeviser*
Olrik, Axel, ed. *Danske Folkeviser i udvalg.* 2 vols. Copenhagen: Gyldendal, 1899–1909.

*Danske folkeæventyr*
Grundtvig, Svend, ed. *Danske folkeæventyr.* 3 vols. Copenhagen: Reitzel, 1876–1884.

*DS*
Tang Kristensen, Evald, ed. *Danske Sagn.* 6 vols. Århus & Silkeborg: Zeuner, 1892–1901.

*DSÆ*
Olrik, Axel, ed. *Danske sagn og æventyr fra folkemunde.* 2 vols. Copenhagen: Foreningen "Fremtiden", 1913–1918.

*Dänische Volkslieder*
Warrens, Rosa, trans. *Dänische Volkslieder der Vorzeit.* Hamburg: Hoffman and Campe, 1858.

*Die deutsche Heldensage* (1897) (1913)
Jiriczek, Otto, ed. *Die deutsche Heldensage.* Leipzig: Göschen,

1897; 2nd ed. 1913.

*Deutsche Sagen*
Grimm, Brüder, ed. *Deutsche Sagen*. 3 vols. Berlin: Nicolaische Verlagsbuchhandlung, 1891.

*Den ældre Edda*
Hansen, Olaf, trans. *Den ældre Edda*. Copenhagen: Pio, 1911.

*Edda Snorra Sturlusonar*
Finnur Jónsson, ed. *Edda Snorra Sturlusonar*. Reykjavik: Sigurður Kristjánsson, 1907.

*Eddica Minora*
Heusler, Andreas, and Wilhelm Ranisch, eds. *Eddica Minora*. Dortmund: Ruhfus, 1903.

*English and Scottish Popular Ballads*
Sargent, Helen Child, and George Lyman Kittredge, eds. *The English and Scottish Popular Ballads, Edited from the Collection of Francis James Child*. Boston and New York: Houghton and Mifflin 1883–1898.

*Eskimoiske Eventyr og Sagn*
Rink, Hinrich J., ed. *Eskimoiske Eventyr og Sagn*. 2 vols. Copenhagen: Reitzel, 1866.

*Fagrskinna* (1847)
Munch, P. A., and C. R. Unger, eds. *Fagrskinna. Kortfattet norsk konge-saga fra slutningen af det tolfte eller begyndelsen af det trettende aarhundrede*. Kristiania [Oslo]: Malling, 1847.

*Fagrskinna* (1902–1903)
Finnur Jónsson, ed. *Fagrskinna. Nóregs kononga tal*. Samfund til udgivelse af gammel nordisk litteratur 30. Copenhagen: Møller, 1902–1903.

*Flateyjarbók*
Vigfússon, Guðbrandr, and C. R. Unger, eds. *Flateyjarbók. En Samling af norske Konge-Sagaer med indskudte mindre, Fortællinger om Begivenheder i og udenfor Norge samt Annaler*. 3 vols. Kristiania [Oslo]: Malling, 1860–1868.

*Folkesagn og Folketro i Ods Herred*
Andersen, Lars, ed. *Folkesagn og Folketro i Ods Herred*. Copenhagen: Lehmann & Stage, 1918.

*Folkesangen paa Færøerne*
Thuren, Hjalmar, ed. *Folkesangen paa Færøerne*. Copenhagen: Høst, 1908.

*Vore Folkeviser*
Steenstrup, Johannes, ed. *Vore Folkeviser fra Middelalderen*. Copenhagen: Klein, 1891.

*Fornmanna sögur*
Hið norræna fornfræða félag, ed. *Fornmanna sögur*. 12 vols. Copenhagen: Popp, 1825–1837.

*Færöiske Kvæder*
Hammershaimb, V. U., ed. *Færöiske Kvæder*. 2 vols. Copen-

hagen: Berlings Bogtrykkeri, 1851–1855.
*Færöiske Ordsprog*
Hammershaimb, V. U. "Færöiske Ordsprog." *Antiquarisk Tidsskrift* (1849–1851): 271–340.
*Færøiske Quæder*
Lyngbye, Hans Christian, ed. *Færøiske Quæder om Sigurd Fofners bane og hans Æt.* Randers: Elmenhoff, 1822.
*Færøsk anthologi*
Hammershaimb, V. U., ed. *Færøsk anthologi.* Copenhagen: Møller, [1886]–1891.
*Genesis*
Gunkel, Hermann, trans. *Genesis übersetzt und erklärt.* 3 vols. Göttingen: Vandenhoeck and Ruprecht, 1910. Leipzig: Teubner, 1907–1912.
*GldM*
Grundtvig, Svend, ed. *Gamle danske Minder i Folkemunde.* 3 vols. Copenhagen: Iversen, 1854–1861.
*Grönlandske sagn*
Thalbitzer, William, ed. *Grönlandske sagn om Eskimoernes fortid.* Stockholm: Cederquist, 1913.
*Heimskringla*
Finnur Jónsson, ed. *Heimskringla. Nóregs konunga sögur af Snorri Sturluson.* Samfund til udgivelse af gammel nordisk litteratur 23. 4 vols. Copenhagen: Møller, 1893–1900.
*Helge*
Øhlenschlæger, Adam G. *Helge.* Copenhagen: Brünnich, 1814.
*Historiegubbar*
Bondeson, August, ed. *Historiegubbar på Dal deras sagor och sägner.* Stockholm: Bonnier, 1886.
*Holger Danske*
Ingemann, Bernhard S., ed. *Holger Danske.* Copenhagen: Reitzel, 1893.
*Hrólfs saga kraka*
Finnur Jónsson, ed. *Hrólfs saga kraka og Bjarkarímur.* Samfund til udgivelse af gammel nordisk litteratur 32. Copenhagen, Møller, 1904.
*Die Geschichte von Hrolf Kraki*
Herrmann, Paul, trans. *Die Geschichte von Hrolf Kraki.* Torgau: Jacob, 1905.
*JFm*
Tang Kristensen, Evald, ed. *Jyske Folkeminder.* 13 vols. Copenhagen, 1871–1897.
*Kalevala* (1835)
Lönnrot, Elias, ed. *Kalevala.* Helsingfors, 1835.
*Kalevala* (1907–1908)
Ohrt, Ferdinand, C. P., trans. *Kalevala.* 2 vols. Copenhagen: Gyldendal, 1907–1908.

*Krøniker fra Valdemarstiden*
Olrik, Jørgen, trans. *Krøniker fra Valdemarstiden.* Copenhagen: Schønberg, 1900-1901.
*Landnámabók*
Finnur Jónsson, ed. *Landnámabók. Hauksbók. Sturlubók. Melabók.* Copenhagen: Thiele, 1900.
*Lappiske eventyr og folkesagn*
Qvigstad, J., and G. Sandberg, eds. *Lappiske eventyr og folkesagn.* Kristiania [Oslo]: Cammermeyer, 1887.
*Ljómur*
Jensen, R. "*Ljómur,* et færøisk, gudeligt kvad." *Aarbøger for Nordisk Oldkyndighed og Historie* (1869): 311-338.
*Lyriske digte*
Hauch, Johannes Carsten. *Lyriske digte.* Copenhagen: Reitzel, 1854.
*Natursagen*
Dänhardt, Oskar, ed. *Natursagen.* 4 vols. Leipzig: Teubner, 1907-1912.
*Norröne skrifter*
Bugge, Sophus, ed. *Norröne skrifter af sagnhistorisk indhold.* 3 vols. Kristiania [Oslo]: Brøgger & Christie, 1864-1873.
*Norske Folkeeventyr* (1852)
Asbjørnsen, P. Chr., and Jørgen Moe, eds. *Norske Folkeeventyr.* Kristiania [Oslo]: Dahl, 1852.
*Norske Folkeeventyr* (1871) (1876)
Asbjørnsen, P. Chr., and Jørgen Moe, eds. *Norske Folkeeventyr.* Copenhagen: Gyldendal, 1871; 2nd ed. 1876
*Norske Folkeeventyr* (1914)
Berge, Rikard, ed. *Norske Folkeeventyr.* Kristiania [Oslo]: Cappelen, 1914.
*Norske folkeviser*
Landstad, Magnus Brostrup, ed. *Norske folkeviser.* Kristiania [Oslo]: Tönsberg, 1853.
*Saga Olafs Konungs ens Helga*
Munch, P. A., and C. R. Unger. eds. *Saga Olafs Konungs ens Helga: udförligere saga om Kong Olaf den Hellige efter det ældste fuldstændige pergaments haandskrift i det Store Kongelige Bibliothek i Stockholm.* Kristiania [Oslo]: Werner & Co., 1853.
*Old English Ballads*
Gummere, Francis Barton, ed. *Old English Ballads.* Boston: Ginn & Co., 1894.
*Örvar-Odds saga*
Boer, R. C., ed. *Örvar-Odds saga.* Leiden: Brill, 1888.
*Petit romancero*
Puymaigre, Théodore J. B., ed. *Petit romancero.* Paris: Librairie de la Société Bibliographique, 1878.

*Poetiske Skrifter*
Paludan-Müller, Frederik, ed. *Poetiske Skrifter.* 8 vols. Copenhagen: Reitzel, 1878–1879.
*Popular Tales of the West Highlands*
Campbell, J. F. ed. *Popular Tales of the West Highlands.* 4 vols. London: Gardner, 1890–1893.
*Primavera y flor de romances*
Wolf, Fernando José, ed. *Primavera y flor de romances.* Berlin: Asher, 1856.
*Præsteindberetninger*
Nielsen, Oluf, ed. *Ribe Stifts Beskrivelse 1638. Indberetninger fra Stiftets Præster til Dr. O. Worm. Danske Samlinger* 4:2 (1874–1876): 1–125.
*Den danske Rimkrønike*
Nielsen, Holger. ed. *Den danske Rimkrønike.* Copenhagen: Thiele, 1895–1911.
*Rímnasafn*
Finnur Jónsson, ed. *Rímnasafn. Samling af de ældste islandske rimer.* 2 vols. Samfund til udgivelse af gammel nordisk litteratur 35. Copenhagen: Møller, 1905–1922.
*Rolandskvadet*
Ritto, O. P., trans. *Rolandskvadet.* Copenhagen: Bojesen, 1897.
*Le romancéro populaire*
Doncieux, George, ed. *Le romancéro populaire de la France.* Paris: Bouillon, 1904.
*Sagen, Märchen und Lieder*
Müllenhoff, Karl V., ed. *Sagen, Märchen und Lieder der Herzogthümer Schleswig-Holstein und Lauenburg.* Kiel: Schwerssche Buchhandlung, 1845.
*Sakses Danesaga*
Olrik, Jørgen, trans. *Sakses Danesaga.* 4 vols. Copenhagen: Gad, 1908–1912.
*Saxonis Grammatici Historia Danica*
Müller, Peter E., and Johannes M. Velschow, eds. *Saxonis Grammatici Historia Danica.* 2 vols. Copenhagen: Gyldendal, 1839–1858.
*Schwedische Volkslieder*
Warrens, Rosa, trans. *Schwedische Volkslieder der Vorzeit.* Leipzig: Brockhaus, 1857.
*Segner fraa Bygdom*
Det norske samlaget, ed. *Segner fraa Bygdom.* 3 vols. Kristiania [Oslo], 1871–1879.
*Sicilianische Märchen*
Gonzenbach, Laura, trans. *Sicilianische Märchen.* Leipzig: Engelmann, 1870.
*Skg*
Tang Kristensen, Evald, ed. *Skattegraveren.* 12 vols. Kolding: Jørgensen, 1884–1889.

*Skjaldedigtning*
  Finnur Jónsson, ed. *Den norsk-islandske skjaldedigtning.* Vols
  1A–2A (transcription) and 1B–2B (corrected text). Copenhagen:
  Gyldendal, 1908–1915.
*Sturlunga saga* (1878)
  Gudbrand Vigfusson, ed. *Sturlunga saga including the Islen-
  dinga Saga of Lawman Sturla Thordsson and other Works.* 2
  vols. Oxford: Clarendon, 1878.
*Sturlunga saga* (1904)
  Kålund, Kr., trans. *Sturlunga saga i dansk oversættelse.* 2 vols.
  Copenhagen and Kristiana [Oslo]: Gyldendal, 1904.
*Sturlunga saga* (1906–1911)
  Kålund, Kr. ed. *Sturlunga saga.* 2 vols. Copenhagen & Kris-
  tiania [Oslo]: Gyldendal, 1906–1911.
*Sven Aggesøns værker*
  Gertz, M. Cl., trans. *En ny text af Sven Aggesøns værker
  genvunden paa grundlag af Codex Arnæmagnæanus 33, 4to.*
  Copenhagen: Gyldendal, 1916.
*Svenska Folkböcker*
  Bäckström, Per Olof, ed. *Svenska Folkböcker.* 2 vols. Stock-
  holm: Bohlin, 1845–1848.
*Svenska folke-sagor och äfventyr*
  Hyltén-Cavallius, Gunnar Olof, and George Stephens. *Svenska
  folk-sagor och äfventyr.* 2 vols. Stockholm: Bohlin, 1844–1849.
*Svenska Fornsånger*
  Arwidsson, Adolf Iwar, ed. *Svenska Fornsånger:* 3 vols. Stock-
  holm: Norstedt, 1834–1842.
*Sønderjydske folkesagn*
  Ohrt, Ferdinand, C. R., ed. *Udvalgte Sønderjydske folkesagn.*
  Copenhagen: Schønberg, 1919.
*Tales of the Punjab*
  Steel, Flora Annie, ed. *Tales of the Punjab.* London & New
  York: Macmillan, 1894.
*Widsith*
  Chambers, Raymond Wilson, ed. *Widsith. A Study in Old
  English Heroic Legend.* Cambridge: Cambridge Univ. Pr., 1912.

Studies:

Aagard (1802)
  Aagard, Knud. *Physisk, oeconomisk og topografisk beskrivelse
  over Thye.* Viborg: Forfatterens Forlag, 1802.
Aarne (1910)
  Aarne, Antti. *Verzeichnis der Märchentypen. FF Communi-
  cations* 3 (1910).
Aarne (1913a)
  Aarne, Antti. *Leitfaden der vergleichenden Märchenforschung.
  FF Communications* 13 (1913).

Aarne (1913b)
    Aarne, Antti. *Die Tiere auf der Wanderschaft. FF Communications* 11 (1913).
Aarne (1914a)
    Aarne, Antti. *Übersicht der Märchenliteratur. FF Communications* 14 (1914).
Aarne (1914b)
    Aarne, Antti. *Der tiersprachenkundige Mann und seine neugierige Frau. FF Communications* 15 (1914).
Ahlström (1895)
    Ahlström, Axel. "Om Folksagorna." *Svenska Landsmålen* 11:1 (1895): 5–86.
Ambrosiani (1907)
    Ambrosiani, Sune. *Odinkultens härkomst.* Stockholm: Cederquist, 1907.
Anderson (1923)
    Anderson, Walter. *Kaiser und Abt. FF Communications* 42 (1923).
d'Arbois de Jubainville (1883–1902)
    d'Arbois de Jubainville, Henry. *Cours de Littérature Celtique.* 5 vols. Paris: Fontemoing, 1883–1902.
Barbeau (1915)
    Barbeau, Charles M. *Huron and Wyandot Mythology.* Ottawa: Government Printing Bureau, 1915.
Beatty (1914)
    Beatty, Arthur. "Ballad, Tale, and Tradition: A Study in Popular Literary Origins." *Publications of the Modern Language Association of America* 29. New Series 22 (1914): 473–498.
Bédier (1895)
    Bédier, Joseph. *Les fabliaux.* Paris: Bouillon, 1895.
Bergström (1905)
    Bergström, L. "Heliga tal och Olyckstal." *Nordisk tidskrift för Vetenskap, Konst och Industri* (1905): 493–509.
Bertram (1915)
    Bertram, Agnete. "De tre Helligaftener. En studie i folkelig fortællestil." *Edda* 3 (1915): 101–115.
Beyer (1791)
    Beyer, Seyer Mahling. *En geographisk-historisk og oeconomisk, physisk-antiqvarisk Beskrivelse over Bringstrup og Sigersted Sogne ved Ringsted.* Sorø, 1791.
Boas (1895)
    Boas, Franz. *Indianische Sagen von der Nordpacifischen Küste Amerikas.* Berlin: Asher, 1895.
BP
    Bolte, Johannes, and Georg Polivka. *Anmerkungen zu den Kinder und Hausmärchen der Brüder Grimm.* 5 vols. Leipzig: Dieterische Verlagsbuchhandlung, 1913–1932.
A. Bugge (1904–1906)
    Bugge, Alexander. *Vikingerne. Billeder fra vore forfædres*

*liv.* 2 vols. Copenhagen & Kristiania [Oslo]: Gyldendal, 1904–1906.

Bugge (1881–1889)
Bugge, Sophus. *Studier over de nordiske Gude- og Heltesagns Oprindelse.* Kristiania [Oslo]: Cammermeyer, 1881–1889.

Bugge (1890–1892)
Bugge, Sophus. "Røveren ved Gråsten og Beowulf." *Dania* 1 (1890–1892): 233–236.

Bugge (1891)
Bugge, Sophus. "Harpens Kraft. Et Bidrag til den nordiske Balladedigtnings Historie, forfattet under Medvirkning af Professor Moltke Moe." *Arkiv för nordisk filologi* 7 (1891): 97–141.

Bugge (1896)
Bugge, Sophus. *Helge-digtene i den ældre Edda deres hjem og forbindelser.* Copenhagen: Gad, 1896.

Bugge (1900)
Bugge, Sophus. "Mythiske Sagn om Halvdan Svarte og Harald Haarfagre." *Arkiv för nordisk filologi* 16 (1900): 1–37.

Bugge (1907)
Bugge, Sophus. *Populær-videnskabelige Foredrag: efterladte arbeider.* Kristiania [Oslo]: Aschehoug, 1907.

Chadwick (1912)
Chadwick, H. Munro. *The Heroic Age.* Cambridge: Cambridge Univ. Pr., 1912.

A. Christensen (1916)
Christensen, Arthur. "Trebrødre- og tobrødre-stamsagn: en studie i sammenlignende sagnforskning." *Danske Studier* 13 (1916): 45–86.

A. Christensen (1917)
Christensen, Arthur. "Lidt om vandrende Motiver i Evald Tang Kristensens Molbo- og Aggerbohistorier." *Danmarks Folkeminder* 17 (1917): 52–62.

Christensen (1906)
Christensen, Georg. "H. C. Andersen og de danske folkeeventyr." *Danske Studier* 3 (1906): 103–112.

Christiansen (1915)
Christiansen, Reidar Th. "Nogen iagttagelser over et par 'episke love' indenfor to eventyrgrupper (Aarnes Märchentypen 332 og 613)." *Danske Studier* 12 (1915): 71–89.

Cox (1895)
Cox, Marian R. *An Introduction to Folklore.* London: Nutt, 1895.

Dahlerup (1896)
Dahlerup, Verner. *Det danske sprogs historie i almenfattelig fremstilling.* Copenhagen: Salmonsen, 1896.

Dennett (1897)
Dennett, R. E. "Notes on the Folklore of the Fjort." *Publications of the Folklore Society* 41 (1897): 1–24.

Dessoir (1906)
Dessoir, Max. *Aesthetik und allgemeine Kunstwissenschaft in*

den Grundzügen dargestellt. Stuttgart: Enke, 1906.

Diels (1897)
Diels, H. "Über Anaximanders Kosmos." Archiv für Geschichte der Philosophie 10 (1897): 228–237.

Diels (1902)
Diels, H. "Ein orphischer Demeterhymnus." Festschrift Theodor Gomperz dargebracht zum siebzigsten Geburtstage am 29. März 1902. Vienna: Hölder, 1902. 1–15.

Ellekilde (1917)
Ellekilde, Hans. "Bjørnemanden." Festskrift til Evald Tang Kristensen paa hans halvtredsaarsdag som folkemindesamler den 31 december 1917. Ed. Gunnar Knudsen. Copenhagen: Schønberg, 1917. 192–237.

Ellekilde (1919)
Ellekilde, Hans. "Nyt fra æventyr-forskningen." Danske Studier 16 (1919): 162–179.

Ellekilde (1923)
Ellekilde, Hans. "Levn." Salmonsens Konversations Leksikon 15. Copenhagen: Schultz, 1923. 744.

Erslev (1892)
Erslev, Kristian. Grundsætninger for historisk Kildekritik. Copenhagen: Erslev, 1892.

Erslev (1902–1904)
Erslev, Kristian. "Nils Kjeldsen den 28. Februar 1864." Historisk Tidsskrift 7:4 (1902–1904): 145–270.

Erslev (1911)
Erslev, Kristian. Historisk teknik. Den historiske undersøgelse fremstillet i sine grundlinier. Copenhagen: Erslev, 1911.

Fausbøl (1909)
Fausbøl, J. "En Slægts Historie i Rurup og Mandbjerg samt Fortællinger om Forholdene der." Sønderjydske Aarbøger 10 (1909): 23–78.

Fechner (1876)
Fechner, Gustav T. Vorschule der Aesthetik. 2 vols. Leipzig: Breitkopf & Härtel, 1876.

Feilberg (1886–1914)
Feilberg, H. F. Bidrag til en ordbog over jyske almuesmål. 4 vols. Copenhagen: Thiele, 1886–1914.

Feilberg (1892–1894a)
Feilberg, H. F. "Hvorledes opstår sagn i vore dage?" Dania 2 (1892–1894): 81–125.

Feilberg (1892–1894b)
Feilberg, H. F. "Tallene i folkets brug og tro." Dania 2 (1892–1894): 185–220.

Feilberg (1894)
Feilberg, H. F. "Wie sich Volkmärchen verbreiten." Am Ur-Quell 5 (1894): 165–169, 215–218, 239–241, 272–275.

Feilberg (1898)
Feilberg, H. F. "Gåder." *Aarbog for Dansk Kulturhistorie* (1898): 10–76.
Feilberg (1899)
Feilberg, H. F. "Ilden—Arnen—Hjemmet." *Aarbog for Dansk Kulturhistorie* (1899): 36–75.
Feilberg (1904)
Feilberg, H. F. *Jul.* 2 vols. Copenhagen: Det Schubotheske forlag, 1904.
Feilberg (1914)
Feilberg, H. F. *Sjæletro.* Copenhagen: Schønberg, 1914.
Feilberg (1915)
Feilberg, H. F. *Skabelsessagn og flodsagn.* Copenhagen & Kristiania [Oslo]: Gyldendal, 1915.
Feilberg (1920)
Feilberg, H. F. "Holger Danske og Antikrist." *Danske Studier* 17 (1920): 97–125.
Fritzner
Fritzner, Johan. *Ordbog over Det gamle norske Sprog.* 3 vols. Kristiania [Oslo], 1886–1896.
van Gennep (1908–1914)
van Gennep, Arnold. *Religions mœurs et legendes: essais d'ethnographie et de linguistique.* 5 vols. Paris: Mercure, 1908–1914.
Gerould (1908)
Gerould, Gordon H. *The Grateful Dead: the history of a folk story.* London: Nutt, 1908.
Gravlund (1911–1914)
Gravlund, Thorkild. *Dansk Folkekarakter: Sjællændere og Jyder.* 2 vols. Copenhagen: Schønberg, 1911–1914.
Gravlund (1916)
Gravlund, Thorkild. *Landsmands Lov: Folkelige iagttagelser.* Copenhagen & Kristiania [Oslo]: Gyldendal, 1916.
Gravlund (1917)
Gravlund, Thorkild. *Dansk Bygd.* Copenhagen & Kristiania [Oslo]: Gyldendal, 1917.
Gr
DFS 9
Grundtvig (1867)
Grundtvig, Svend. *Udsigt over den nordiske oldtids heroiske digtning. Tre forelæsninger.* Copenhagen: Gyldendal, 1867.
Grundtvig (1881)
Grundtvig, Svend. *Elverskud.* Copenhagen: Thiele, 1881.
Hackman (1904)
Hackman, Oskar. *Die Polyphemsaga in der Volksüberlieferung.* Helsingfors: Frenckell, 1904.
Hallström (1912)
Hallström, Gustaf. "Kättil okristen." *Meddelanden från*

*Östergötlands Fornminnesförening.* Ed. O. Klockhoff. Linköping: Östgöta Correspondentens Boktryckeri, 1912. 33–43.

Hart (1907)
Hart, Walter Morris. *Ballad and Epic. A Study in the Development of the Narrative Art.* Studies and Notes in Philology and Literature 11. Boston: Ginn & Co., 1907.

Hartland (1891)
Hartland, Edwin Sidney. *The Science of Fairy Tales: An Inquiry into Fairy Mythology.* London: Scott, 1891.

Hartland (1894–1896)
Hartland, Edwin Sidney. *Legend of Perseus.* 3 vols. London: Nutt, 1894–1896.

Hellquist (1903–1906)
Hellquist, Elof. *Studier öfver de svenska sjönamnen. Bidrag till kännedom om de Svenska landsmålen ock Svensket folkliv* 20. Stockholm: Norstedt, 1903–1906.

Heusler (1901)
Heusler, Andreas. "Die altnordische Rätsel." *Zeitschrift des Vereins für Volkskunde* 11 (1901): 117–149.

Heusler (1902a)
Heusler, Andreas. "Die Lieder der Lücke im Codex Regius der Edda." *Germanistische Abhandlungen Hermann Paul zum 17 März 1902 dargebracht.* Strassburg: Trübner, 1902. 1–98.

Heusler (1902b)
Heusler, Andreas. "Der Dialog in der altgermanischen erzählenden Dichtung." *Zeitschrift für deutsches Altertum und deutsche Literatur* 46 (1902): 169–284.

Heusler (1905)
Heusler, Andreas. *Lied und Epos in germanischer Sagendichtung.* Dortmund: Ruhfus, 1905.

Heusler (1908)
Heusler, Andreas. *Die gelehrte Urgeschichte im altisländischen Schrifttum.* Berlin: Verlag der königlichen Akademie der Wissenschaften, 1908.

Hjelholt (1917)
Hjelholt, Holger. "Kultur og folkeminder." Rev. of *Hemmabyarna. Världsbetraktelser i femton kapitel* by Hans Larsson. *Danske Studier* 14 (1917): 156–157.

Holmström (1919)
Holmström, Helge. *Studier över svanjungfrumotivet i Volundarkvida och annorstädes.* Malmö: Maiander, 1919.

Jacobsen (1913)
Jacobsen, J. P. *Heros og helgen.* Copenhagen & Kristiania [Oslo]: Gyldendal, 1913.

Jensen (1871)
Jensen, R. "Rettelser til Oversættelsen af Ljómur." *Aarbøger for Nordisk Oldkyndighed og Historie* (1871): 227–228.

Jónsson (1894–1902)
Jónsson, Finnur. *Den oldnorske og oldislandske litteraturs historie.* 3 vols. Copenhagen: Gad, 1894–1902.
Jónsson (1899)
Jónsson, Finnur. "Sagnet om Harald hårfagre som Dovrefostre." *Arkiv för nordisk filologi* 15 (1899): 262–267.
Jónsson (1907)
Jónsson, Finnur. *Den islandske litteraturs historie.* Copenhagen: Gad, 1907.
Jørgensen (1912)
Jørgensen, Ellen. "Djævelen i Vitskøl kloster." *Danske Studier* 9 (1912): 15–17.
Kauffmann (1902)
Kauffmann, Fr. *Balder, Mythus und Sage, nach ihren dichterischen und religiösen. Elementen untersucht.* Strassburg: Trübner, 1902.
Ker (1897)
Ker, William P. *Epic and Romance. Essays on Medieval Literature.* London: Macmillan, 1897.
Kierckebye (1866–1867)
Kierckebye, J. "Ribe Bisp og Byhyrde for Kong Valdemar." *Jyske Samlinger* 1 (1866–1867): 165–172.
Kristensen (1907)
Kristensen, Marius. "Abbeden og hans kok." *Danske Studier* 4 (1907): 145–146.
Kristensen (1914)
Kristensen, Marius. "Til Johannes Ewalds Orlogssang." *Danske Studier* 11 (1914): 97–103.
J. Krohn (1888)
Krohn, J. "Die Entstehung der einheitlichen Epen im allgemeinen." *Zeitschrift für Völkerpsychologie und Sprachwissenschaft* 18 (1888): 59–68.
Krohn (1888)
Krohn, Kaarle. *Bär (Wolf) und Fuchs. Eine nordische Tiermärchenkette.* Helsingfors: Druckerei der Finnischen Litteratur-Gesellschaft, 1888.
Krohn (1903–1910)
Krohn, Kaarle. *Kalevalan runojen historia.* 7 vols. Helsingfors: Seuran Kirjapainon, 1903–1910.
Krohn (1910)
Krohn, Kaarle. "Über die finnische folkloristische Methode." *Finnisch-ugrische Forschungen* 10 (1910): 33–43.
Krohn (1912)
Krohn, Kaarle. Rev. of *Altgermanische Religionsgeschichte* by Richard M. Meyer. *Göttingische gelehrte Anzeigen* (1912): 193–223.
Köhler (1898–1900)
Köhler, Reinhold. *Kleinere Schriften zur neueren Literaturge-*

*schichte, Volkskunde und Wortforschung.* 3 vols. Berlin: Felber, 1898-1900.

Lang (1885)
    Lang, Andrew. *Custom and Myth.* London: Longman, Green & Co., 1885.
Larsson (1912)
    Larsson, Hans. *Hemmabyarna. Världsbetraktelser i femton Kapitel.* Stockholm: Bonnier, 1912.
Larsson (1914)
    Larsson, Hans. *Poesiens logik.* Lund: Gleerup, 1914.
Lehmann (1914)
    Lehmann, Alfred. *Die Hauptgesetze des menschlichen Gefühlslebens.* Leipzig: Reisland, 1914.
von der Leyen (1899)
    von der Leyen, Friedrich. *Das Märchen in den Göttersagen der Edda.* Berlin: Reimer, 1899.
von der Leyen (1902)
    von der Leyen, Friedrich. "Kleine Studien zur Deutschen Mythologie." *Germanistische Abhandlungen,* ed. Hermann Paul. Strassburg: Trübner, 1902, 143-166.
von der Leyen (1908)
    von der Leyen, Friedrich. *Der Gefesselte Unhold: eine mythologische Studie.* Prague: Prager Deutsche Studien, 1908.
von der Leyen (1916)
    von der Leyen, Friedrich. "Aufgaben und Wege der Märchenforschung." In *Aufsätze zur Kultur-und Sprachgeschichte vornehmlich des Orients Ernst Kuhn zum 70. Geburtstage am 7. Februar 1916 gewidmet von Freunden und Schülern.* Ed. L. Scherman and C. Bezold. Munich: Breslau, 1916, 400-412.
Liestöl (1918)
    Liestöl, Knut. "Litterære eventyr og segner i folketraditionen." *Maal og Minne* (1918): 89-105.
Lindholm (1884)
    Lindholm, P. A. *Hos Lappbönder.* Stockholm: Bonnier, 1884.
Lund (1908)
    Lund, Astrid. "Indiansk sagndigtning og de episke love." *Danske Studier* 5 (1908): 175-188.
Lundell (1903-1906)
    Lundell, J. A. *Bidrag til Kännedom om De Svenska Landsmålen ock Svenskt Folkliv. Svenska Landsmålen* 20:1 (1903-1906).
Løffler (1876a)
    Løffler, J. B. "Vestervig Kloster og Liden Kirstins Grav." *Aarbøger for Nordisk Oldkyndighed og Historie* (1876): 1-52.
Løffler (1876b)
    Løffler, J. B. "Et Sagn fra Faareveile Kirke." *Illustreret Tidende* 18, 10 December 1876: 1.
von Lövis (1912)
    von Lövis, August A. *Der Held im deutschen und russischen*

*Märchen.* Jena: Diederich, 1912.

Mannhardt (1875–1877)
Mannhardt, Wilhelm. *Antike Wald- und Feldkulte.* Berlin: Gebrüder Borntraeger, 1875–1877.

Mansikka (1909)
Mansikka, Viljo J. *Über russische Zauber-formeln mit Berüchsicktigung der Blut- und Verrenkungssegen.* Helsinki: Druckerei der Finnischen Literaturgesellschaft, 1909.

Meier (1909)
Meier, John. *Werden und Leben des Volksepos.* Halle: Niemeyer, 1909.

Meyer (1906a)
Meyer, Richard M. *Deutsche Stilistik.* Munich: Beck, 1906.

Meyer (1906b)
Meyer, Richard M. *Kriterien der Aneignung.* Leipzig: Teubner, 1906.

Meyer (1906c)
Meyer, Richard M. "Mythologische Fragen." *Archiv für Religionswissenschaft* 9 (1906): 417–428.

Meyer (1913)
Meyer, Richard M. "Die Zwangsläufigkeit literarischer Formen." *Internationale Monatsschrift für Wissenschaft, Kunst und Technik* 7 (1913): 707–720.

Moe (1895)
Moe, Moltke. "Æventyri paa vandring." *Syn og Segn* 1 (1895): 87–115.

Moe (1906)
Moe, Moltke. "Finnerne i gamle historiske sagn." *Topografisk-Statistisk Beskrivelse over Finmarkens Amt* 2 (1906): 581–665.

Moe (1908a)
Moe, Moltke. "Finnkongjens dotter." *Sproglige og historiske afhandlinger viede Sophus Bugges minde.* Kristiania [Oslo]: Aschehoug, 1908. 263–267.

Moe (1908b)
Moe, Moltke. "Overnaturlige væsener og overtro." *Topografisk-Statistisk Beskrivelse over Nordlands Amt* 2. Ed. Amund Helland. Kristiania [Oslo]: Aschehoug, 1908. 415–543.

Moe (1909)
Moe, Moltke. "Det mytiske tænkesæt." *Maal og Minne* (1909): 1–16.

Moe (1914)
Moe, Moltke. "Episke grundlove." *Edda* 2 (1914): 1–16, 233–249.

Moe (1915)
Moe, Moltke. "Episke grundlove." *Edda* 4 (1915): 85–126.

Moe (1917)
Moe, Moltke. "Episke grundlove." *Edda* 7 (1917): 72–88.

P. Müller (1817–1820)
Müller, Peter E. *Sagabibliothek med Anmærkninger og indle-*

*dende Afhandlinger.* 3 vols. Copenhagen: Schultz, 1817–1820.

P. Müller (1823)
    Müller, Peter E. *Critisk Undersögelse af Danmarks og Norges Sagnhistorie eller om Troværdigheden af Saxos og Snorros Kilder.* Copenhagen: Popp, 1823.

Müller (1892–1894)
    Müller, Theodor A. "En folkloristisk Methode og Theori." *Dania* 2 (1892–1894): 229–251.

Neckel (1910)
    Neckel, Gustav. "Etwas von germanischer Sagenforschung." *Germanisch-Romanische Monatschrift* 2 (1910): 1–14.

Nielsen (1892–1894)
    Nielsen, O. "Bemærkninger om Nutidens danske Folkesagn." *Dania* 2 (1892–1894): 35–48.

Nutt (1899)
    Nutt, Alfred. *Celtic and Mediæval Romance.* Popular Studies in Mythology, Romance and Folklore 1. London: Nutt, 1899.

Nyrop (1883)
    Nyrop, Kristoffer. *Den oldfranske Heltedigtning.* Copenhagen: Reitzel, 1883.

Nyrop (1901)
    Nyrop, Kristoffer. "Elverskud." *Dania* 8 (1901): 211–220.

Nyrop (1907)
    Nyrop Kristoffer. *Toves tryllering.* Copenhagen: Gyldendal, 1907.

Ohrt (1916)
    Ohrt, Frederik C. P. "Wodans eller Kristi ridt." Rev. of *Die finnischen und nordischen Merseburgerspruches* by Reidar Th. Christiansen. *Danske Studier* 13 (1916): 189–193.

Olrik (1886)
    Olrik, Axel. "Middelalderens vandrende spillemænd i Norden og deres visesang." *Opuscula Philologica* (1886): 1–11.

Olrik (1889)
    Olrik, Axel. "Om Sønderjyllands folkeviser." *Sønderjydske Aarbøger* 1 (1889): 246–296.

Olrik (1890–1892a)
    Olrik, Axel. "Dansk Folkemindeliteratur 1891." *Dania* 1 (1890–1892): 253–260.

Olrik (1890–1892b)
    Olrik, Axel. "Tre danske folkesagn. 1. Et Starkadssagn fra Sønderjylland. 2. Tislundstenen. 3. Dannevirke og Dronning Tyre." *Dania* 1 (1890–1892): 135–153.

Olrik (1890–1892c)
    Olrik, Axel. "Røveren ved Gråsten og Beowulf." *Dania* 1 (1890–1892): 236–245.

Olrik (1891)
    Olrik, Axel. Rev. of *Studier over de nordiske Gude-Heltesagns*

*Oprindelse* 1:3 by Sophus Bugge. *Arkiv för nordisk filologi* 7 (1891): 86–89.

Olrik (1892)
Olrik, Axel. "Märchen in Saxo Grammaticus." *Zeitschrift des Vereins für Volkskunde* 2 (1892): 117–123.

Olrik (1892–1894)
Olrik, Axel. *Kilderne til Sakses Oldhistorie.* 2 vols. Copenhagen: Wroblewski, 1892; Gad, 1894.

Olrik (1894a)
Olrik, Axel. "Bråvallakvadets kæmperække. Tekst og oplysninger." *Arkiv för nordisk filologi* 10 (1894): 223–287.

Olrik (1894b)
Olrik, Axel. "Skjoldungasaga i Arngrim Jonssons Udtog." *Aarbøger for Nordisk Oldkyndighed og Historie* (1894): 83–164.

Olrik (1895)
Olrik, Axel. "Lunds Sprogkundskab og Opfattelse af Folkeoverleveringer." *Hr. L. Lund og "Professorerne."* Copenhagen: Erslev, 1895. 43–48.

Olrik (1898)
Olrik, Axel. "Tvedelingen af Sakses kilder, et genmæle." *Arkiv för nordisk filologi* 14 (1898): 47–93.

Olrik (1899)
Olrik, Axel. "Amledsagnet på Island." *Arkiv för nordisk filologi* 15 (1899): 360–376.

Olrik (1901)
Olrik, Axel. "Odinsjægeren i Jylland." *Dania* 8 (1901): 139–173.

Olrik (1902)
Olrik, Axel. "Om Ragnarok." *Aarbøger for Nordisk Oldkyndighed og Historie* (1902): 157–291.

Olrik (1902–1914)
Olrik, Axel. *Om Ragnarok.* 2 vols. Copenhagen: Gad, 1902–1914.

Olrik (1903a)
Olrik, Axel. Rev. of *Balder, Mythus und Sage, nach ihren dichterischen und religiösen Elementen untersucht* by Fr. Kauffmann. *Dania* 10 (1903): 181–184.

Olrik (1903b)
Olrik, Axel. "Sivard den digre, en vikingesaga fra de danske i Nordengland." *Arkiv för nordisk filologi* 19 (1903): 199–223.

Olrik (1903–1910)
Olrik, Axel. *Danmarks heltedigtning. En oltidsstudie.* 2 vols. Copenhagen: Gad, 1903–1910.

Olrik (1904a)
Olrik, Axel. "E. T. Kristensen som skattegraver." *Dansk folketidende* 45 (1904): 358–359.

Olrik (1904b)
Olrik, Axel. "Kong Lindorm." *Danske Studier* 1 (1904): 1–34.

Olrik (1905)
Olrik, Axel. "Tordenguden og hans dreng." *Danske Studier* 2 (1905): 129–146.
Olrik (1906a)
Olrik, Axel. "Riboldvisen." Rev. of *Nogle folkeviseredaktioner: Bidrag til visekritiken* by Ernst von der Recke. *Danske Studier* 3 (1906): 40–42.
Olrik (1906b)
Olrik, Axel. "Riboldvisen." *Danske Studier* 3 (1906): 175–221.
Olrik (1907a)
Olrik, Axel. *Nordisk aandsliv i vikingetid og tidlig middelalder.* Copenhagen and Kristiania [Oslo]: Gyldendal, 1907.
Olrik (1907b)
Olrik, Axel. "Forårsmyten hos finnerne." Rev. of *Finnische beiträge zur germanischen mythologie* by Kaarle Krohn. *Danske Studier* 4 (1907): 62–64.
Olrik (1907c)
Olrik, Axel. "Et finsk sidestykke til Baldersagnet." Rev. of *Lemminkäinens tod < Christi > Balders tod* by Kaarle Krohn. *Danske Studier* 4 (1907): 141–142.
Olrik (1907d)
Olrik, Axel. "Sophus Bugge." *Danske Studier* 4 (1907): 180–192.
Olrik (1907e)
Olrik, Axel. "Episke love i Gote-ættens oldsagn." Rev. of *Oldsagn om Godtjod, bidrag til etnisk kildeforsknings metode med særligt henblik på folke-stamsagn* by Gudmund Schütte. *Danske Studier* 4 (1907): 193–201.
Olrik (1908a)
Olrik, Axel. "Nyt fra folkemindeforskningen." *Danske Studier* 5 (1908): 60–64.
Olrik (1908b)
Olrik, Axel. "Episke love i folkedigtningen." *Danske Studier* 5 (1908): 69–89.
Olrik (1908c)
Olrik, Axel. "Finsk og lappisk mytologi." *Danske Studier* 5 (1908): 240–241.
Olrik (1908d)
Olrik, Axel. Rev. of *Oldsagn om Godtjod: vore forfædres land, folk og race* by Gudmund Schütte. *Folklore* 19 (1908): 353–359.
Olrik (1908e)
Olrik, Axel. "Gotiske Heltesagn." *Verdenshistorien i Skildringer og Livsbilleder* 1 (1908): 426–444.
Olrik (1908f)
Olrik, Axel. "Folkedigtningens episke love." *Nordisk tidskrift för Vetenskap, Konst och Industri* (1908): 547–554.
Olrik (1909a)
Olrik, Axel. "Epische Gesetze der Volksdichtung." *Zeitschrift*

*für Deutsches Alterthum* 51 (1909): 1–12.
Olrik (1909b)
Olrik, Axel. "Heltedigtningens udspring." Rev. of *Geschichtliches und Mytisches in der germanischen Heldensage* by Andreas Heusler and "Some disputed questions in the Beowulf-criticism" by Will W. Laurence (*Publications of the Modern Language Association of America 24*). *Danske Studier* 6 (1909): 188–191.
Olrik (1911a)
Olrik, Axel. "En oldtidshelligdom." *Danske Studier* 8 (1911): 1–14.
Olrik (1911b)
Olrik, Axel. "Nyere myteforskning." *Danske Studier* 8 (1911): 37–40.
Olrik (1911c)
Olrik, Axel. "Myterne om Loke." *Festskrift til H. F. Feilberg.* *Danske Studier* 8 (1911): 548–593.
Olrik (1912)
Olrik, Axel. "Glemsomhed." *Danske Studier* 9 (1912): 145–151.
Olrik (1913)
Olrik, Axel. "Ragnarokforestillingernes udspring." *Danske Studier* 10 (1913): 1–283.
Olrik (1914)
Olrik, Axel. "Goter og Tjerkesser i 4de årh. e. Kr." *Danske Studier* 11 (1914): 9–20.
Olrik (1915a)
Olrik, Axel. "Moltke Moe: personlige minder." *Danske Studier* 12 (1915): 1–55.
Olrik (1915b)
Olrik, Axel. *Personal Impressions of Moltke Moe. FF Communications* 17 (1915).
Olrik (1917a)
Olrik, Axel. "Didrik af Bern." *Salmonsens Konversations Leksikon* 6. Copenhagen: Schultz, 1917.
Olrik (1917b)
Olrik, Axel. "Eddamytologien." *Nordisk tidskrift för Vetenskap, Konst och Industri* (1917): 81–93.
Olrik (1919a)
Olrik, Axel. *Folkelige Afhandlinger.* Ed. Hans Ellekilde. Copenhagen & Kristiania [Oslo]: Gyldendal, 1919.
Olrik (1919b)
Olrik, Axel. "Folkeminder." *Salmonsens Konversations Leksikon* 8. Copenhagen: Schultz, 1919.
Olrik (1925)
Olrik, Axel. "Odins ridt." *Danske Studier* 22 (1925): 1–18.
Olrik & Ellekilde (1922)
Olrik, Axel, and Hans Ellekilde. "Keiser-sagnet." *Salmonsens*

*Konversations Leksikon* 13. Copenhagen: Schultz, 1922.

Olrik & Ellekilde (1926–1951)
  Olrik, Axel, and Hans Ellekilde. *Nordens gudeverden.* Copenhagen: Gad, 1926–1951.

H. Olrik (1888)
  Olrik, Hans T. *Knud Lavards liv og gærning.* Copenhagen: Wroblewski, 1888.

J. Olrik (1899–1900)
  Olrik, Jørgen. "Sagnkrøniken i Lundeårbøgerne." *Historisk Tidsskrift* 7:2 (1899–1900): 222–229.

J. Olrik & Olrik (1907)
  Olrik, Jørgen, and Axel Olrik. "Kvindegilde i Middelalderen. En gråmunks vidnesbyrd fra 13de årh." *Danske Studier* 4 (1907): 175–176.

Owen (1904)
  Owen, Mary Alicia. *Folk-lore of the Musquakie Indians.* London: Nutt, 1904.

Paasche (1914)
  Paasche, Fredrik. "St. Michael og hans engle. En studie over den ældre katolske skaldedigtning, Draumkvædet, og særlig Sólarljóð." *Edda* 1 (1914): 33–74.

Panzer (1910–1912)
  Panzer, Friedrich. *Studien zur germanischen Sagengeschichte.* 2 vols. Munich: Beck, 1910–1912.

Petersen (1905)
  Petersen, Carl S. "Fra folkevisestriden." *Danske Studier* 2 (1905): 65–114.

Petsch (1900)
  Petsch, Robert. *Formelhafte Schlüsse im Volksmärchen.* Berlin: Weidmann, 1900.

Pohlmann (1912)
  Pohlmann, G. *De arte qva fabellae Herodoteae narratae sint.* Göttingen: Dietrich, 1912.

Potter (1902)
  Potter, Murray, A. *Sohrab and Rustem, the epic theme of a combat between father and son.* London: Nutt, 1902.

von der Recke (1906)
  Recke, Ernst von der. *Nogle Folkeviseredactioner. Bidrag til Visekritiken.* Copenhagen & Kristiania [Oslo]: Gyldendal, 1906.

Relander (1894)
  Relander, O. *Kuvakielestä vanhemmassa suomalaisessa lyyrillisessä kansanrunoudessa.* Helsinki: Suomalaisen kirjallisuuden seuran kirjapainossa, 1894.

Richter (1889)
  Richter, Fr. "Lithauische Märchen." *Zeitschrift für Volkskunde* 1 (1889): 87–93.

Rohde (1876)
  Rohde, Erwin. *Der griechische Roman und seine Vorläufer.*

Leipzig: Breitkopf & Härtel, 1876.
Rydberg (1886–1889)
Rydberg, Viktor. *Undersökningar i germansk Mythologi.* 2 vols. Stockholm: Bonnier, 1886–1889.
Salin (1903)
Salin, Bernhard. "Heimskringlas tradition om asarnes invandring." *Studier tillägnade Oscar Montelius 9/9 1903 af lärjungar.* Stockholm: Norstedt, 1903. 133–141.
Scherer (1888)
Scherer, Wilhelm. *Poetik.* Berlin: Weidmann, 1888.
Schiern (1840)
Schiern, Frederik. "Et nordisk sagns vandring fornemmelig med hensyn til sagnet om Wilhelm Tell." *Historisk Tidsskrift* 1:1 (1840): 45–111.
Schiødte (1908)
Schiødte, Augusta. "Fortegnelse over enlige stene, hvortil der knyttes navn, sagn eller folketro." *Fra dansk folkemindesamling, meddelelser og spörgsmål.* Ed. Axel Olrik. Copenhagen: Schubotheske Forlag, 1908. 97–113.
Schück (1904)
Schück, Henrik. *Studier i Nordisk literatur- och religionshistoria.* 2 vols. Stockholm: Geber, 1904.
Schütte (1903)
Schütte, Gudmund. "Über die alte politische Geographie der nicht-klassischen Völker Europas." *Indogermanische Forschungen* 15 (1903): 211–336.
Schütte (1907)
Schütte, Gudmund. *Oldsagn om Godtjod: vore forfædres land, folk og race.* Copenhagen: Hagerup, 1907.
Schütte (1917)
Schütte, Gudmund. "Nibelungsagnet." *Edda* 8 (1917): 213–269.
Schütte (1919)
Schütte, Gudmund. *Hjemligt Hedenskab i almenfattelig Fremstilling.* Copenhagen & Kristiania [Oslo]: Gyldendal, 1919.
Schütte (1920)
Schütte, Gudmund. "Vidsid og Slægtsagnene om Hengest og Angantyr." *Arkiv för nordisk filologi* 36 (1920): 1–32.
Schwartz (1893)
Schwartz, Wilhelm. "Volkstümliche Schlaglichter." *Zeitschrift des Vereins für Volkskunde* 3 (1893): 117–130.
Seip (1916)
Seip, Didrik Arup. "Stilen i Bjørnsons bondefortellinger." *Edda* 5 (1916): 1–21.
Severinsen (1917)
Severinsen, P. "Sigar-Sagnets Stednavne hos Saxo." *Aarbog for Historisk Samfund for Sorø Amt* 6 (1917): 3–29.
Sijmons (1906)
Sijmons, B. "Das niederdeutsche lied von König Ermenrichs

tod und die eddischen Hamþésmöl." *Zeitschrift für deutsche Philologie* 38 (1906): 145–166.

Skar (1903–1907)
Skar, Johannes. *Gamalt or Sætesdal.* 2 vols. Kristiania [Oslo]: Eige, 1903; Norli, 1907.

Spinden (1908)
Spinden, Herbert J. "Myths of the Nez Percé Indians." *The Journal of American Folklore* 21 (1908): 13–23.

Steenstrup (1876–1882)
Steenstrup, Johannes. *Normannerne.* 4 vols. Copenhagen: Klein, 1876–1882.

Steenstrup (1897)
Steenstrup, Johannes. "Saxo Grammaticus og den danske og svenske Oldtidshistorie." *Arkiv för nordisk filologi* 13 (1897): 101–161.

von Sydow (1907)
von Sydow, Carl W. "Studier i Finnsägnen och besläktade byggmästarsägner." *Fataburen* (1907): 65–78, 199–218.

von Sydow (1908)
von Sydow, Carl W. "Studier i Finnsägnen och besläktade byggmästarsägner." *Fataburen* (1908): 19–27.

von Sydow (1912)
von Sydow, Carl W. Rev. of *Studien zur germanischen Sagengeschichte* 1 by Friedrich Panzer. *Anzeiger für deutsches Altertum* 35 (1912): 123–131.

von Sydow (1918)
von Sydow, Carl W. *Sigurds strid med Fåvne.* Lunds Universitets Årsskrift, New Series 1, 14:16. Lund: Gleerup, 1918.

von Sydow (1919)
von Sydow, Carl W. *Våra Folkminnen.* Lund: Domförlaget, 1919.

Symons (1900)
Symons, B. "Heldensage." *Grundriss der Germanischen Philologie* 3 (1900): 606–734.

Sørensen (1883)
Sørensen, Søren. *Om Mahabharatas stilling i den indiske literatur.* Copenhagen: Klein, 1883.

Thuren (1910)
Thuren, H. J. *Fra Dansk Folkeminde samling.* Copenhagen: Schønberg, 1910.

Tylor (1871)(1891)
Tylor, Edward B. *Primitive Culture.* 2 vols. London: Murray, 1871, 3rd ed. 1891.

Ussing (1910)
Ussing, Henrik. *Om det indbyrdes forhold mellem heltekvadene i ældre Edda.* Copenhagen: Gad, 1910.

Vedel (1903)
Vedel, Valdemar. *Helteliv. En Studie over Heltedigtningens Grundtræk.* Copenhagen: Nordisk forlag, 1903.

Vedel (1914)
  Vedel, Valdemar. "Den digteriske barokstil omkring aar 1600."
  *Edda* 2 (1914): 17–40.
Vogt (1876)
  Vogt, Friedrich. *Leben und Dichten der deutschen Spielleute im
  Mittelalter.* Halle: Niemeyer 1876.
Wehrhan (1908)
  Wehrhan, Karl. *Die Sage.* Leipzig: Heim, 1908.
Weinhold (1894)
  Weinhold, Karl. "Zur Bedeutung der Zahl Neun." *Am Ur-Quell*
  5 (1894): 1–2.
Weinhold (1897)
  Weinhold, Karl. "Die mystische Neunzahl bei den Deutschen."
  *Abhandlungen der Königlichen Akademie der Wissenschaften
  zu Berlin* 2 (1897): 1–61.
Weiske (1842)
  Weiske, Benjamin G. *Prometheus und sein Mythenkreis.*
  Leipzig: Köhler, 1842.
Weston (1899)
  Weston, Jessie L. *King Arthur and his Knights.* Popular Studies
  in Mythology, Romance and Folklore 4. London: Nutt, 1899.
Weston (1900)
  Weston, Jessie L. *Sir Gawain and the Green Knight.* Popular
  Studies in Mythology, Romance and Folklore 17. London: Nutt,
  1900.
Wiklund (1906)
  Wiklund, K. B. Rev. of *Anteckningar under min vistelse i
  Lappmarken* by Jacob Fellman. *Fataburen* (1906): 246–250.
Wiklund (1908)
  Wiklund, K. B. Rev. of *Finnbyggare* by Valdemar Lindholm
  and *Lappfolk* by P. A. Lindholm. *Fataburen* (1908): 164–168.
Wundt (1908–1912)
  Wundt, Wilhelm. *Völkerpsychologie.* 4 vols. Leipzig: Engel-
  mann, 1908–1912.
Ziegler (1893)
  Ziegler, Theobald. *Das Gefühl. Eine psychologische Untersuch-
  ung.* Stuttgart: Göschen, 1893.
Zimmer (1888)
  Zimmer, H. "Keltische Beiträge." *Zeitschrift für deutsches
  Altertum* 32 (1888): 196–334.
Zimmer (1891)
  Zimmer, H. "Keltische Beiträge." *Zeitschrift für deutsches Al-
  tertum* 35 (1891): 1–172.
Østrup (1888)
  Østrup, J. "Hellige Tal." *Nationaltidende* 22–23 November
  1888.

# Index

AXEL OLRIK was Professor of Folklore at the University of Copenhagen, Denmark, and founder of the Danish Folklore Archives. He specialized in medieval Scandinavian folklore, ballads, legends, and comparative religion. Three of his books have appeared in English: *The Heroic Legends of Denmark, Viking Civilization,* and *A Book of Danish Ballads.*

KIRSTEN WOLF is Associate Professor and Chair of the Department of Icelandic Language and Literature at the University of Manitoba. Her edition of the Old Norse *Gyðinga saga* is forthcoming in the series of the Árni Magnússon Institute in Iceland, and she is co-editor of *Medieval Scandinavia: An Encyclopedia.* She has written articles and reviews on Old Norse and Modern Icelandic language and literature.

JODY JENSEN completed a year of Doctoral research in Denmark on a Fulbright-Hays Fellowship, having obtained an M.A. in Scandinavian Studies at the University of Wisconsin-Madison. She is translating, researching, and writing in Scandinavian and other related fields.